Puritan Family and Community in the English Atlantic World

C000084874

Puritan Family and Community in the English Atlantic World examines the dynamics of marriage, family and community life during the "Great Migration" through the microhistorical study of one puritan family in 1638 Rhode Island.

Through studying the Verin family, a group of English non-conformists who took part in the "Great Migration", this book examines differing approaches within puritanism towards critical issues of the age, including liberty of conscience, marriage, family, female agency, domestic violence, and the role of civil government in responding to these developments. Like other nonconformists who challenged the established Church of England, the Verins faced important personal dilemmas brought on by the dictates of their conscience even after emigrating. A violent marital dispute between Jane and her husband Joshua divided the Providence community and resulted, for the first time in the English-speaking colonies, in a woman's right to a liberty of conscience independent of her husband being upheld. Through biographical sketches of the founders of Providence and engaging with puritan ministerial and prescriptive literature and female-authored petitions and pamphlets, this book illustrates how women saw their place in the world and considers the exercise of female agency in the early modern era.

Connecting migration studies, family and community studies, religious studies, and political philosophy, *Puritan Family and Community in the English Atlantic World* will be of great interest to scholars of the English Atlantic World, American religious history, gender and violence, the history of New England, and the history of family.

Margaret Murányi Manchester is Associate Professor in the Department of History at Providence College, USA. She teaches courses on US history, American women's history, and diplomatic history. Her current research revisits a spy story in Cold War Hungary.

Microhistories

Series editors: Sigurður Gylfi Magnússon and Istyán M. Szijártó

The *Microhistories* series is open to books employing different microhistorical approaches, including global microhistories aimed at grasping world-wide connections in local research, social history trying to find determining historical structures through a micro-analysis, and cultural history in the form of microhistories that relate directly to large or small scale historical contexts. They are interesting stories that bring the everyday life and culture of common people of the past close to the readers, without the aspiration of finding answers to general "big questions" or relating them to the grand narratives of history. The series is open to publishing both theoretical and empirical works, but with a focus on empirical monographs which can communicate stories from the past and capture the imagination of our readers.

Published

The Revolt of Snowballs: A Microhistory, by Claire Judde De Larivière

A Tale of a Fool? A Microhistorical Study of an 18th-Century Peasant Woman, by Guðný Hallgrímsdóttir

Roman Tales: A Reader's Guide to the Art of Microhistory, by Thomas V. Cohen

Puritan Family and Community in the English Atlantic World: "Being Much Afflicted with Conscience", by Margaret Manchester

Five Parishes in late Medieval and Tudor London: Communities and Reforms, by Gary G. Gibbs

Forthcoming

Who Killed Panayot? Reforming Ottoman Legal Culture in the 19th century, by Omri Paz

Puritan Family and Community in the English Atlantic World

Being "Much Afflicted with Conscience"

Margaret Murányi Manchester

Routledge
Taylor & Francis Group

LONDON AND NEW YORK

First published 2019
by Routledge
2 Park Square, Milton Park, Abingdon, Oxon OX14 4RN

and by Routledge
52 Vanderbilt Avenue, New York, NY 10017

Routledge is an imprint of the Taylor & Francis Group, an informa business

First issued in paperback 2021

British Library Cataloguing-in-Publication Data
A catalogue record for this book is available from the British Library

Library of Congress Cataloging-in-Publication Data
Names: Manchester, Margaret Muranyi, 1954- author.
Title: Puritan family and community in the English Atlantic world :
being "much afflicted with conscience" / Margaret Murânyi
Manchester.
Description: Abingdon, Oxon ; New York, NY : Routledge, 2019. |
Series: Microhistories | Includes bibliographical references and
index. |
Identifiers: LCCN 2019007037 (print) | LCCN 2019014570 (ebook)
| ISBN 9780429054860 (eBook) | ISBN 9780367150785
(hardback : alk. paper) | ISBN 9780429054860 (ebk)
Subjects: LCSH: Puritans—Rhode Island—Providence—
History—17th century. | Verin family. | Puritan women—Rhode
Island—Providence—Social conditions—17th century. |
Family violence—Law and legislation—Rhode Island—
Providence—History—17th century. | Married women—Legal
status, laws, etc.—Rhode Island—Providence—History—17th
century. | Sex role—Religious aspects—Puritans. | Freedom of
religion—Rhode Island—Providence—History—17th century. |
Providence (R.I.)—History—17th century. | New England—History—
Colonial period, ca. 1600-1775.
Classification: LCC F82 (ebook) | LCC F82 .M26 2019 (print) |
DDC 974.5/202—dc23
LC record available at https://lccn.loc.gov/2019007037

ISBN: 978-0-367-15078-5 (hbk)
ISBN: 978-1-03-209235-5 (pbk)
ISBN: 978-0-429-05486-0 (ebk)

Typeset in Sabon
by Integra Software Services Pvt. Ltd.

To Bernard, Bernard, Andrew, and Kate with all my love and gratitude.

Contents

Figures

Abbreviations

TNA   The National Archives, Kew, London, England
RIHS   Rhode Island Historical Society, Providence, RI
MHS   Massachusetts Historical Society, Boston, MA
PIL   Peabody Institute Museum and Library, Peabody, MA

Acknowledgements

I first learned about the Verins in a call for interested participants for the Verin Colonial Women's History Project co-sponsored by the Rhode Island Commission on Women and the National Park Service/Roger Williams Memorial Park. In presenting preliminary findings at the Rhode Island and Newport Historical Societies, I was much encouraged by the positive response and helpful commentaries. Heartfelt thanks to my colleagues and friends at Providence College who were so unselfish in sharing their expertise, helping me to refine my arguments, and giving me feedback on the Verin project in its different stages. The Dean of the School of Arts and Sciences and the Committee on Aid to Fund Faculty Research provided sabbatical funding and travel grants, and the research librarians at Phillips Memorial Library were incredibly responsive to my requests for materials. I want to thank my graduate students, especially Mr. Steven Pickford, Dr. Erik Chaput and Nicholas Moran, who combed the archives, searching for passenger lists, genealogical data, church records, colonial papers, etc. to help me build the biographical sketches of the original proprietors. Special thanks go to Dr. Adrian Chastain Weimer, Dr. Edward E. Andrews, Dr. Steven C. Smith, and to Dr. Jeffrey A. Johnson, for their invaluable assistance and support. Thanks to Christopher Judge, Multimedia Producer at PC, who used his drone to take photos of the statue of Roger Williams overlooking the city of Providence. Thanks and appreciation also to Dr. Douglas Little, on whom I have relied for counsel since his mentorship at Clark University—despite the fact that this project is a far cry from US diplomatic history! I very much appreciate our continued friendship and collaboration over the ensuing years.

This project could not have been possible without the support of countless people, especially helpful archivists at the Rhode Island and Massachusetts Historical Societies, the Providence Public Library, the Athenaea in Boston and Providence, and the Peabody Essex Museum and Library. I would also like to thank the archivists at the National Archives and at the Family History Centre in London and at the local records offices in Wiltshire, England.

I would like to acknowledge the anonymous reviewers who initially rejected an early version of these arguments as being "too speculative." Their feedback encouraged me to redouble my efforts to find alternative ways to give voice to a woman like Jane Verin and to clarify my analysis. I thank the anonymous reviewers of this manuscript proposal for their careful and constructive critiques that have rendered this family history more coherent and, I hope you will agree, more persuasive. Thanks to Dr. István Szijártó and Dr. Sigurður Gylfi Magnússon, my co-editors for the Routledge Series on *Microhistories*, who carefully shepherded me through this project.

Finally, I want to say thank you to my family and friends, who have attended my talks, listened to me discuss my ideas, and provided me with unstinting encouragement, including Kate and Mike Fortino, who helped me with a reenactment of "haling his wife with ropes to Salem" on a chilly Thanksgiving weekend. I am blessed and fortunate indeed. Lastly, any errors in this manuscript are my own.

Introduction

The Verins—a family "much afflicted with conscience"

The brief entry for the Providence town meeting on May 21, 1638, reads, "It was agreed that Joshua Verin upon the breach of a couvenant for restraining the liberty of consciensce shall be withheld from the liberty of voting till he shall declare [to] the contrary."[1] It had only been three years earlier, during the winter of 1635/1636, that the puritan divine, Roger Williams, fled Massachusetts Bay Colony and made his way to what would become Providence, Rhode Island. There he set up a "shelter for persons distressed for Conscience." Among those who accompanied him was one Joshua Verin, his wife, Jane, and his mother-in-law, the Widow Reeves.

Two years later, in an undated letter in early May, Williams wrote to Massachusetts Bay Governor John Winthrop asking for advice concerning "… one unruly person" whose speech, Williams believed, threatened "… no other than the Raping of the Fundamentall Liberties of the Countrey," which he believed should be "dearer to us than our Right Eyes."[2] Apparently, a disagreement had broken out between him and Joshua Verin, whose house lot abutted his, because Williams later complained that Verin had refused to join them in prayer for at least a year and had further forbidden his wife, Jane, from joining in as well. When she disobeyed her husband, Verin had "… trodden her under foote tyrannically" to the point that Jane Verin's neighbours feared "… with his furious blowes she went in danger of her life."[3] Williams describes Jane Verin as a "gracious & modest woman," whom Verin was unable to draw into the same "ungodliness." In his letter to Winthrop dated May 22, 1638, Williams reports that Verin had a "fowle & slanderous & brutish carriage." Further, after being disenfranchised by his neighbors in Providence, he had haled "his wife with ropes to Salem" where she continued to be troublesome as their differences "yet stand." Williams adds that she was willing to stay and live with her husband, or elsewhere, "where she may not offend."[4] This appears to be the first time that a wife's liberty of conscience, independent of her husband's, was upheld in the English colonies. This historic event raises some interesting questions that will serve as the basis for this study. Given the violence of the Joshua Verin's discipline of his wife, why did the people of Providence charge Joshua Verin with violating his wife's liberty of conscience? Why not charge him with putting his wife in "danger of life"? The dynamics of the controversy clearly raised issues of religion and authority within the puritan patriarchy and within the institution of marriage.

The Verins and family history

Family history is particularly useful here, in that one can focus on the way in which members of this family lived their own history while being active participants in larger national and international historical developments. The Verins were English nonconformists who took part in the "Great Migration" in the first half of the seventeenth century. Their family history is a fascinating and multi-faceted one. Like other English emigrants, the story of the Verin family shows the mobility of the English Atlantic world. Joshua and Jane Verin settled in Salem, moved to Providence, and returned to Salem. Later, Joshua Verin sold his property in Massachusetts and started anew in the Barbados, like many of his English compatriots. This microhistorical study of one family reveals that, like other nonconformists who challenged the established Church of England before emigrating, they continued to face important personal dilemmas brought on by the dictates of their conscience even after their arrival in the English colonies. Families split over issues of conscience, maintaining order in the family household, and governance of the commonwealth.

The family is also very much a social construction; that is, it must be understood within its specific cultural and historical context. For this reason, much attention will be given to determining how puritans them- selves understood the institution of marriage and the role of men and women within it. Like their relationship with God, Puritans considered marriage to be covenantal. They ordered their society and familial relations on clear principles based on their understanding of the scripture. *Both* Joshua and Jane Verin were devout Christians; *both* believed they were acting in accordance with their conscience—Joshua Verin in trying to govern his unruly wife and Jane Verin in trying to follow her Biblically- inspired conscience that led her, as a consequence, to challenge her hus- band's authority over her. In order to understand Joshua and Jane Verin's actions, one needs to understand puritan theology, especially as it applied to marriage and family; additionally, investigating the history of family law, particularly as it relates to issues of family violence, helps the reader to understand the divisions among the proprietors of Providence when it came to responding to Verin's brutal carriage toward his wife.

The puritans were a diverse group of devout English immigrants who braved censure, discrimination, and even death in England because of their opposition to policies in the Church of England. When they arrived in New England, they had an unprecedented opportunity to create and recre- ate lives in the American wilderness. They attempted to create a Christian utopia, communities of "Visible Saints" who tried to live out their faith according to the Scriptures and the advice of their ministers. What did it mean to be a devout puritan? To what extent did their lives in these new communities reflect their values and beliefs? And to what degree did their lived experiences challenge those ideals? What happened when, inevitably, conflicts arose? Using the experiences of the extended Verin family and the marital relationship of Joshua and Jane Verin enables the modern reader to answer some of these questions.

Given that the vast majority of English who moved to New England during these two waves of migration were puritans, one would expect that all those who had fled persecution would hold to the same set of Calvinist belief and the practice that derived from their interpretation of the scripture. After all, they were all people of conscience. But, in fact, the diversity of belief among puritans in colonial New England is vital to understanding the fissures that developed not only within the Verin family, but also within the larger community in the new world. In particular, Chapter One explores these religious differences. There is a high degree of correlation that emerges when once compares the list of those who might have been pre-disposed to be sympathetic to Jane Verin and their subsequent changes in religious affiliation. Roger Williams and John Clarke, for example, were later among the co-founders of the First Baptist Church in America. Later, some of the earliest settlers of Providence became Quakers, a group whom even the tolerant Williams could hardly abide. Both the Baptists and the Quakers would support an individual's right to conscience, even as their beliefs and practices challenged the orthodoxy of Congregationalist New England. That religious diversity is explored in depth and helps explain the differences in England and between Salem, Boston and Providence; central among these was the question of freedom of conscience and the issue of state-enforced orthodoxy which was at the heart of a series of pamphlet wars between Williams and some of the puritan ministers of Massachusetts Bay, including Nathanial Ward and Cotton Mather.

Anne Hutchinson is well known in puritan and early colonial history for her defiance of ministerial authority in Massachusetts Bay and her leadership of what came to be known as the Antinomians. Like Anne Hutchinson, Jane Verin, too, was a woman of conscience who was willing to defy those who would exert governorship over her. The Antinomian Crisis, a controversy sparked in part by disagreements over doctrine, has a direct bearing on the Verin decision. Hutchinson and some of her followers had connections to the townspeople of Providence, and they arrived in Portsmouth, RI months before the vote on Joshua Verin. For example, Richard Scott, was an original proprietor of Providence and was married to her sister, Katherine. Understanding Hutchinson's role in Rhode Island is important in that it illuminates Williams' seemingly contradictory views on women. So, while he supported a woman's right to conscience and helped Ann Hutchinson to obtain a land grant in Portsmouth, he rejected her claim that she had the right to prophesy. Jane

Verin's story exemplifies the stories of many other unknown English women who were nonconformists willing to challenge male authority. The biographical sketches of the founding women of Providence in Chapter Two reveal that these women were far more numerous than previously thought.

The many Puritanisms

One of the central paradoxes of puritanism is the fact that these "Saints" believed that divine revelation connected them directly with God in an often-intimate relationship. Despite the role of ministers, sermonizers, the magistrates and the larger community in creating a Christian order that accorded with the Scriptures, that relationship brought about by conversion was still highly personal. Tensions inevitably arose. *Any* individual, regardless of sex or class, could be chosen by God for salvation. That is a fundamentally egalitarian belief in a society that was unequal. So, too, tensions developed in a society that viewed marriage as largely reciprocal, but that ordered its social and political relations in a hierarchy. Jane Verin's experiences overlap these two key questions. Clarifying that social and political ordering of puritan New England is also essential to understanding the Verin decision. So again, the historian must navigate between the microhistorical study of one family and the larger historical narrative.

In the case of Joshua and Jane Verin, a married couple who later followed the Reverend Roger Williams to Rhode Island, Jane's obedience to her conscience led her to disobey her husband and to Joshua Verin's "brutal carriage" toward his wife. This split the Providence community into those who supported Jane Verin's right to a liberty of conscience independent of her husband and those who believed Joshua Verin was obeying *his* conscience in disciplining his wife, even if it endangered her life. Those in the community who were sympathetic to Joshua Verin later split from Roger Williams and founded other settlements in Rhode Island. Ultimately, Rhode Island's Charter of 1663 used gender-neutral language in affirming complete liberty of conscience.

This family history is the lens through which one can examine the differences among the puritan divines on issues relating to family violence, domestic disturbances and the best means of maintaining order in both puritan families (also considered to be commonwealths) and within the larger community. The Massachusetts Body of Liberties of 1641 was the first to prohibit wife beating in the English-speaking world. The lack of strict enforcement in the ensuing years testifies to the ambivalence among the English regarding the appropriate level of force that a husband could use in exercising "governorship" of his spouse.

A note about methodology

Few people have ever heard of the Verins; Jane Verin left no letters, diary or other personal documents and disappears from the historical record after 1640 (when she was ejected from the First Church of Salem for her continued challenges to its legitimacy). Joshua Verin appears in church and court records in both New England and in the Barbados, where he eventually settled prior to his death. The Verin decision occurred in 1638, several years before Rhode Island adopted a legal code and set up a court system to administer justice. As such, the case of the Verins set no legal precedent that can be traced through subsequent legal history as a way to determine whether, for example, women in Rhode Island lost or gained status over the course of the seventeenth century. The questions raised by their experience are too intriguing to accept simply that "there is nothing there." The methodology used to reconstruct their story, then, includes searching for genealogical and legal records at county and national archives in England, passenger lists, court and town records, early histories of the New England plantations, plot and house maps, rosters of church memberships, among other sources to develop biographical and genealogical sketches of each person who was in Providence at the time of the Verin decision. Those biographical sketches are then analyzed to trace the web of connections that connected the Verins to their neighbours in Wiltshire, England, Salem, Massachusetts, Providence, RI, and the Barbados. This information, assembled from disparate sources, will serve as the foundation for creating a genealogical history of the Verins and their larger puritan community. Chapter One, for example, reconstructs the lives of the original male proprietors who joined Williams and who were present in Providence at time of Verin's hearing. Constructing individual biographies brings to light similarities in their experiences. The grand narratives of the puritan settlement of the English Atlantic world focus on their difficulties and persecutions in England brought on by their willingness to defy the authority of the Church of England (and thus also the Crown) in following their religiously inspired consciences; once in the colonies, the historical studies distinguish the diverse patterns of settlement, the doctrinal and theological differences that emerged, and the ways in which puritan ministers and magistrates attempted to preserve their utopian experiment in the wilderness. Other historians have stressed the ways in which puritan settlers established political and social institutions that ultimately contributed to the development of democracy in the Americas. In attempting to answer the questions raised by the case of the Verins, the historian moves back and forth between the grand narrative and the microhistory. Studying the family history of the larger Verin family shows the way in which individuals, families and communities (such as Providence) were influenced by the forces shaping their worlds (as identified in the grand narratives). Further, the Verins themselves contributed in discrete ways to the construction of that larger narrative. So, for example, the decisions made by the proprietors regarding Jane Verin's plight had implications for the Charter for Rhode Island that was issued in 1663, which affirmed for all its citizens an unimpeded right to liberty of conscience. *All* of the first settlers of Providence were separatist puritans. That alone does not explain why some voted to deprive Joshua Verin of the franchise. In the case of the early Providence founders, using the biographical method illuminates their origins, family connections and experiences and can help the reader understand why the majority supported Williams. The men of Providence were not unanimous in their censure of Verin. Thus, William Arnold argued strenuously that when he consented to Williams' dictate that no man should be molested for his conscience, he never intended that it "should extend to the breach of any ordinance of God, such as the subjugation of wives to their husbands, etc., and gave divers reasons against it." And this chapter explores the underlying tensions, including land disputes, that were exacerbated by the disagreements about how to respond to Verin's physical beatings of his wife. Shortly afterward, Arnold and others who dissented on the Verin decision removed themselves from Providence and organized a new settlement in Pawtuxet.

Women and the historical record in the early modern era

One of the problems historians must confront is that of reconstructing events when records are incomplete or written by unreliable witnesses. Aside from the fact that much evidence from the seventeenth century has been destroyed as a result of wars, fires and other disasters, women in the early modern era are often "invisible" because of their legal status as *femme couverte*. This meant that, upon marriage, a woman lost her legal identity independent of her husband's. Of the historical evidence about the puritans that has been preserved over the centuries, much of it was written by puritan ministers, who naturally tended to make judgements through the prism of their belief and value systems. Remember that Jane Verin appears in the records, but she does not speak directly. One would assume that, because she left no diary or letters, it will be impossible to discern her thoughts and feelings about her experiences. Historians of the early modern era frequently grapple with these gaps in knowledge; microhistorians must also contend with the problem of evidence. The historian's task is to approach the topics indirectly through the reconstruction as much as possible of the context in which the principle actors in Jane and Joshua Verin's drama were active. How can one give voice to an unknown woman such as Jane Verin? At different times she was called pious, gracious and modest. What did that mean at the time? In Chapter Two, I consider tracts written by puritan theologians about appropriate behavior for women. They disagreed, especially on the extent to which a husband could discipline an unruly wife. The use of female-authored petitions can reveal what women contemporaneous to Jane Verin were saying about both their hopes and aspirations and the reality of their lives. Jane Verin was a member of the First Church of Salem—she appears in the membership roll. That meant that she must have testified to a faith experience in order to be admitted to the congregation. That record is not available; however, the conversion narratives of William and Elizabeth Adams, who arrived in Massachusetts Bay around the same time as the Verins, are available, as is "The call of Christ unto thirsty Sinners ...," a sermon preached by the Reverend Thomas Allen. Taken together, one can get a sense of how puritan ministers instructed their flocks on the path to conversion (and salvation); and one can compare William and Elizabeth's personal accounts to explore gendered differences to faith. These all can be used to shed light on what might have inspired Jane Verin's beliefs and actions. Further, a variety of sources, including passenger lists, court records, probate records and wills, church records, town records, diaries, rosters of church memberships, etc. are helpful in reconstructing the lives of the early female settlers of Providence. Upon examining the bibliographical sketches of the women of Providence, one can conclude that female challenges to the puritan social order were far more prevalent than has been previously acknowledged. The case of Jane Verin and many of the women featured in Chapter Two attest to this fact. Using context setting and approaching the topic from a variety of sources and perspectives enables the historian to ascertain what can be known for sure. We know for certain, for example, that there were approximately 50 persons living in Providence in May of 1638. We can determine, based on the plot maps and town records, where each lived in relation to the other. We know too that they met roughly every two weeks to discuss matters of mutual concern and to make decisions relating to governance of their small community. Further, it is clear that several among them met much more frequently to pray together, read and reflect on the scripture, and to hear the sermons of Rev. Williams. The existing sources also attest to disagreements that had arisen regarding relations with the Indians, disputes over land and how best to structure their government. These facts confirm the *intimacy* of this tiny community living, working and praying together. Everyone could not help but know everyone else; therefore, it is impossible for the residents not to have known about Joshua Verin's violent carriage toward his wife. The biographical sketches of the men who followed Roger Williams to Providence provide vital clues as to who was among the majority that voted to censure Joshua Verin. The available resources, including correspondence, petitions and official records reinforce both the facts and the educated guesses. Further, the biographical sketches of the women who founded Providence provide further vital clues as to how or why their male kinfolk voted as they did. Throughout the discussion that follows, I will try to answer the following questions: What are the facts of the case? What can we state to be true with a great deal of certainty? Where can we speculate based on the available evidence? Despite the problems of evidence, this family history seeks to make personal the larger historical forces at work. At the individual and at the family level, then, we can begin to see both how difficult and how remarkable was the arc of puritan history. Developing an understanding of the 1638 decision of the townspeople of Providence about this one couple is an opening to comprehending the larger issues that men and women on both sides of the Atlantic continued to confront years later.

As a complement to the reconstruction of events using a quantity and variety of primary sources mentioned previously, there exists a wealth of scholarship on the puritans, the founding of New England, the English Atlantic world, and their connections to the foundations of American religious liberty and republican government. Scholars have not always agreed, and the debates have been vigorous over the centuries since the founding of Plymouth, Massachusetts Bay, and Rhode Island. A thorough examination of the secondary literature provides a variety of frameworks within which to understand the experiences of the central actors in this family and community drama. A good example of this dynamic is included in Chapter Two. Once the biographical sketches of the women who founded Providence are compiled, one becomes instantly aware of the gaps in certain knowledge. However, an analysis of the existing data reveals ties that bound some of these women together in common cause—ties that sometimes extended back to England before migration, and forward in time to Salem and Boston. As puritan women, they as a group shared common experiences both in England and in Massachusetts. Further, in addition to their Calvinism and their status as "Visible Saints," their willingness to defy authority in response to the dictates of their conscience bound them together, especially when their husbands shared and/or supported their activism. Thus, the intimacy of community life in Providence (noted earlier), coupled with the results of the detailed analysis of their individual stories, supports the conclusion that several of these women, including Jane Verin and her mother, the Widow Reeves, formed a kind of spirit group. The existing work of other historians working in related fields can then be used to reinforce these conclusions. So, for example, other historians have done detailed analyses of puritan piety, sentiment and practice. Others have focused on women's roles in English religious life, while still others have narrowed their studies to examine the agency of puritan, Baptist or Quaker women. These studies validate the conclusions drawn in this study; and the details of this study both personalize and bring to light some of the themes emphasized in the larger meta-narratives. In other words, the relationship between the two is symbiotic, and the movement between the primary and secondary sources and between the microhistorical study and the grand narratives will hopefully render this analysis more credible and persuasive.

Women's agency in the early modern era

It was only male property-owners who were heads of household who could be admitted into the "fellowship of vote." Although it was the men of

Providence who had the power and authority to decide Joshua Verin's fate, women very much played a decisive role in the outcome. Joshua's violence is important as it represents the ultimate, basic power relationship between men and women. That Joshua could force march his wife back to Salem argues against female agency; Jane's refusal to attend services after their return to Salem argues for it. I developed the following methodology in order to answer this question with greater certitude: the key puritan ministers and theologians must be identified and their different positions regarding the position of women within Puritan patriarchy, the possibility of women being among the "elect" or "Visible Saints," the issue of female prophesying, and changing attitudes regarding domestic abuse must be clarified. Women's roles in puritan churches must be investigated to shed light on Jane Verin and her behavior. One can also examine female-authored petitions and pamphlets as a way of getting at the differences between the ideals of puritan community life and the lived experience. The prescriptive literature, such as *A Womans Counsell*, provides the reader with insights on the kind of advice women gave to their daughters and female kin and the way in which they structured their social world. Clearly, the Widow Reeves and Jane Verin had a strong and supportive mother–daughter relationship. The available facts and timeline of events attest to this. The female-authored conduct guides such as *A Womans Counsell* provide us with a window to examine what the women themselves considered important in leading a good and moral life. One approach used in our analysis is to compare the actual behavior of Jane Verin and the Widow Reeves with that counselled by another mother to her daughter. This kind of analysis makes it possible to make sense of both Jane Verin's continued defiance of her husband when it came to her conscience *and* the decision to remain with her husband, in spite of his brutal carriage. The female-authored petitions to courts and colonial assemblies, in contrast, clearly indicate women's expectations by examining their petitions about male kin who had failed to meet those expectations. These themes are developed in Chapter Two.

Moving back and forth between this microhistory and the larger puritan and/or English narrative reveals that, at a very early and formative stage in the colony's history, the Verin case forced Williams and other residents in Providence to confront the very issues which were perceived to be undermining the quiet and calm of England and New England: namely, the right to dissent within the Church of England, the issue of liberty of conscience, the differing positions within puritanism on the issue of domestic violence, the place of women in puritan social and religious life, and the role of civil government in responding to these developments. Having left England to escape these divisive issues, they found themselves confronting the same in New England. Many women in the colony, given their previous experiences defying authority in defense of individual conscience, might through their spouses and male relatives, exert both a tacit and an indirect influence on male decision-makers that could result in the community condemning Joshua Verin for his disrespect of Jane Verin.

The townspeople of Providence were divided on the extent to which a wife's liberty of conscience, even when challenging her husband's authority, could be tolerated. This debate was at the root of a far larger debate regarding whether or not a church state system, in which civil and ecclesiastical power reinforced one another, or a complete separation of church and state was the best means of securing liberty of conscience and maintaining civil order. Further, like the puritan divines who attempted in their ministerial and prescriptive literature to advise their readers on the best way of maintaining order and stability in puritan marriages, the voters of Providence were also split on how much family violence they would tolerate. While the Massachusetts Body of Liberties of 1641 criminalized wife beating and the Rhode Island Charter of 1663 granted complete liberty of conscience to its citizens, in practice, the deep differences of opinion on women's right to religious liberty and their husbands' right to discipline them continued to roil in the English Atlantic world.

Notes

1 Providence (R.I.) Record Commissioners (1892–1915), *The Early Records of the Town of Providence*, Vol. I (Providence: Snow & Farnham, City Printers, 1892), Rhode Island Historical Society (hereafter cited as RIHS), 4.
2 Glenn W. LaFantasie, ed., *The Correspondence of Roger Williams*, Volume I, 1629–1653 (Providence, RI: Rhode Island Historical Society, 1988), RIHS (hereafter cited as *The Correspondence of Roger Williams*), 154. LaFantasie believes the unruly person refers to J. Verin whose case would come before the town later in the month.
3 *The Winthrop Papers*, Vol. IV, 1638–1644 (Boston: Massachusetts Historical Society, 1944), 31 (hereafter cited MHS). See also Howard M. Chapin, *Documentary History of Rhode Island: Being the History of the Towns of Providence and Warwick to 1649 and of the Colony to 1647* (Providence: Preston & Rounds, Co., 1916), 72.
4 *The Winthrop Papers*, Ibid.

1 "Gone to New England for conscience sake"

Family history as New England history

Jane Verin left no journals, letters, or other personal documentation, but she appears in church and court records and in the correspondence of Roger Williams and others. Joshua Verin appears in these and in Salem town records; his letters also appear in Providence town records. Despite the paucity of sources, there are elements of their history that one can determine with a great deal of certainty. Using a variety of sources, including birth, marriage and death records, wills and probate records, church membership rosters, passenger lists, court records, correspondence, town and plantation records, and early histories of the New England colonies, the skeleton of a family sketch begins to emerge. This chapter will reconstruct as much as possible the circumstances of the Verin family within the English Atlantic world, based on facts ascertained from the available sources, and place their experiences within the context of English migration.

The Verins

The Verin family hailed from New Sarum (later called Salisbury), in Wiltshire, England. Records indicate that the family had lived in and around Salisbury for many generations.[1] The male members of the family were tradesmen. Philip Verin and his brother, Hugh, were ropers and actively involved in the Joiners Guild in Salisbury.[2] Philip and Dorcas Verin married ca. 1615.[3] Although both Philip and Hugh owed money to the guild in 1616, by 1618, Philip was a chamberlain, enrolling apprentices for the guild. In 1622, Philip narrowly missed election as warden, coming in third of thirteen candidates for the two one-year positions.[4] Several male members of the Verin family took up the profession; Thomas Verin, whose will was probated on May 24, 1658 in Deptford, England, listed it as his occupation.[5] The passenger list of the *James* includes Philip and his son, Joshua Verin, who is also identified as a roper.[6] The fact that Joshua is listed indicates that he was an adult. The passenger list includes "53 men, youths, boys, besides wives and children of divers of them" and identifies them as "late of New Sarum."[7] Philip Verin took a large extended family with him, including his wife Dorcas, their eldest son Philip, a wheelwright, and his wife Joanna, their sons Nathaniel and Hilliard, and Joshua and his wife Jane.[8]

At some point before their departure for New England, the Verin family joined with other non-conformists (as puritans were then known). On July 15, 1626, Joshua's older brother, Philip, married Joanna Cash.[9] The marriage license identifies her as a 23-year-old spinster and daughter of Elizabeth, a widow.[10] At the time, non-conformists frequently obtained a license because this necessitated appearing in church only once as opposed to having the banns read in church three times, a practice required by the Church of England. There is no surviving license or certificate for marriage between Joshua and Jane Verin either in England or New England. However, it can be assumed that they were married sometime prior to their arrival in Salem in June 1635, because they were, with their parents and siblings, listed as members of the First Church of Salem.[11]

There is no information available about Jane's origins or, indeed, even her surname. Her mother was the Widow Reeves, but it is unknown whether that was a first or second marriage. Several women were excommunicated from the First Church of Salem for following Roger Williams, among them the Widow Reeves, Jane Verin, Margery Holliman, and Mary Oliver. Jane Verin continued to defy the religious authorities, even after her return to Salem. Records from the Quarterly Court in Salem note that on Christmas Day, 1638 "Jane, wife of Joshua Verrin, [was] presented for absence from religious worship." Hugh Peter, pastor of the First Church of Salem, requested time to confer with her again, most probably to try to dissuade her from her continued defiance. The Widow Reeves was censored by the Church of Salem for refusing to hear the word and for refusing to acknowledge the churches of Massachusetts as true churches. She was a landowner in early Providence, her lot being north of Joshua and Jane Verin's land (two house lots up from Roger Williams and his family).

While many congregations followed their ministers to the New World, the Verins, although they were actively involved in their church *after* their arrival in Plymouth, appear to have emigrated for both religious and economic reasons. None of the ministers or other church leaders from either St. Edmund's or St. Thomas parishes in Salisbury during this time appears on any of the passenger lists, nor did any of the clerics receive licenses to pass beyond the seas.[12] However, the Reverend John Avery, a preacher of "good repute" who arrived in Boston with his wife and children, hailed from Wiltshire. A closer connection can be found in the case of Anthony Thatcher. Thatcher, his wife, and their four children, too, came from Salisbury. They embarked on the *James* in 1635. Prior to their departure, Anthony had served as a curate in 1631 and 1634 to his brother, Peter Thatcher, the rector of St. Edmonds. Anthony Thatcher was a non-conformist who had lived in Holland prior to his departure for New

England.[13] St. Edmond's is the parish where Joshua Verin and all of his siblings were baptized.

Plymouth Colony was founded in 1620 by English separatists, also called Pilgrims, who settled in and around Cape Cod. William Bradford served as the governor for the first 30 years of its founding; his *History of Plimoth Plantation*, remains an important source for understanding the early history of these colonies and the rivalries that emerged. Salem (derived from the Hebrew word for Peace) is the second oldest settlement in New England, founded in 1626 by Roger Conant. Starting in 1628, the colony at Salem was led by Governor John Endecott.[14] Two years later, they were joined by puritans under the leadership of John Winthrop; beginning in 1630, members of the "Great Migration" arrived first at Salem, and then moved northward to establish permanent settlements in Boston and elsewhere along the Shawmut Peninsula in what would later be named Massachusetts Bay. The Verin family stayed in Salem. The patriarch of the family, Philip Verin, was made a freeman of the Massachusetts colony on September 2, 1635; and in the following year, he received a grant of 160 acres in Salem.[15] Being a freeman meant that Verin was considered a full citizen of the colony. These satisfied conditions of church membership (and hence guaranteed voting rights); only freemen had the right to hold public office or vote in town meetings. Joshua Verin received a land grant for a two-acre house lot on February 6, 1635.[16] The renewal of the Church covenant signed at Salem in 1637 promises that the signatories would "walk with our brethren & sisters in ... Congregation, with all watchfulness & tenderness ..."[17] It was signed by 85 men and 79 women, including Dorcas Verin, Philip Verin's wife (and mother of Joshua).

The entry for Joshua Verin in James Savage's *Genealogical Dictionary of the First Settlers of New England* describes Verin as "a favorer of Roger Williams" who went to Providence in 1637, where his "w[ife] made some trouble there, came back, and in few [years he followed ... her]."[18] In fact, Savage erred as it was Jane, not Joshua, who was the reason the Verins came to Providence. As mentioned earlier, records indicate Joshua arrived in New England in June 1635 on the *James* with his parents and siblings. Joshua, his father, and his brother Hilliard all became landowners, members of the First Church of Salem, and held various positions of authority in Salem.[19] While both Joshua and Jane were admitted to communion in the First Church of Salem, in the two years prior to their arrival in Providence, several sources indicate that Jane Verin and her mother, Margery Reeves, were among the female activists who "refused to worship with the congregation from 1635 to 1638 and the latter two women denied that the churches of the Bay colony were true churches."[20] Apparently, Joshua Verin was a non-Separatist Congregationalist, while his wife was a committed Separatist. In England and Massachusetts Bay, an unregenerate could go to church, but not receive communion. These frequently included women and children. Williams went one step further, arguing that unregenerate Christians could not even attend church.[21] Indeed, he believed that men and women should not pray together unless both were regenerate.[22] Williams was a charismatic and persuasive preacher. In his journal, John Winthrop confirms that Roger Williams had been so influential in Salem, that

> many there (especially of devout women) did embrace his opinions and separated from the Churches ... he has drawn about twenty persons to his opinion ... [they] went all together out of our jurisdiction and precinct, into an Island, called Read-Iland ... and there they live to this day ... but in great strife and contention.[23]

It seems some members of their congregation had returned to England and while there, they had attended services in the Church of England. Once they returned to Salem, these travellers were allowed once again to receive communion.[24] Williams and his followers condemned these practices, among others, as corrupt.

As a result of this and other criticisms, Roger Williams, having been banished by the authorities in Massachusetts Bay and fearing imminent arrest, made his way to what would become Providence on land he had purchased from the Narragansett Indians. Williams later recalled that he had been "unkindly & unchristianly (as I believe) driven from my howse & land & wife & children (in the midst of N. England winter)."[25] According to John Winthrop, Williams and about 20 followers "intended to erect a plantation about the Narragansett Bay."[26] Joshua Verin certainly counted himself among the "six which came first."[27]

A plot map of the early township reveals Verin purchased the house lot abutting Williams' property in 1636; Verin and the others who accompanied Williams were among the original proprietors of the new settlement. Jane Verin's mother, the Widow Reeves, purchased the lot that abutted them on the other side in 1638.[28] About a year after following Williams to Providence, Verin had some kind of falling out with his neighbor, because he stopped attending prayer services. In his letter to John Winthrop, Roger Williams notes that Joshua Verin had "refused to hear the word with us ([for which] we molested him not for) this twelve month."[29] Williams complains about Verin's behaviour, calling him "unruly."[30] Further, Verin's speech threatened, according to Williams, "... no other than the Raping of the Fundamentall Liberties of the Countrey," which he believed should be "dearer to us than our Right Eyes."[31] Jane Verin continued her defiance of authority by disobeying her husband and attending prayer services with Roger Williams and the other faithful. As a consequence, Williams reports Verin had trodden this "gracious & modest woman," under his feet to the point where he and the Verins' other neighbours feared that "... with his furious blowes she went in danger of her life."[32]

In his letter to Winthrop dated May 22, 1638, Williams reports that as a result of Verin's "fowle & slanderous & brutish carriage," the town had voted to disenfranchise him.[33] The entry in the Providence Town records, however, notes only that Verin had violated the covenant by "restraining the liberty of consciencse [sic]" and makes no mention of the violence he had perpetrated upon his wife as a reason for excluding him "from the liberty of voting."[34]

Joshua Verin adamantly rejected the authority of the freeholders both to interfere in his marriage and to disenfranchise him. He vowed he would "have justice."[35] Further, after the actions of his neighbours in Providence, he returned to Massachusetts Bay.[36] According to Williams, he haled "his wife with ropes to Salem," leaving behind their property.[37] Williams notes she continued to be troublesome in Salem, as their differences "yet stand."[38] He adds that she was willing to stay and live with her husband, or elsewhere, "where she may not offend."[39]

In stark contrast to his experiences in Providence, Joshua Verin received several grants of land after his return to Salem.[40] He also served in a variety of capacities at the First Church of Salem.[41] For example, on July 7, 1644, Joshua Verin was assigned to check on church attendance and attentiveness.[42] Clearly, he and his family remained members in good standing in both the town and church community. On December 3, 1647, the Church asked another member of the Verin family to speak with congregation members who were "under the Churches admonition for scandalous sin."[43] His brother, Hilliard, also served as county clerk. Verin evidently supported the right and duty of the church to enforce morality in

Figure 1.1 Reenactment, *He haled his wife with ropes to Salem*, M. Manchester

Salem. Jane Verin, however, continued to challenge the legitimacy of the Puritan hierarchy. Court records note that on October 4, 1638, she was "referd [sic] to Salem,"[44] and on December 25, 1638, Jane Verin was presented in court at Salem for absence from religious worship, shortly after her husband received a substantial land grant.[45] Church records indicate that Jane Verin was removed from the First Church of Salem on January 7, 1640.[46] This demonstrates that she continued to act on her conscience and to challenge the magistracy. Sometime in the interim, Joshua Verin sold his house to Zacheus Curtis. A note dated November 2, 1646, in the records of the Quarterly Court indicates that Curtis received a land grant from the town of Salem near the house he had bought of Joshua Verin at Brooksby.[47] In subsequent years, Verin made numerous efforts to receive compensation for his land in Providence, arguing that the land was lawfully his and therefore recoverable. In his letter to the town, Verin finds it "contrary to law, reason, and etiquette" that the town fathers would dispose of his property without his consent, exhorting them not to deal "worse with me that we dealt with the Indians."[48] During the next several years, he made several more fruitless attempts to get compensation for his property.

The issue of liberty of conscience also divided the larger Verin family. For example, Joshua Verin's brother and sister-in-law also challenged the authority of the First Church of Salem and later suffered admonishment, removal from the church, and physical punishment for their beliefs.[49] Between 1660 and 1663, for example, Philip Verin and his wife Joanna were presented many times for nonattendance at public worship; Phillip was also called to court to answer for "seditious and treasonable words against the government, in saying that they had murdered the dear saints and servants of God." Ultimately, Philip was set by the heels in stocks in November 1663 for denying the country's power to force any to come to the public worship.[50] Clearly, others beside Jane were willing to challenge both the civil and religious authorities in following their conscience. The entire Verin family was afflicted.

Like many during this era, Englishmen often moved several times within the English Atlantic world. In the case of Joshua Verin, remember that he, after having settled in Salem, removed himself to Providence, and then returned to Salem. Eventually, he resettled in the Barbados by September 1663. He appears on the register of St. James Parish, Barbados on December 20, 1679. Records reveal that he owned ten acres of land and eleven slaves.[51] This indicates that he had been accepted into the new congregational community there. He married Agnes Simpson at St. Michael's, Barbados on October 7, 1694, shortly before he died on March 15, 1695. The matter of Joshua Verin's lands resurfaced again in the spring of 1719. The town received a petition from Thomas and Agnes King of St. James parish, Barbados. Agnes King, the widow of Joshua Verin, was the executrix of his will. The couple appointed William Browne of Boston to represent them in their efforts to recover or receive compensation from the "estate of the above mentioned Joshua Verin deceased."[52] Jane Verin and her mother, the Widow Reeve, disappear from the historical record.

Like the extended Verin family, numerous non-conformists left England rather than submit to practices within the Church of England which they found reprehensible. A pamphlet published in London in 1630 entitled *The Planters' Plea*, strongly asserts a religious aim for the planting of the New England colonies, describing it as "a fit country for the seating of a colony for the propagation of religion."[53] The author argues that New England is particularly fit precisely because its soil is so poor, inviting those who "desire that Piety and godliness shall prosper accompanied with sobriety, justice, and love, let them choose a Country such as this is—which may yield sufficiency with hard labor and industry."[54] In a petition to the Privy Council in November 1632, Edward Winslow, an agent for the planters in New England, listed reasons for the colonists leaving England, noting that "disliking many things in practice here in respect of Church ceremony," they choose to leave rather than be accounted "troublers of it."[55] The Reverend John Cotton later reaffirmed this motivation when he observed, "the body of the members whom we receive, do in general profess, the reason of their coming over to us was, that they might be freed from the bondage of such humane inventions and ordinances as their souls groaned under ..."[56]

Who were the puritans?

Understanding the basic tenets of puritan theology, no less than their world view, provides the context for the disturbances in the relations between Joshua and Jane Verin. Ultimately, their marriage reflects in microcosm the larger stresses experienced by the communities of English settlers attempting to live out their faith in New England. These English transplants were devout Calvinists whose religious convictions had brought them increasingly into conflict with both the Church of England and the English Crown. Essentially accepting the Augustinian view of man's sinful nature, these followers of Calvin believed that human beings, because of their absolute depravity, were powerless to bring about their own salvation. God, in his mercy, selected or preordained those who would be saved and those who would suffer eternal damnation. Once chosen, these "elect" would be overcome with an irresistible call from God to repent and reform their lives in order to come closer to Christ.

Calvinism is a covenantal theology; the New Testament represented God's new covenant with his followers. Worship, therefore, was regulated according to the tenets of the New Testament. All of congregants were exhorted to read the Scriptures in order to hear the word of God directly. The Reverend John Geree published *The Character of an Old English Puritan, or Non-Conformist* in 1646. It presents a clear synopsis of the main tenets of Puritan theology and worship.

The Old English Puritan was such an[sic] one, that honored God above all, and under God gave everyone his due. His first care was to serve God, and therein he did not what was good in his own, but in God's sight, making the word of God the rule of his worship. He reverenced Authority keeping within its sphere, but durst not under pretence[sic] of subjection to the higher powers, worship God after the traditions of men.[57]

A strong sense of order is revealed in this passage. Everyone operates within his or her sphere, subject directly to the word of God, as opposed to the traditions of men. Thus, right interpretation of the Scripture was essential to right living. Later, Geree notes that, for the puritan, religion is an "engagement to duty." By this he means that every Christian must, in whatever station he or she is, be the best possible person. Thus, "best Christians should be best husbands, best wives, best parents, best children, best masters, best servants, best magistrates, best subjects, that the doctrine of God might be adorned, not blasphemed."[58] Puritanism balanced respect for the individual conscience with preservation of the well-being of the community. Geree notes that although the "first care was in the examination of himself: yet as an act of office or charity, he had an eye on others. He endeavored to have the scandalous cast out of communion."[59] This would explain why Roger Williams and his neighbours, while allowing Joshua Verin the right to exercise his conscience by not attending prayer services, stepped in as a community when Verin tried, with his "brutal carriage," to draw his wife into the same ungodliness with him.

Geree's pamphlet also provides valuable insights into how puritans formed congregations. According to their interpretation of the Scripture, the purest churches were those governed by elders, what Geree called an "aristocratical model" which he distinguished from a monarchical (by bishops) or democratical (by the people) model. Churches could admit none except those who "feared God; and in laboring those there were borne it in, might be born again into God." Many of the elements of worship laid out in John Geree's pamphlet formed the basis of puritan congregationalism and communitarianism. Notice the parallels Geree draws between the family and the church community: "He set up discipline in his family, as he desired it in the church, not only reproving but restraining vileness in his. He was conscientious of equity as well as piety knowing that unrighteousness is abomination as well as ungodliness."[60] Maintaining order in the family mirrored efforts to do the same within the church community; and this meant eliminating sinful behavior from both.

The nonconformists had come to view the Roman Catholic Church as absolutely corrupt and the focus of evil in the world, often referring to the church as "whorish." Their efforts to purify the Church of England of its popish influences resulted in persecution, including imprisonment, fines, and other sorts of officially sanctioned harassment. As a result, some fled to the Netherlands and many others attempted to flee to the New World, where they hoped they might live out their faith unmolested. William Bradford, in his *History of Plymouth Plantation, 1606–1646*, describes the effects of these injuries: "Religion hath been disgraced, the godly grieved, afflicted, persecuted, and many exiled, sundry have lost their lives in prisons and otherways."[61] According to Bradford, the Puritan Divine William Perkins exhorted the devout to repent, pointing out that although the Calvinists had been attempting to reform the Anglican Church from within, "in England at this day the man or woman that begins to profess Religion and to serve God, must resolve with himself to sustain mocks and injuries even as though he lived amongst the enemies of Religion."[62] Like William Perkins, many puritans, both separatist and non-separatist, had concluded that England was no longer a fit or safe place to actualize their new covenant with God.

Their hope was to establish a kind of Christian utopia. The covenantal and communitarian beliefs are apparent in "A Model of Christian Charity," a sermon delivered by Governor John Winthrop while still on the *Arabella* prior to their arrival in 1630. Professing themselves to be fellow members of Christ, he emphasizes that "it is by a mutual consent, through a special overvaluing providence" that this band of puritans "seek out a place of cohabitation and consortship under a due form of government both civil and ecclesiastical."[63] In other words, they were forming a covenant whose purpose was to promote the common good and whose form would include both civil and religious authority. From the earliest moments, then, the purpose is clear. Their goal was to set up a pure, uncorrupted Christian community to serve the Lord and to work for their salvation. Winthrop uses the metaphor of marriage to describe the nature of this covenantal relationship and to lay out both the rights and responsibilities, the curses and the blessings of that contract when he states,

> First, in regard of the more near bond of marriage between Him and us, wherein He hath taken us to be His, after the most strict and peculiar manner, which will make Him the more jealous of our love and obedience. So He tells the people of Israel, you only have I known of all the families of the earth, therefore will I punish you for your transgressions.[64]

As the "elect," they must live as saints. In effect, they had ratified this contractual relationship, and the Lord "will expect a strict performance of the articles contained in it."[65]

The "Model of Christian Charity" publicly commits this community of Puritans "to do justly, to love mercy, to walk humbly with our God."[66] If they obey and live for one another and if they put the common good ahead of private gain, they will enjoy the blessings of God's favor and they shall be as a "city upon a hill." A recent analysis has also emphasized

Winthrop's stress on reciprocal affections, labelled "puritan sympathy," as essential to the success of this venture.[67] Another study has argued that the concept of "brotherly affection" stressed by Winthrop reflects a patriarchal order based on sentimental relations. While women were important to the ultimate success of the puritan experiment in New England, Winthrop, it is argued, assumed the "city upon a hill" would be populated by "godly patriarchs joined together in 'brotherly love.'"[68] Further, self-conscious and purposeful, Winthrop and his followers recognized that if they failed to live according to God's precepts or in some other way were to "deal falsely with our God in this work we have undertaken," not only would God withdraw his favor from them, but they would be "made a story and a by-word through the world."[69] It is clear, even at this early stage, that enforced orthodoxy will be the rule. Failure was unacceptable. At the same time, however, it is important to note that the Puritans distinguished between the "True Church," that is the community of believers as God sees it that is invisible to humans, and the "Visible Church." Were New England churches that had not separated themselves from the Church of England corrupted or defiled as a result? Disputes arose both in England and the New England colonies about questions of Church membership: Who should be admitted to communion? What about those who professed to be Christians but had not testified to a faith experience—were they entitled to pray with the elect? Later, some, like Roger Williams and others, also raised questions regarding infant baptism. The Baptists and Quakers further complicated these debates.

Inspired by the Scripture, the newly arrived puritans created congregations led by their elected ministers, those deemed the ablest to explicate the word of God or to guide individuals in their attempts to reform and live exemplary Christian lives. Their focus was on Christian duty—to live out their faith to the best of their ability, each according to his or her station. This would explain the fidelity that the Verins and some 20 others showed to Roger Williams, the minister whom they were willing to following into the wilderness.

Early laws sought to regulate behavior to preserve Christian godliness. Thus, laws could punish civil infractions as well as religious infractions, such as taking the Lord's name in vain. Attendance at church was required by law, and tax revenues were used to support the churches. The interaction of civil and ecclesiastical functions can also be seen in the way the government supported the church. In order to be accepted into a congregation, a puritan needed to testify to a faith experience or demonstrate evidence of conversion. Only full church members could vote. Michael Winship emphasizes the purposefulness of Winthrop and his peers in creating a "godly republic" to serve Massachusetts congregationalism. In addition to purifying the membership of the congregated churches, restricting the right to vote to church members "purified the political nation of the ungodly."[70] Rather than seeing these community-based values as an infringement upon the rights of the individual, puritans cherished liberty, which they viewed as "a pre-condition to the construction of godly community—the opportunity to fuse Christian piety with service to the public good."[71] It is evident that the majority of the English families, at least in the early years of emigration, took their Christian duty very seriously. "Communal peace and reciprocal charity were the ends of liberty, not alternatives to the protection of individual freedom."[72] As one study points out, it was no accident that until 1672, "the title page of the code book [of the General Court] often carried a quote from Romans 13:12—'Whosoever therefore resisteth the power, resisteth the ordinance of God: and they that resist shall receive to themselves damnation.'"[73] Another analysis examines court depositions to determine the extent to which seventeenth-century New Englanders acted as their "brothers' keepers."[74] Privacy was difficult to achieve, and most agreed that it was in the interests of the community to maintain good relations with one's neighbors.

The Puritans were by no means a homogenous group. The differences among these Congregationalists are an important factor in understanding the rift that would develop not only between Jane and Joshua Verin, but within the larger extended Verin family. The Separatists who founded Plymouth acted on their conscience and withdrew from the national church to protest what they considered its oppression and corruption. Earlier, many of them had fled from England and set up a small community of believers in Holland. The majority of the puritans who immigrated to Massachusetts Bay, on the other hand, were non-separatist Congregationalists. Prior to their departure from England, many of them continued to take communion in the church. At the time of their departure, John Winthrop and others wrote a farewell, addressed to "Reverend Fathers and Brethren," in which they stressed that it was their honor to call the Church of England "our dear mother"; they parted their native country with "much sadness of heart and many tears in our eyes."[75]

Cotton Mather would later assert that Roger Williams was so intent on this separation that he refused "... to *communicate* with the church of Boston, because they would not make a public and solemn declaration of repentance for their communicating with the church of England, while they were in the realm of England."[76] According to Mather's analysis, Williams was "violent" in his insistence that the civil magistrate might not punish breaches of the first table in the laws of the Ten Commandments.[77] In other words, for Williams, separatism included both official separation of the churches of New England from those of the Church of England *and* a separation of the civil and ecclesiastical functions among their governors.

Patterns of English migration

The Verins were representative of other emigrants who left Wiltshire County in the west of England for the New World. There are two distinct phases to the Great Migration: the first phase (from 1628 to 1634) when the number of emigrants was relatively few and the second phase (from 1634–1640) which brought in the bulk of immigrants and has been called the "Laudian Migration," named for the period after 1633 when Archbishop Laud began his systematic persecution of English Puritans.[78] Roger Williams arrived in the first wave of immigration, but the Verin family arrived during the latter phase.

While the profile of the typical Wiltshire emigrant in the 1630s would have been male and single, a "substantial minority" was married couples travelling with their children. Most of them were young, ranging in age from 16 to 30. The unmarried migrants were usually servants or urban artisans, drawn primarily from Wiltshire's two largest urban centers, Salisbury (New Sarum) and Marlborough. Nearly 60 per cent were related to one or more of their fellow colonists either directly or through marriage, demonstrating that "kinship ties were strong among the group bound for New England."[79] A survey of the economic conditions in Wiltshire county during the sixteenth and seventeenth centuries reveals that a downturn in the western broadcloth industry was not the primary motivating force for Wiltshire emigration as only 10 per cent of the 1630s group listed occupations in the textile or textile-related trades. Instead, the dramatic growth of Wiltshire's towns because of natural increase and in-migration (as attested by court records) are key to understanding why Wiltshire County was such a numerically significant source of emigrants. It became more and more difficult as artisans and craftsman competed to find work in the crowded towns. Further, a majority of Wiltshire's emigrants were from communities "whose inhabitants had already demonstrated a willingness to break with the bonds of community."[80] At that time, "Wiltshire towns and pasture-farming regions, centers of seventeenth-century emigration, were also centers of seventeenth-century religious radicalism."[81] This reinforces an earlier study that concluded that given the "unusually strong appeal of non-conformity to town dwellers and artisans," it would not be surprising or unusual to find that the "disgruntled tradesman" and the disgruntled puritan were often one and the same.[82] Prior to the English Civil War, migrants had to provide the royal authorities an oath of loyalty to the crown and of conformity to the established church prior to their departure. Though many surely avoided this process, well over 2000 names were recorded in such a manner.[83] An analysis of these lists, in particular those from 1637, demonstrates the interconnectedness of economic and religious motivations as most were both tradesmen and nonconformist puritans. Other sources support this link. For example, one official in Suffolk lamented to Archbishop Laud that anyone who failed in business or found himself unable to pay a debt could simply "cry religion" and move to New England. Later, John Cotton would remark on the "inadvertent Puritan" who came to New England for reasons other than religious, and then discovered "that grace, which they sought not for."[84] The men of the Verin family were all tradesman, and they were all non-conformist puritans.

The Verins were typical of the other passengers on the *James*; while Philip and Joshua both listed their occupation as roper, Joshua's brother Philip was a wheelwright, and Hilliard Verin was a scrivener and merchant.[85] Some of the other occupations listed on the passenger list include maltster, weaver, taylor [sic], and surgeon. The punitive measures taken against English puritans made it difficult for them to make a living and follow their conscience. For this reason, one observer noted "... there be many here that incline much to that country." These included "young men of rare gifts, who cannot get any lawful entry, as also professors of good means who labor to keep themselves pure and undefiled."[86] Roger Williams himself, writing to the daughter of his mentor, Sir Edward Coke, affirms this as the reason for his emigration. "It was as bitter as death to me ... when Bishop Laud pursued me out of this land, and my conscience was persuaded against the national Church and ceremonies, and bishops ..."[87] Even the gentry were affected. Sir Henry Vane "as good as lost his eldest son ... who is gone to New England for conscience sake."[88] There were family connections among these as well, the most obvious being the entire extended Verin family that made the trip on the *James*. Edmund Batter, a maltster was born in 1608 in New Sarum. He was related to the Verins by marriage as he was Hilliard Verin's brother-in-law.[89] Both he and another New Sarum passenger, Thomas Antrum, a weaver, were relatively well-to-do—each brought a servant with them.[90]

The male members of the Verin family, including Joshua, his father, and his brother Hilliard, all became landowners, members of the First Church of Salem, and held various positions of authority in Salem.[91] While both Joshua and Jane were admitted to communion in the First Church of Salem, in the two years prior to their arrival in Providence, Jane and her mother, following the example of their minister, Roger Williams, refused to worship with the congregation and later denied the churches of the Bay Colony were true churches because they had not separated from the Church of England.[92] Apparently some members of their congregation had returned to England and, while there, had heard ministers and received communion in the Church of England. Once they returned to Salem, these travellers were allowed once again to receive communion.[93] Williams and his followers condemned these practices as corrupt. Williams was a charismatic and persuasive preacher. Williams' contemporaries agreed that he was beloved. "In Salem every person loved Mr. Williams. All valued his friendship."[94] According to the nineteenth century historian, Charles Upham, the congregants of the First Church of Salem were loyal and steadfast in their support of Williams, even after he had been admonished and then banished for his challenges to the authority of the magistracy. Upham asserts the people of Salem

adhered to him long and faithfully ... And when at last he was sentenced by the General Court to banishment from the colony, on account of his principles, we cannot but admire the fidelity of that friendship which prompted many members of his congregation to accompany him in his exile and partake of his fortunes when an outcast upon the earth.[95]

It is entirely possible that the Verins left Salem because they were about to face the consequences of *Jane Verin's* challenges to the ministry in Salem. In fact, once in Providence, it was *Joshua Verin* who refused to attend religious services. In his letter to John Winthrop, Roger Williams notes that Joshua Verin had "refused to hear the word with us ([for which] we molested him not for) this twelve month."[96] Jane continued her defiance of authority by disobeying her husband and attending prayer services with Roger Williams and the other faithful, suffering a life-threatening beating as a consequence.

In defying church authorities in Salem, and later defying her husband's authority in Providence, Jane Verin not only challenged puritan notions about appropriate behaviour for women, but her actions threatened to undermine the very basis of family and community structure. Gender was central to understanding a person's rightful place in puritan society; in their theology as well as in their social and spatial arrangements, New Englanders were "people of the word."[97] By making sermons the center-piece of ritual life, "Puritan thinkers demanded heightened respect for the voices of godly ministers, that is, for the voices of eminent men."[98] Thus, when a woman like Jane Verin challenged the legitimacy of the First Church in Salem or of the other Bay Colony churches, she also challenged the authority of the male hierarchy who supported them.

Stephen Foster defines puritanism as a continuing interaction among magistrates, ministers, and laity dedicated to creating a godly society by imposing their version of social and ecclesiastical discipline on their neighbors.[99] In order to accomplish this, the puritans set up a state church system. Roger Thompson, a British historian, agrees that the English puritans were essentially reacting against the anti-Calvinist measures of Archbishop Laud. He argues "they emigrated to conserve the purer, pre-Laudian faith and liturgy, and to return to the primitive."[100] His study of 2,000 Anglian emigrants to New England during the 1630s has found that

[T]he great majority had come from long-settled ancestries and person-ally stable backgrounds. The trauma of uprooting and transatlantic relocation was minimized by their moving almost exclusively in groups, by their personal and resident longevity in New England and by their rapid sinking of roots there. They were, quite literally, settlers. Few of the different occupational groups betrayed a zest for modern-ization. Preservation of traditional norms and values was the aim of their errand into the wilderness.[101]

These migrants were backward looking, wishing to recreate the early Christian communities—they were traditionalists who wished to restore traditions that had been befouled by the corruption in the Church of England. In New England, in fact, Puritans had "the possibility of ideological control unimaginable in England" and could "attempt to achieve a previously theoretical commitment to uniformity through state power."[102] Civil power reinforced ecclesiastical authority. "Civil government, the Puritans believed, became an absolute necessity after the fall of man. The sin of the first Adam had so vitiated human nature that family governors could not be trusted to maintain the order that God had commanded."[103] These structures of control were not well established in the Providence community which was still in its infancy.

A new community in Providence

According to Roger Williams' recollection, he gave permission to William Harris, "then poor and destitute," John Smith (banished also), Francis Wickes, and a lad of Richard Waterman's named Thomas Angell to accompany him to Providence.[104] Although it is not entirely clear whether Jane or Joshua Verin initiated the decision to accompany Roger Williams in his exile, remember that Verin counted himself among the "six which Cam[e] first."[105] In a community in its early stages of formation, Joshua Verin would encounter many other non-conformist men whose viewpoints and experiences would determine their level of sympathy toward him.

Roger Williams purchased the land for his new settlement from two local sachems, Canonicus and Miantinomi, sometime in the spring of 1636, although the earliest record of this transaction does not appear in the records until a memorandum dated March 24, 1637/1638.[106] According to one estimate, there were 24 men, women, and children in the settlement by September of 1636.[107] There he and his small company cleared land, farmed, and engaged primarily in trade with the local Indians. The deed contains the list of thirteen original proprietors.[108]

The structure of this early community reflected the commitment to Christian liberty by these early Providence settlers, who relied on equality to roster a sense of community.[109] The first land distribution of house lots, fields, and commons, was divided equally among the proprietors. A study of the transformation of the law and economy in early America distinguishes between the head right system of land distribution in the southern colonies and the type of concentrated settlement that was promoted in New England by granting large tracts of land to proprietors who would then allocate the land to male heads of households. This distribution of house and farm lots, as well as rights to pasturage on common lands to the so-called "original proprietors" tended to the formation of towns.

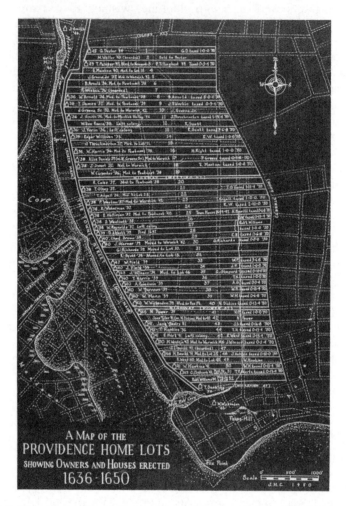

Figure 1.2 "Providence Home Lots, 1636–1650, Providence," VMO11_02_01043, John Hitchens Cady Research Scrapbooks Collection, Courtesy of Providence Public Library

Often, covenants were signed laying out in specific language the economic and civic rights associated with land ownership.

> In time, the arrival of new settlers who could purchase land but not shares in the proprietorship and the coming of age of sons of proprietors who similarly were excluded from the benefits of proprietorship—the most valuable of which was the right to share in future land distributions—caused significant problems for town governance and citizenship.[110]

In a letter to John Winthrop during late summer 1636, Williams points out that the colony had neither a patent nor any magistracy. What little government that existed tended to be very informal. He notes, for example, that "Hitherto, the masters of families have ordinarily met once a fortnight and consulted about our common peace, watch, and with mutual consent have finished all matters with speed and peace."[111] At this point, this meant that unmarried property owners had no political voice in the affairs of the community. Many of the single men and some of the men who had arrived in Providence after the original six began to clamor for a greater influence in the community's political and economic life. These were supported in principle by some of the married "masters of households" such as Joshua Verin. Williams writes that Verin had "openly in Towne meeting more than once professed to hope for and long for a better Government then the Country hath yet ..."[112] Bowing to the "murmurings of after comers,"[113] Williams wrote up a civil compact on August 20, 1637, signed by thirteen male inhabitants, that reads as follows:

> We whose names are hereunder, desirous to inhabit in the town of Providence, do promise to subject ourselves in active or passive obedience, to all such orders or agreements as shall be made for public good of our body, in an orderly way, by the major consent of the inhabitants, masters of families, incorporated together into a town fellowship, and such others whom they shall admit unto them only in civil things.[114]

By promising to obey all agreements that were made for the common good, the signatories bound themselves to a civil compact, in this case the "town fellowship." Williams later recalled that this action had brought the original proprietors into "a oneness by arbitration."[115] The puritan emphasis on covenants is very much evident in the crafting of this civil arrangement. It should also be noted that of these original thirteen, five men were unmarried in the summer of 1638.[116] Marital status was an important factor in determining the status and place of a Puritan man in seventeenth-century New England. Civil and domestic authority were joined as a result of the marriage covenant—men assumed "governorship" of their households (note the use of the term "masters" of families in the Covenant of 1637) *and* became fully enfranchised.[117] Several of the younger, single men, many of whom had found it difficult to earn a living because of their non-conformist beliefs, were eager to shelter in Providence, but soon they began to pressure Williams to admit them into his "fellowship of purchase." According to several accounts, William Harris led this contingent. Williams bowed to pressure and agreed that "the place should be for such as were destitute (especially for Conscience Sake)."[118] By October 1638, Williams conveyed land he had received from the sachems to twelve people, an act which also admitted them into the fellowship of vote.[119] The town began to take shape; 52 house lots had been laid out along the Great Salt Marsh. Each proprietor also received a six-acre lot for planting and other lots were designated for pasturage.[120]

The proprietors

Biographical sketches of some of these "first comers" can be useful in understanding why a majority of them supported Roger Williams in condemning Verin's behaviour and agreeing to his disenfranchisement. Their origins, family connections, and experiences can, conversely, also help the reader understand why some opposed Roger Williams and disagreed with the punishment meted out to Verin. The records indicate only that a "majority of them" voted to discard Verin of his civil freedom. This fact is indisputable, but the exact names of those who voted against and those who voted in support of this action are unknown. It remains for the historian to put together as comprehensive set of facts as possible regarding the proprietors. Discerning patterns, connections, and relationships amongst them will enable us to guess, with some accuracy, as to who voted for Joshua Verin and who was predisposed to agree with Roger Williams and Jane Verin.

Thomas Angell was born on May 1, 1618, in St. Albans, London, the son of James Angell. He was thirteen years old when he embarked on the *Lyon* in 1631 as an apprentice to Roger Williams. Likewise, he accompanied Roger Williams to Providence in 1636, having spent the previous winter at Seekonk. He was a signer of the Compact of 1637.[121] He was twenty years old and unmarried in the summer of 1638 when the Verin case was being considered. He married Alice Ashton on April 10, 1643, with whom he had two sons and five daughters. His sister-in-law, Mary, was married to Thomas Olney. His lot abutted the Olney holding on the south.[122] The Olneys were close friends and supporters of Roger Williams and well respected and influential both in Massachusetts Bay and in Providence. By 1655, Angell appeared as one of the freemen and was appointed constable. He died sometime before September 18, 1694, when his will was proved.[123] Given his close association with Roger Williams, it can be safely assumed that Angell would have supported his mentor in the Verin matter, had he been able to vote.

William Arnold was born in 1587 in Cheselbourne, Dorset to Nicholas and Alice (Gully) Arnold. He married Christanna Peak by 1611 in the Ilchester Parish, Somerset.[124] They had four children between 1611 and 1622. They emigrated to Massachusetts in 1635, setting sail from Dartmouth on May 1 and arriving in New England on June 24, 1635. They settled first in Hingham, where Arnold received a house lot of two acres on September 18, 1635.[125] According to Providence Town Records, Arnold was one of the original six who accompanied Roger Williams to Providence and one of the original proprietors.[126] The family history written by his son, Benedict, dates the family's arrival in Providence on April 20, 1636. Arnold clearly supported Williams' position on the separation of churches; Winthrop placed him in the group of those who had left Massachusetts so as "not to offend God in order to please men."[127] A biographical sketch prepared by the New England Historic Genealogical Society reveals Arnold had education sufficient to compose lengthy letters in support of his positions in land disputes.

Not all of the men supported Roger Williams on the decision to disenfranchise Joshua Verin; it was a contentious and divisive issue. An entry in John Winthrop's journal describes William Arnold as "a witty man of their company" who argued strenuously that when he consented to Williams' dictate that no man should be molested for his conscience, he never intended that "it should extend to the breach of any ordinance of God, such as the subjugation of wives to their husbands, etc. and gave divers reasons against it."[128] Arnold repeated his assertion that they had all left Massachusetts because "they would not offend God to please men." He asked, would they "now break an ordinance and commandment of God to please women?"[129] Arnold also took issue with the argument that Joshua Verin had denied his wife her liberty of conscience, arguing rather, that it wasn't Jane Verin's desire to "go so oft from home, but only Mr. Williams and others." He was rather directly criticizing Williams' influence over Jane Verin. Arnold concluded by declaring that censuring Verin for denying his wife's liberty of conscience violated their own rules, "for what Verin did that he did out of conscience."[130] Although Arnold was a separatist Congregationalist, he did not support Jane Verin's defiance of her husband's authority. Later, Williams wrote to Governor Winthrop complaining about Joshua Verin and William Arnold who had, according to Williams, "most falsely and slanderously ... complotted together ... many odious accusations in writing."[131] Williams assumed their goal was to render him "odious both to the king's majesty" and to Winthrop himself.[132]

Shortly after the Verins and the Widow Reeves returned to Salem, several of these dissenters removed themselves from Providence and organized a new settlement in Pawtuxet later in 1638. These included William and Benedict Arnold and their families, William Harris, William Carpenter, and Robert Coles.[133] One can surmise that these men would have agreed with William Arnold's objections to the censure of Joshua Verin. They probably also agreed with Joshua Verin on the need for a more orderly government. On July 27, 1640, William Arnold was one of those who signed the "constitution" of Providence; and by 1642, these same men attempted to place Pawtuxet back under the jurisdiction of Massachusetts Bay. Perhaps they agreed with Joshua Verin that it was desirable to have more government than they presently enjoyed. Governor Winthrop wrote a letter to "our neighbors of Providence" on October 28, 1642, in which he asserts,

... whereas William Arnold of Patuxet [sic] and Robert Cole & others have lately put themselves & their families, lands & estates under the protection & government of this jurisdiction & have since complained to us that you have since (under pretense of a late purchase from the Indians gone about to deprive them of their lawful interest confirmed by 4 years' possession, & otherwise to molest them: We thought good therefore to write to you on their behalf to give you notice that they and their lands etc., being under our jurisdiction, we are to maintain them in their lawful right.[134]

It appears that Roger Williams and his supporters sought to punish those who opposed them, including Joshua Verin and William Arnold, by rescinding their rights to land ownership. This precipitated a hailstorm of controversy. Arnold (and Verin) was subsequently involved in numerous land disputes with his former neighbors in Providence. The colonial records for Providence and Rhode Island and Williams' correspondence are replete with references to these disputes over the next several decades, as well as numerous purchases and sales of property in Pawtuxet and Providence. Arnold was still living in Pawtuxet when King Phillip's War broke out in 1675. William Arnold would not leave his home, despite the pleas of his neighbors who wanted him to take refuge either in Providence with his son Benedict, or at some other safe haven. Ultimately, his son Stephen went to see him and convinced him to take refuge with his garrison. The Historic and Genealogical Records place his death somewhere "... after the beginning of King Phillip's war and before November 3, 1677," when, Benedict Arnold, described himself as "eldest son and heir of William Arnold late of Pautexett in the said Colony deceased."[135]

William Arnold's oldest son, Benedict, was born in England on December 21, 1615. He married Damalies, the daughter of Stukely Wescott (one of the other original proprietors) on December 17, 1640, with whom he had numerous sons and daughters.[136] According to legend, Benedict Arnold became the richest man in the colony, benefitting enormously from his "thorough acquaintance with the manners as well as language of the aborigines" which resulted in his becoming the "most effective auxiliary in negotiations with them."[137] He served in a number of elected posts, including President of the colony. As mentioned earlier, he removed his family to Pawtuxet, along with his father and others who had disagreed with Williams and his supporters regarding the Verin decision and about the distribution of land. It is unclear whether or not the fact that he was married to Stukely Wescott's daughter has any bearing on his stance on the issue. But almost certainly, family loyalty would have played a key role in Benedict Arnold's decision to support Joshua Verin.

Like Joshua Verin, William Carpenter was also a Wiltshire lad, having been born around 1610 in Amesbury, the son of Richard Carpenter. He arrived in New England some time in 1635. Some of the records indicate he married Elizabeth Peake Arnold, the daughter of William Arnold in 1635.[138] He was in Providence by 1637, when he received a land grant.[139] There is no evidence that the two families were acquainted prior to their departure from England. The couple had six children. He was an original member of the First Baptist Church and signed the Compact of 1640. He and his family moved to Pawtuxet in 1642. He was elected an Assistant in 1665 and took the oath of allegiance in 1666. He died in Pawtuxet on September 7, 1685. On the one hand, the fact that he was one of the original members of the First Baptist Church would indicate sympathy for Jane Verin's right to act on her conscience. On the other hand, as a member of William Arnold's extended household, and as a master of a household himself, it can be assumed that William Carpenter joined his father-in-law in opposition to Roger Williams and his supporters in the matter of the Verins, perhaps because he too preferred to preserve the established order.

Robert Cole was born around 1605 and arrived in Roxbury with the "first company" of the Winthrop fleet in 1630. He was later fined 5 marks for drinking too much aboard ship.[140] Once arrived, he was admitted to the Roxbury Church as member number eight and as a freeman on May 18, 1631. He married Mary Cole sometime in 1630, as she was admitted to the church as member number 34.[141] Despite being elected as a representative of Roxbury to the General Court in 1632, Cole struggled with alcohol abuse. He was cited several times for public drunkenness. Indeed, in March of 1633, he was temporarily disenfranchised for his intemperance.[142] This clearly was a burden on his wife as revealed in the following passage: "God also wrought upon her heart ... after coming to N.E., but after her husband's excommunication & falls she did too much favor his life, by reason of his unsettledness & removing from place to place."[143]

Cole appears to have reformed his life sometime prior to his wife's death. He received a land grant of 300 acres in Salem on December 28, 1635.[144] There he must have met Roger Williams, for James Savage's entry for Cole indicates that when he "went at last to Providence, was reform[ed] in earnest."[145] He is identified as "one of the principal men of Providence on December 22, 1636, when Roger Williams sold his Indian deed to the town's inhabitants." In 1637, he married his second wife, Mary Hawkshurst, with whom he had four sons and two daughters. He appears on the list of proprietors of Pawtuxet on October 8, 1638. He went on to become one of the founders of the First Baptist Church. He died before October 18, 1654.[146]

One would assume that Cole would have supported Roger Williams in the Verin decision, given the apparent influence that Williams had on Cole's reformation and new life. Additionally, given his future role in the founding of the Baptist church, one would expect him to be sympathetic to Jane Verin's plight. But it appears Cole disagreed with his mentor about the Verins. As evidenced by the records of the Arnold dispute with

Williams, Cole agreed with William Arnold and his supporters, moved his family to Pawtuxet, and later joined with them in their attempt to place Pawtuxet back under the jurisdiction of Massachusetts Bay—a clear rejection of Williams' authority. Although his position regarding Joshua Verin is ambiguous and subject to interpretation, one can surmise that for Robert Cole, maintaining order trumped sympathy for any individual woman.

John Greene was born in Gillinghan, Dorset. He was a surgeon who practiced in Salisbury, Wiltshire. He arrived in Boston in 1635 with his wife and five children on the *James*, the same ship as the Verin family.[147] In 1637, he was fined for speaking "contemptuously" to the magistrates. Subsequently, he became one of the original proprietors of Providence, living two house lots north of the Widow Reeves, Jane Verin's mother. He married Alice Beggarly Daniell, who also appears on the map of Providence Home Lots. One source accuses him of "marr[y]ing wife of Beggerly, who had no divorce."[148] He joined the First Baptist church, and in 1642, became one of the original proprietors of Warwick. According to Savage's *Genealogical Dictionary*, Greene "partook largely in the exertions of Gorton and his friends to obtain security for their worldly as well as spiritual rights." He went to London in 1644 to negotiate successfully for Narraganset, of which Warwick was the chief settlement. He died in later December 1658.[149]

It is highly likely that John Greene supported the decision to discipline Joshua Verin for his violent behavior toward his wife. Like Jane Verin, he had already been punished in Massachusetts Bay for challenging the magistracy. As a surgeon who lived in close proximity to the Verins, he would have been one of the first to be called to deal with her severe injuries. Given his subsequent decision to join the Baptist Church, which indicates his fundamental agreement with the right of the individual to liberty of conscience, including that of women, it would be surprising if he did *not* support Williams in his censure of Verin.

The brothers, William and Thomas Harris, came from Bristol. William Harris was born in 1609. Both brothers were on the *Lyon* in 1631, the same as Roger Williams. Both arrived in Providence in the spring of 1636, among the original proprietors. According to Roger Williams' recollection, William Harris was destitute and pressured Williams to grant him an allotment. As mentioned earlier, William Harris was among those who "pretending Religion, wearied me with his desire."[150] It was in accordance with this resolution that, in October 1638, Williams executed to twelve persons, including William Harris, a conveyance of the land received from the sachems, "unto my loving friends and neighbors ... and such others as the major part of us shall admit into the same fellowship of vote with us."[151] Each of these twelve "first-comers" paid thirty shillings "towards a town stock," and it was further agreed that Roger Williams should have thirty pounds as a "loving consideration and gratuity" for his "great charge and travel" in the matter. Of this he received "£28 in broken parcels in five years."[152]

It is probable that the brothers disagreed about what do about Joshua Verin. Records indicate that Thomas Harris was whipped in 1658, claiming the liberty to speak in assembly and preaching Quakerism. Thus, he would most likely earlier have supported Jane Verin's liberty of conscience and been considered part of Roger Williams' faction. He, together with Roger Williams and Thomas Olney, was chosen a judge of the Justices Court in 1665.[153] In contrast, William Harris moved to Pawtuxet and joined with William Arnold, opposing Roger Williams on the Verin issue. William Harris was at the center of a "bitter controversy" that resulted in the division of all the planters into two factions, one of which moved to Warwick.[154] One of the issues, apparently, was who would have the right to land at Pawtuxet, situated between Warwick and Providence; more specifically, the dispute involved William Harris, who declared himself to be "Always Ready, to divide, because, by division, of the same, Each man, shall possess, his Own. 2ly, And be, in the better, Capacity, to possess."[155] In a series of transactions with local Narragansett sachems, Harris extended the boundaries of the grant that Roger Williams had verbally negotiated years earlier. Further, his deeds applied English legal and economic terms to the definitions of ownership and transfer. Under the terms of the new deeds, the local Indians would no longer have rights to the use of the land.[156] In 1669, Roger Williams clarified the terms of the original agreements signed with the sachems. In a series of letters written in 1669, he emphasized that it was his special relationship with the Narragansett sachems, based on living with them, learning their language, and trading with them, that enabled him to acquire the land at Providence and Pawtucket in the first place.[157] In his letter, Williams defends his understanding of the bounds of the land grant he had received: "by the Sachems' grant to me of an abundant Sufficiency to myself and my Friends. I never understood infinite and boundless matters, no nor 20 miles, but what was accounted sufficient for any plantation or Towne in the Country."[158]

William Harris, like many of his peers, appealed for redress of his grievances frequently throughout the seventeenth century, mostly in disputes over land.[159] An Assembly of Commissioners and an Inquest or Jury arrived in Providence in November 1677 to hear Harris's complaint against Williams. In his answer to the charges, Williams laments the fact that "a self- seeking contentious fool, who has long afflicted this town and colony, should now, with his unreasonable and unjust clamor afflict" the Council with his contentious behavior.[160] He points out that the Commissioners had been satisfied with his version of the events.[161] Williams also notes that it was his "soul's desire" to do the natives good.[162] Moreover, it was out of pity that he gave William Harris permission to accompany him to Providence. His letter stresses that God had furnished him with "advantages which Wm. H. nor scarce any in New England had."[163] In his version of the events, Williams recalls that he had yielded to Harris and others' pressure to admit them "into [the] fellowship of my purchase." So, everyone who was admitted paid 30s toward a town stock for Providence. He furnished the same opportunity for the Pawtuxet holding, pointing out that "for then that monstrous bound or business of upstream without Limits, was not thought of."[164] The Assembly of Commissioners exonerated Williams of the charges. According to one legal scholar, the right to appeal a decision or judgment by a governing body "signaled the acceptance of authority—whether of God, the governor, or, more questionably, the English—in return for the promise of a just decision."[165] If this is true, then Harris clearly rejected Roger Williams' claims to authority, disagreeing with him not only about Joshua Verin, but over issues of law and land as well. In fact, he left for England in 1678 to "support the cause of Pautuxet[sic] proprietors," embarking from Boston on the *Unity*. Unfortunately for Harris, he was seized by pirates and sold into slavery in Barbary. Despite his advanced age (he was 68 years old at the time), he was not redeemed until a year later. He made his way across Spain and France, arriving at the London house of his friend, John Stokes, in 1680, only to die three days later.[166] Roger Williams most likely did *not* mourn his passing.

Ezekiel Holliman was born in Tring, County Hertford. He arrived first to Dedham in 1634 and then moved to Salem.[167] He was fined in 1638 for not attending church and preaching heresy. He is listed as one of the original proprietors of Providence where he married his second wife Mary, widow of Isaac Sweet, sometime in 1638. His wife, sometimes called Margery, too, had been cast out of the Church at Salem, "perhaps for carrying out the opinions of her husband."[168] He baptized Roger Williams and was one of the founding members of the First Baptist Church. According to Savage, his wife Margery was of the "same condemnation." By 1640, he had moved to Portsmouth (where Anne Hutchinson and her fellow Antinomians had settled) and where he operated a grist mill and "other works on the Potowomut ... burnt by the Indians in Philip's War, 1675."[169] Both Holliman and his wife-to-be were willing to challenge the magistracy in Salem, just like Jane Verin. It is also evident that Holliman was the type of husband who not only condoned, but endorsed, his wife acting on her conscience. He had also supported her when her conscience led her to challenge the ministers of their congregation in Salem. In fact, the Hollimans not only knew Jane Verin and her mother, but as mentioned earlier, Margery Holliman was named, along with Margery Reeves (Jane Verin's mother) as having "refused to worship with the congregation from 1635 to 1638 and the latter two women denied that the churches of the Bay colony were true churches."[170] The Hollimans would certainly have been more sympathetic to Jane Verin's plight as opposed to Joshua Verin. Their ultimate conversion to the Baptist faith would also signal their willingness to support a woman like Verin, who acted on her individual conscience.

Thomas James was born in Lincolnshire around 1593 and baptized on October 5, 1595. He was the son of John and Alice James. He received his degrees from Cambridge at Emmanuel College and preached in Lincoln County.[171] He married his second wife, Elizabeth, sometime before 1632. Along with two sons from his first marriage, the young couple immigrated to the New World on the *William and Francis* on June 5, 1632, settling first in Boston where they were both admitted to the Boston church as members numbers 149 and 150.[172] In October, they received permission to participate in the organizing of a new church at Charlestown, the same church where their first son, John, was baptized on January 9, 1632/3. Thomas James was the first pastor of the new Charlestown church. According to the records, some of the members of the congregation began to "question their fact of breaking from Boston," an argument that grew to "such a principle of conscience among them," that even when other ministers were called in to mediate, no agreement could be reached.[173] John Winthrop describes James as a "melancholic man, and full of causeless jealousies." His temperament was so bad that, according to Winthrop, that he had a severe falling out with his congregants.[174]

Winthrop's journal entry indicates that the congregants wanted to avoid "extremities," but "if he persisted, etc. the church should cast him out."[175] One account states that "a spirit of discord or jealousy was so active, that as early as March 1636 he was dismissed."[176] Apparently his uncompromising position had offended many of his brethren. James and his family moved to Providence some time in 1637. During that year, Providence town records show that Roger Williams had laid out the lines for grass and meadow lands and house lots, including for "our neighbor James."[177] His Providence neighbours seem to have had a kinder view of him. William Harris described him as "a man of learning and wisdom."[178]

According to the records, James also had some medical knowledge.[179] The James family sold their property in Providence to William Field on March 20, 1639, and they moved to New Haven where he was granted a lot in November 1639, followed by freeman status in 1640.[180] In 1642, James was one of several ministers doing missionary work in Virginia, before returning to England. He died in Needham Market, Suffolk in February 1682, his wife Elizabeth having predeceased him. When it comes to the matter of Joshua and Jane Verin, James is of interest for several reasons. Having been a member of the Boston Church, he and his wife would have been acquainted with William and Mary Oliver, Robert and Phillipa Harding, William and Mary Dyer, and Richard and Jane Hawkins. These families had all been admonished by their churches in England and would in 1638 come to Rhode Island with the Antinomians after being banished from the church in Massachusetts. Given his difficulties with his parishioners in Charlestown, it is not unreasonable to assume he was uncompromising in his views on nonconformism and rejection of any church that had not completed separated itself from the English church, a view which Jane Verin shared. Further, as a physician, he might well have been called together with John Greene to minister to Jane Verin after her husband beat her so severely. Given that James was described as a "physician, a strong friend of Williams, [and] a good servant in the cause of humanity," it is highly likely that Mr. James would have voted to disenfranchise Joshua Verin.[181] In addition, James was one of the founding members of the First Baptist Church; his Baptist leanings might also have predisposed him to be sympathetic to Jane Verin. Ultimately, Thomas James spent a year in Virginia as a missionary; he returned to England to serve as a minister at Needham in County Suffolk, where he lived the remainder of his days. He died in 1687 at the age of 85.

Thomas Olney was born in St. Albans, Hertfordshire, England on June 6, 1600, the son of Thomas and Mary (Small) Olney.[182] He married Mary Ashton on September 16, 1629. He was a shoemaker by trade. He received a "Permit to Emigrate to New England" on April 2, 1635 and arrived on *The Planter* to Salem in 1635 with his wife, and their children Thomas and Epenetus, ages three and one.[183] By all accounts, Thomas Olney was well respected by his peers. He was appointed surveyor shortly after his arrival and made a freeman in 1637. That same year, Salem Quarterly Court records indicate that he served as a member of the jury. Their third child, Nebabiah, was baptized in 1637. Felt's *Annals of Salem* places both Thomas and Mary among the followers of Roger Williams. The General Court convened on March 12, 1638 and arraigned Ezekiel Holliman "for not attending public worship, and influencing others to imitate his example." Francis Weston, Richard Waterman, Thomas Olney and Stukely Westcott were also required to appear at the next session. The following year (in July 1639), the Reverend Hugh Peters, pastor at the First Church of Salem, sent a letter to the church at Dorchester, informing their brethren that they had excommunicated Roger Williams, John Throckmorton, Thomas Olney and Stukely Westcott, with their wives, and Mary Holliman and Widow Reeves "because they refused admonition, and denied that the churches of the Bay were true churches."[184] The records clearly include both Olney and his wife as challengers to the Magistracy. Like Jane Verin and her mother, they were both Separatist Congregationalists, a position that would have put them in contention with Joshua Verin.

Olney accompanied Roger Williams and became one of the founders of Providence. There Olney continued to serve the community; he was the first treasurer of the colony. He was a signer of the first compact, appears on the deed Roger Williams prepared in October of 1638, and later served as Assistant for the town of Providence, a judge of the Justices court, and as an emissary to Massachusetts Bay in 1656 to resolve the dispute over the Pawtuxet lands. He cofounded the Baptist Church in Providence where the Historical Catalog of the Members of the First Baptist Church lists him as the third pastor. He also continued his profession of shoemaking. The inventory of his estate taken after his death sometime in the summer of 1682 includes many shoemaking materials. Included among his books are a Bible, Ainsworth's *Anotations, A Concordance*, and Fisher's *Ashford Dispute*.[185] Henry Ainsworth, the author of *Anotations*, was the leader of a separatist congregation at Amsterdam. Born in 1571, he has been described as "a fine type of the Elizabethan puritan—learned, sincere, earnest, and uncompromising." He and Roger Williams were acquainted. According to the Dictionary of National Biography, Ainsworth was associated with the "Brownists," a group of independent Calvinists who were the ancestors of the Congregationalists, and who would defend the liberty of congregations to order their affairs. Ainsworth defended the separated churches as the true Visible Churches and their ministers as the true ministers of Christ.[186] The fact that Ainsworth's book appears in Olney's probate inventory strongly supports the view that Olney would have opposed Joshua (and supported Jane) Verin.

Richard Waterman was born and married in England; there is little information available about his parentage or background. The family history names him as one of the founders of Salem, having arrived in 1629, before Governor Winthrop's fleet. He served in several official capacities in Salem between 1632 and 1636, including as a canoe inspector and on a Petit Jury. All sources indicate that at some point he became a follower of Roger Williams and followed him to Providence. Roger Williams lists him among the original proprietors, those who desired a shelter for persons distressed for conscience; he received a confirmation of land for a lot on the southeast corner of Waterman and Benefit Streets on June 10, 1637. He and his wife, Bethiah, had several children: Mehitable (born 1630) and Nathaniel (born August 20, 1637). Bethiah was pregnant with their third child at the time of the Verin dispute; Resolved was born in July 1638. Waterman signed the Compact of 1640. He was later found guilty of being "erroneous, heretical, and obstinate" by the General Court in May of 1644. He died on December 3, 1680, in Providence.[187]

It appears that although a majority of the free holders agreed with Roger Williams about Joshua Verin's violation of his wife's liberty of conscience and the use of disenfranchisement as the appropriate sanction, not all of these, however, agreed on the appropriateness of depriving Verin of his property. Richard Waterman's son, Nathaniel, would later sign a petition protesting the town's action.

The antinomians in Rhode Island

The rise of Antinomianism attests to the diversity of belief among the puritans in England and New England.[188] Considered radical and heretical by mainstream puritan clergy, the Antinomians believed that under the gospel dispensation of grace, moral law is of no use or obligation because faith alone is necessary to salvation. Remember that congregations were communities of believers—those who had testified to their faith experience and who were known as "the Elect." Believing they had entered into a covenant with God, in return for accepting Christ, they (hoped) and expected they would be granted salvation. Some ministers urged these "justified saints" to devote themselves to charity and other good works as a sign of their having been called. Led by Anne Hutchinson, a midwife and spiritual advisor to other women, these radical puritans challenged those ministers who preached a version of the "covenant of works" to their congregations, and they insisted on faith alone as the means to salvation.[189] As a result, John Winthrop and the clergy and magistrates increasingly viewed Hutchinson and her followers, because of their rejection of a socially established morality, as threats to the civil and religious order.[190] In fact, Winthrop considered Hutchinson the most dangerous, stating, "the last and worst of all, which most suddenly diffused the venome of these opinions into the very veines and vitals of the People in the Country, was Mistrus Hutchinsons double weekly-lecture."[191] The Hutchinsons had followed the Reverend John Cotton to Massachusetts Bay Colony. They were members of the Alford congregation. In England, this congregation believed it should be responsible for choosing and paying for their minister. But in Massachusetts Bay, the Company leadership appointed all ministers and paid their salaries. The Alford faction tried to organize a separate church but could not gain official recognition. As a result, they began to meet privately. The Hutchinsons' home was often used for private worship services; her brother-in-law, the Reverend John Wheelwright, frequently preached at their farm.

Winthrop claimed that fifty to sixty people (and sometimes as many as eighty) attended her talks, "seducing … almost all parts of the Country, round about."[192] Ultimately, the puritan church state had to respond to twin challenges: the threat posed to the social order by the Antinomians and other dissenters and the danger to the patriarchy posed by activist females who stepped outside the acceptable boundaries of gendered norms. While women often made up a majority of worshippers in puritan congregations, they were expected to defer to their ministers.[193]

Anne Hutchinson was found guilty of not only heresy, but also of conduct unbecoming a woman. Winthrop viewed Anne Hutchinson's dissent as a challenge to "family order, sexual morality, and the subordination of women to men."[194] The puritan response to these threats was enforced conformity. She was excommunicated and exiled. On February 19, 1638, two of Anne Hutchinson's supporters, John Coggeshall and William Aspinwall, wrote to Roger Williams inquiring about the availability of land. He agreed to provide them a land grant, and shortly after, on March 17, 1638, 19 men signed an agreement forming a civil compact and departed for Portsmouth, Rhode Island shortly before Anne Hutchinson's official banishment on March 22, 1638. Anne Hutchinson left for the Rhode Island colony six days later (March 28, 1638).[195] Among the Antinomian exiles in Rhode Island were men who had been admonished, disarmed, excommunicated, banished and otherwise silenced—such was the perception of the threat they posed. Some, like William Aspinwall, had arrived in New England with the first wave of Puritans in 1630, while others, like John Clarke, were more recent arrivals. A direct relationship between the Antinomians and the Providence plantation already existed as manifested in the connection by marriage between Richard Scott (an original proprietor as noted earlier) and Anne Hutchinson's sister. Equally noteworthy is the fact that several prominent Antinomian exiles and their wives and families were already in Rhode Island, months *before* the townspeople of Providence decided on the Verins. As followers of Anne Hutchinson, it is highly likely that these would have been sympathetic to Jane Verin as one who followed her conscience and as a woman who had, in following the dictates of her conscience, been willing to challenge the very same kinds of authorities who had exiled them. Even though these newcomers did not vote in Providence, their ideas most certainly would have been discussed, if not endorsed.

Disputes over land

Joshua Verin adamantly rejected the right of the freeholders in Providence to disenfranchise him. Williams notes that Verin demanded that he would "have justice, (as he clamors) at other Courts."[196] Shortly after the decision, the Verins returned to Salem, leaving behind their property. In subsequent years, Verin made numerous efforts to receive compensation for his land, arguing that the land was lawfully his and therefore recoverable. In his letter to the town, Verin finds it "contrary to law, reason, and etiquette" that the town fathers would dispose of his property without his consent, exhorting them not to deal "worse with me that we dealt with the Indians."[197] The town replied that in the event Verin would come to court and prove his right, the "Towne will do him justice."[198] Daniel Abbott challenged this decision. In a lengthy protest Abbott calls the entire proceedings "preposterous" and "contrary to equity."[199] He took umbrage at the town's failure to compensate Joshua Verin for his property. He especially took issue with the town's decision, a decision he called "unrighteous," to try to force Verin to return to Providence to defend his claim.[200] Finally, at a town meeting in January 1675, records show the town voted to grant John Whipple

in the behalf of Joshua Veren for[mer] inhabitant of the town of Providence that the said John Whipple may have all such Lands as are due
to the said Veren Laid out to him for the use of said Verin Appointed
by the attorney of the Verin.[201]

Richard Arnold and Nicholas Power were granted the right to receive
portions of Verin's land in payment for their legal services. By April of
1675, the town reversed its earlier decision, voting that "Joshua Veren
hath no Right in this town of providence, and therefore deny John Whipple to draw a paper for the dividing of any Land in the Behalf of the said
Joshua Veren."[202] This decision was not without controversy. Several residents officially protested the town's decision to deny Verin his lands. It is
interesting to note that some of these men who would most likely have
voted *against* Verin in the matter of his physical abuse of his wife, *did* support him in the matter of property.[203] A month later, John Whipple tried
to pay the town sum of 50 shillings on behalf Joshua Verin. The town,
however, refused to accept Verin's money, stating that "Verin hath no
right to Land in this town."[204] Verin continued to appear in town records
as having original rights to town lands although he was unsuccessful in
gaining compensation.[205] It is clear from the description of the preceding
series of events that the founders of Providence, while they would take vigorous action to defend a person's liberty of conscience, took one's property
rights equally seriously.

Post-script

In stark contrast to Verin's experiences in Providence, he and his family
clearly remained members in good standing in both the town and church
community in Massachusetts. As noted earlier, Joshua Verin received several grants of land after his return to Salem.[206] He also served in a variety
of capacities at the First Church of Salem.[207] Verin clearly supported the
right and duty of the Church to enforce morality in Salem. Jane, however,
continued to challenge the legitimacy of the Puritan hierarchy. Court
records note that on October 4, 1638, she was "referd[sic] to Salem,"
meaning she had to appear before the Court of Assistants to answer to
charges of defying ministerial authority.[208] On December 25, 1638, Jane
Verin was presented in court at Salem for absence from religious worship,
shortly *after* her husband received a substantial land grant.[209] Church
records indicate that Jane Verin was removed from the First Church of
Salem on January 7, 1640.[210] This demonstrates that Jane Verin continued
to act on her conscience and to challenge the magistracy.

Joshua Verin, after having settled in Salem, removed himself to Providence,
and then returned to Salem. Like many during this era, Englishmen often
moved several times within the English Atlantic world. Founded just
a few years prior to Massachusetts Bay, the Barbados was settled in 1625 by

30 persons arriving on the *William and John*.[211] The rapid growth of the population attests to the fertility of the lands, particularly for the cultivation of sugar cane.[212] An autobiography by one of the original proprietors, Edward, Earl of Clarendon, asserts both an economic and a religious motive for the settlement of Barbados. Clarendon notes the original settlers had "repaired thither as to a desolate place, and had by their industry obtained a livelihood there, when they could not with a good conscience stay in England."[213] In contrast, one historian argues the first settlers of Barbados were a "class of society in which morals and virtue are seldom met," who differed from their compatriots who settled in New England in their motivations for settlement. He describes them as "ruthless and unprincipled," motivated not by their Christian virtues, but rather "the desire of enriching themselves by any means at their command."[214] A report by Sir Richard Dutton, Governor-in-Chief, indicates St. James Parish was composed of 204 families and householders, including 999 free persons, 210 indentured servants, and roughly 3,582 slaves.[215] Joshua Verin had resettled in the Barbados by September 1663. He appears on the register of St. James Parish, Barbados on December 20, 1679. Records reveal that he owned ten acres of land and 11 slaves.[216] This indicates that he had been accepted into the new congregational community there. He married Agnes Simpson at St. Michael's, Barbados on October 7, 1694, shortly before he died on March 15, 1695. While Jane Verin and her mother disappeared from the historical record, Joshua Verin reappeared (by way of his executrix) several times in continued disputes over the disposition of his lands.

A woman's liberty of conscience was a divisive issue in Massachusetts Bay as reflected in the colony's response to Anne Hutchinson's leadership of the Antinomians. A wife's right to follow her conscience in defiance of her husband's wishes also divided the Providence community, as evidenced by the fissures that developed in the aftermath of disagreements over the Verin decision. These, added to already simmering tensions regarding land and civil order, contributed to further splintering of the settlers in Providence and Rhode Island Plantations, as revealed by the decisions of the Arnold family and others to remove themselves to Pawtuxet and subsequently their efforts to return to the jurisdiction of Massachusetts Bay. Further, acting on one's conscience not only caused strife within the Verin marriage, but also within the extended Verin family. The divisions in the Verin family reflect the disagreements that roiled the peace of Plymouth and Massachusetts Bay colony. Joshua Verin clearly disagreed with his wife on the status of the New England churches relative to England as he remained a congregant; he ultimately resorted to beatings to discipline her. Puritan men were expected to exercise "governorship" over their wives. In New England, when marital discord threatened social harmony, neighbors, ministers, and magistrates would intervene in the interests of restoring peace. In other words, civil and ecclesiastical authorities were charged with maintaining order. Records indicate that Jane Verin challenged the authority of her ministers even before she left

Salem. Yet, there is no evidence that Joshua Verin physically abused his wife during this time. It is only in Rhode Island, where these tools for maintaining social order were poorly developed, that Joshua Verin beat his wife. Upon their return to Salem, Jane Verin continued to defy her ministers. Yet, there is no further evidence of any continuing mistreatment by her husband. Instead, church authorities stepped in to discipline Jane Verin, ultimately barring her from continued church membership.

Joshua Verin's brother and sister-in-law probably sided with Jane in that they, too, challenged the authority of the First Church of Salem and later suffered admonishment, removal from the church, and physical punishment for their beliefs.[217] Decades after the Verins returned to Salem, Joshua's brother Philip and his wife Joanna (Jane) were presented at court many times for nonattendance at public worship; and Philip continued to deny the country's power to force any to come to the public worship—an action that resulted in him being publicly hung by the heels.[218]

One analysis of Anglo-American puritans stresses that they were English Protestants whose commitment to conventional attitudes and values were especially strong. "Their internalized predestinarian theology, and support for a preaching ministry and for broad campaigns of godly reformation, were broadly shared among English elites and amounted to a consensual commitment to order and authority."[219] These English puritans were naturally conservative, and it was only in face of the "rise of a distinctive ecclesiastical establishment hostile to evangelical Calvinism, backed by Charles I," that radicalized them from conformist to oppositional views.[220] This would seem to fit the character of Joshua Verin, a man very much concerned with maintaining order. He despaired of the lack of order and effective government in Rhode Island as he despaired of maintaining order in his own household. Despite severe methods, he was unable to control completely his religiously inspired activist wife.

Notes

1 See John B. Threlfall, "The Verin Family of Salem, Massachusetts," *The New England Historical and Genealogical Register* (Boston: The Historical Society, April 1977), Massachusetts Historical Society (hereafter cited as MHS).
2 The Register of St. Edmund's Parish, New Sarum (Salisbury), England shows that Hugh Verin was buried on November 30, 1617. The will was proved in 1618. Wiltshire and Swindon Record Office, Reference #P4/1618/15, Wiltshire, England.
3 Clarence A. Torry, *New England Marriages Prior to 1700, New England Marriages Prior to 1700* (Baltimore, MD: Genealogical Publishing Co., 2004), 767.
4 Charles Haskins Alderman, JP, *The Ancient Trade Guilds and Companies of Salisbury,* (Salisbury, England: Bennett Brothers, Printers, 1912), 344–354, The National Archives (hereafter cited as TNA), Kew, London, England.
5 Probate 11/278, May 24, 1658, Deptford, Kent, TNA.

6 Charles E. Banks, *Topographical Dictionary of 2885 English Emigrants to New England, 1620–1650*, edited, indexed and published by Elijah Ellsworth Brownell (Philadelphia: Bertram Press, 1937), 295. See also Michael Tepper, ed., *Passengers to America: A Consolidation of Ship Passenger Lists from the New England Historical and Genealogical Register* (Baltimore: Genealogical Pub. Co, 1978), 46. NOTE: Verin left from the town of Hampton, England.

7 Charles Henry Pope, *The Pioneers of Massachusetts: A Descriptive List, Drawn from the Records of the Colonies, Towns, and Churches, and other Contemporaneous Documents* (Baltimore, MD: Genealogical Publishing Co., Inc., 1998), 471.

8 Ibid.

9 The names Jane and Joanna were often used interchangeably, a fact that renders the records somewhat confusing.

10 Marriage Register, Males Only, 1570–1812 (Veron, Number 626), Dorset Record Office, Blandford Forum, Dorset.

11 Richard D. Pierce, ed., *The Records of the First Church in Salem* (Salem, MA: Essex Institute, 1974), 4.

12 Hugo Williams was rector of St. Edmunds parish from 1613 until 1623, followed by Petrus Thatcher. Johannes Read was the Curate. William Albright was rector of St. Thomas during the 1620s. Their names do not appear in the *Exchequer: King's Remembrancer: Registers of Licenses to Pass Beyond the Seas*, nor in the *Calendar of State Papers Colonial—America and West Indies, Overseas Record Information*, 32, Vol. I: 1574–1660 or in *American and West Indian Colonies before 1782, Overseas Record Information*, 51, Secretary of State for Southern Department, TNA.

13 Sidney Perley, *The History of Salem, Massachusetts*, Vol. I, 1626–1637 (Salem, MA: Sidney Perley, 1924), 296.

14 Salem, Massachusetts: Historical Profile, at "Salem Still Making History," Accessed December 4, 2018, www.salem.com/city-clerk/pages/historical-profile.

15 *Town Records of Salem, Massachusetts* (Salem, MA: The Essex Institute, 1868), Vol. I, 5 and 7, Peabody Institute Library, Peabody, MA (hereafter cited as PIL).

16 *Town Records of Salem, 1634–1659*, Essex Institute—Historical Collections, Second Series, Vol. I, Part I (Salem, 1868), 9, PIL.

17 David Pulsifer, "Extracts from Records kept by the Rev. John Fiske during his Ministry at Salem, Wenham, and Chelmsford," Historical Collections of the Essex Institute (Vol. I, #2, May 1859), Salem, 1859, 37–39, PIL.

18 Michael Tepper, ed., *Passengers to America: A Consolidation of Ship Passenger Lists from the New England Historical and Genealogical Register* (Baltimore: Genealogical Pub. Co, 1978), 46. NOTE: Verin left from the town of Hampton, England. See also James Savage, *Genealogical Dictionary of the First Settlers of New England, Showing Three Generations of Those Who Came Before May 1692 on the Basis of Farmer's Register*, Originally Published Boston, 1860–1862, Vol. IV, 371.

19 Joshua was the son of Philip and Dorcas Verin. Both Philip and Joshua's brother Hilliard were freemen and members of the First Church of Salem. Each held a variety of appointed offices in Salem; Hilliard was clerk of the Salem Quarterly Court.

20 Lyle Koehler, *A Search for Power: The "Weaker Sex" in Seventeenth-Century New England* (Champaign, IL: University of Illinois Press, 1980), 217. See also Winthrop, *The Journal of John Winthrop 1630–1649*, Richard S. Dunn, James Savage & Laetitia Yeandle, eds. (Cambridge, MA: The Massachusetts Historical Society, 1996), Vol. I, 162, 168, and Joseph B. Felt, *Annals of Salem, from its first settlement* (Salem, MA: W & SB Ives, 1827), Vol. II, 573 and 576.

21 Perry Miller, ed., *The Complete Writings of Roger Williams*, Vol. III (New York: Russell & Russell, 1963), 225. See also, Edmund Morgan, *The Puritan Dilemma: The Story of John Winthrop* (Boston: Little Brown, 1958), 115–133.

22 James Savage, ed., John Winthrop, *The History of New England from 1630–1649*, Vol. I (Boston: Little Brown, 1853), 194.

23 *Journal of John Winthrop*, 163–164.

24 The quotation continues, "for this cause that some of their members goeinge [sic] into England did hear the ministers there, & when they came home, the Churches heere [sic] held communion with them." *The Journal of John Winthrop*, 163–164.

25 Letter, Roger Williams to Major Mason, dated June 22, 1670, in *Letters of Roger Williams, 1632–1682, Now First Collected*, John R. Bartlett, ed. (Providence: The Narragansett Club, 1874), 335.

26 *Journal of John Winthrop*, Vol. I, 209.

27 Letter, Joshua Verin to Town of Providence, dated November 21, 1650. In *Documentary History of Rhode Island*, Howard M. Chapin, ed. (Providence, RI: Preston & Rounds, Co, 1916), 11.

28 "Providence Home Lots, 1636–1650, Providence," VMO11_02_01043, John Hitchens Cady Research Scrapbooks Collection, Providence Public Library, Providence, RI.

29 Glenn W. La Fantasie, ed. *The Correspondence of Roger Williams*, Vol. I, 1629–1653 (Providence, RI: Rhode Island Historical Society, 1988), RIHS, 156.

30 Ibid., 154. La Fantasie believes the unruly person refers to J. Verin whose case would come before the town later in the month.

31 Ibid.

32 *Winthrop Papers*, Vol. IV, 1638–1644 (Boston: Massachusetts Historical Society, 1944), 31, MHS. See also Chapin, *Documentary History of Rhode Island*, 72.

33 Letter, Roger Williams to John Winthrop, May 22, 1638, in *Winthrop Papers*, Vol. I, 209.

34 Providence (R.I.) Record Commissioners (1892–1915). *The early records of the town of Providence*, Vol. I (Providence: Snow & Farnham, City Printers, 1892), RIHS, 4.

35 *Winthrop Papers*, Ibid.

36 According to Howard Chapin, this occurred sometime between May 21, the date of his trial, and June 10, a record confirming land ownership in which Verin is not named one of the neighbors. *Documentary History of Rhode Island*, Vol. I, 75–76.

37 Ibid.

38 *Town Records of Salem, Massachusetts*, Vol. I, 1634–1659, Essex Institute, Historical Collections, Second Series, Vol. I, Part I (Salem, MA: The Essex Institute, 1868). (PIL) Town records indicate that Verin received a two-acre house lot on February 6, 1635, 9. On August 29, 1638, he was granted a 10-acre lot, and on November 21, 1638, he received a 40-acre land grant, 73 and 97. See also Felt, *Annals of Salem*, Vol. I, 2nd Edition (Boston: W&SB Ives, 1845), 170.

39 *Winthrop Papers*, Ibid.

40 *The Records of the First Church in Salem*, 144. PIL.

41 Ibid.

42 Sidney Perley, *The History of Salem, Massachusetts*, Vol. II, 1638–1670 (Salem, MA: Sidney Perley, 1926), 165.

43 Joshua Verin's brother, Hilliard, served as clerk of Essex County. See Michael Tepper, *Passengers to America*, 134.

44 John Noble, supervisor, *Records of the Court of Assistants of the Colony of Massachusetts Bay 1630–1692*. Boston: Massachusetts Historical Society, 1904. Quarter Court held at Boston on October 4, 1638, 79, MHS.

45 *Records of Quarterly Court*, Essex County, Vol. I, 10, PIL.
46 *The Records of the First Church in Salem*, 10.
47 Sidney Perley. *The History of Salem, Massachusetts*, Vol. II, 180.
48 *Town Records of Providence*, Vol. 15, 37.
49 Jane Verin was removed on May 2, 1640. *The Records of the First Church in Salem*, 9.
50 George F. Dow, ed., *Records and Files of the Quarterly Courts of Essex County, Vol. III, 1662–1667* (Essex, MA: Essex Institute, 1913), 111, 116, 117 and 223.
51 He appears on the list of *English Settlers in Barbados, 1637–1800*. Available at Ancestry.com; accessed October 15, 2016, http://search.ancestry.com/cgi-bin/sse.dll?db=barbadossettlers_ga&h=57272&ti=0&indiv=try&gss=pt().
52 Petition dated March 25, 1719, recorded on June 20, 1721. *Providence Town Records*, 9, 27–29.
53 Quoted in Sanford H. Cobb, *The Rise of Religious Liberty in America: A History* (New York: MacMillan Company, 1968), 154. NB: The original English spellings have been retained as much as possible.
54 Ibid.
55 W. Noel Sainsbury, Esq., ed., *Calendar of State Papers, Colonial Series, 1574–1660* (London: Longman, Green, Longman, & Roberts, 1860), Vol. VI, 157. Non-conformists insisted on receiving communion standing, rather than kneeling, a practice which Anglican ministers refused to endorse. See also a letter from G. Garrard to Lord Conway, September 18, 1635 in *Calendar of State Papers Colonial—America and WestIndies, Overseas Record Information, 32*, Vol. I, 1574–1660 and Vol. VIII, 214, TNA.
56 Quoted in David D. Hall, "The Experience of Authority in Early New England," *The Journal of American and Canadian Studies*, No. 23, 2005, 12.
57 John Geree, *The Character of an Old English Puritan, or Non-Conformist* (London: W. Wilson, 1646), 1.
58 Ibid.
59 Ibid.
60 Ibid.
61 William Bradford, *History of Plymouth Plantation, 1606–1646*, Vol. 6, William T. Davis, ed. (New York: William Scribner & Sons, 1908), 26.
62 Ibid., 28.
63 John Winthrop, "A Model of Christian Charity," 1630, University of Virginia; accessed March 2, 2012, http://religiousfreedom.lib.virginia.edu/sacred/charity.html. See also Abram C. Van Engen, *Sympathetic Puritans: Calvinist Fellow Feeling in Early New England* (New York: Oxford University Press, 2015), especially Chapter I, "Puritan Sympathy," in which Van Engen analyzes Winthrop's "Model of Christian Charity" and argues "Christ's active fellow feeling modeled the affections all Christians should possess." Van Engen argues this sympathy was essential to the social order by linking the affections of fellow puritans together in their enterprise in the wilderness, noting, "the experience of separating out from the broader profane multitude heightened the bonds of love, the sympathy of saints." 48–49.
64 Ibid.
65 Ibid.
66 Ibid.
67 Van Engen, *Sympathetic Puritans*, ibid.
68 Matthew J. Reardon, "A Fraternity of Patriarchs: The Gendered Order of Early Puritan Massachusetts," *Historical Journal of Massachusetts*, 42(2), Summer 2014, 124.

69 Ibid.
70 Michael P. Winship, *Godly Republicanism: Puritans Pilgrims, and a City on a Hill* (Cambridge, MA: Harvard University Press, 2012), 199.
71 Mark McGarvie and Elizabeth Mensch, "Law and Religion in Colonial America," in *The Cambridge History of Law in America*, Vol. I—Early America (1580–1815), eds., Michael Grossberg and Christopher Tomlins (New York: Cambridge University Press, 2008), 335.
72 Ibid.
73 Ibid. Although she deals primarily with the eighteenth century in her analysis, Elaine Forman Crane analyzes the ways in which legal culture permeated people's everyday lives. See especially Chapter III: "Leave of or Else I would Cry Out Murder: The Community Response to Family Violence in Early New England," in *Witches, Wife Beaters, and Whores: Common Law and Common Folk in Early America* (Ithaca, NY: Cornell University Press, 2011). In this chapter, she explores the community responses to family violence based on an analysis of eight Rhode Island cases spanning the eighteenth century.
74 M. Michelle Jarrett Morris analyzes sex and family dynamics by examining court cases relating to fornication, rape, and bastardy, and other cases of sexual misconduct in Massachusetts. See *Under Household Government: Sex and Family in Puritan Massachusetts* (Cambridge, MA: Harvard University Press, 2013).
75 Quoted in Cobb, *The Rise of Religious Liberty in America*, 151.
76 Cotton Mather, *Magnalia Christi Americana; or The Ecclesiastical History of New-England* (Hartford: Silas Andrus & Son, 1853), Vol. II, 496. Mather calls the chapter on Roger Williams, "Little Foxes; or the Spirit of Rigid Separation in One Remarkable Zealot."
77 Mather, *Magnalia Christi Americana*, 496.
78 Robert C. Anderson, "Communications: On English Migration to Early New England," *New England Quarterly*, 59(3), September 1986, 407. In the same edition, Virginia Dejohn Anderson argues in "Religion, the Common Thread," that a large number of the adult emigrants in her study group had demonstrable links with the Puritan movement, usually because they had gotten into trouble for their beliefs," 420. She concludes that the emigrants *did* pay heed to their material welfare, "but they did so in a way that emphasized their religious commitment...in other words...what others have identified as economic *causes* of the Great Migration were instead economic *concerns* that the settlers subsumed within their larger religious world view," 421.
79 Anthony Salerno, "The Social Background of Seventeenth-Century Emigration to America," *Journal of British Studies*, 1979, 29(1), 33. Salerno used ships' passenger lists and other English records to determine the name, age, occupation and family information in creating a profile of the typical Wiltshire emigrant grant to the colonies.
80 Ibid., 52. Salerno agrees with T.H. Breenand Stephen Foster who in an earlier work attempted a systematic analysis of the mass of ordinary settlers who moved to New England during the 1630s. Breen and Foster found that a significant number of the migrants were grouped into relatively small nuclear families consisting of two parents, a few children, and sometimes one or two servants. Men and women were about equal in number. Breen and Foster reject the traditional either/or dichotomy of either religion or economics as an essentially meaningless distinction. Instead, they argue that one must examine both economic and religious influences as important, "each to a degree dependent upon individual circumstances." T.H. Breen and Stephen Foster, "Moving to

the New World: The Character of Early Massachusetts Immigration," *William and Mary Quarterly*, 3rd Series, 1973, 30(2).

81 Salerno, Ibid.

82 Breen and Foster, "Moving to the New World: The Character of Early Massachusetts Immigration," 192–195.

83 Ibid.

84 Ibid., 203–208.

85 Perley, *The History of Salem, Massachusetts*, Vol. I, 304.

86 May 8, 1634, letter Joseph Ker to Thomas Leviston [extract from Domestic Correspondence, Car I], *Calendar of State Papers*, Vol. VIII, 178. TNA.

87 Quoted in *Gertrude Selwyn Kimball, Providence in Colonial Times* (Boston: Houghton Mifflin Co., 1912), 8.

88 September 18, 1635, letter G. Garrard to Lord Conway. Garrard notes that Vane's son "likes not the discipline of the Church of England, none of our ministers will give him the sacrament standing, and no persuasions of the Bishops nor Authority of his parents will prevail with him." {Extract, Domestic Correspondence, CarI], *Calendar of State Papers*, Vol. VIII, 214, TNA.

89 Perley, *The History of Salem, Massachusetts*, Vol. I, 304.

90 Batter brought a servant named John Small and Antrum brought a servant named Thomas Browne. Ibid., 279–296.

91 Joshua was the son of Philip and Dorcas Verin. Both Philip and Joshua's brother Hilliard were free men and members of the First Church of Salem. Each held a variety of appointed offices in Salem; Hilliard was clerk of the Salem Quarterly Court.

92 Lyle Koehler, *A Search for Power: The "Weaker Sex" in Seventeenth-Century New England* (Champaign, IL: University of Illinois Press, 1980), 217. Williams' followers at Salem were Jane Verin, Mary Oliver, Margery Reeves, and Margery Holliman. They "refused to worship with the congregation from 1635 to 1638 and the latter two women denied that the churches of the Baycolony were true churches." See also Winthrop, *Journal* I 162 and 168, and Felt, *Annals of Salem* II (Boston: W&SB Ives, 1845), 573 and 576. NB: These women were all present in Providence at the time of the Verin decision.

93 The quotation continues, "for this cause that some of their members goeinge [sic] into England did heare the ministers there, & when they came home, the Churches heere [sic] held communion with them." John Winthrop, *The Journal of John Winthrop*, 163–164.

94 Quoted in John Hopkins Morison, *A Sermon, Preached at the Installation of Rev. George W. Briggs, as Pastor of The First Church in Salem, January 6, 1853* (Salem, MA: Gazette Press, 1853), 39.

95 John Winthrop, *The Journal of John Winthrop 1630–1649*, Richard S. Dunn, James Savage & Laetitia Yeandle, eds. (Cambridge, MA: Massachusetts Historical Society, 1996), 163–164, MHS.

96 *The Correspondence of Roger Williams*, Vol. I: 1629–1653, 156.

97 Jane Kamensky, "Talk Like a Man: Speech, Power, and Masculinity in Early New England," *Gender and History*, 8(1), April 1996, 27.

98 Ibid.

99 Stephen Foster, *The Long Argument: English Puritanism and the Shaping of New England Culture 1570–1700* (Chapel Hill, NC: Omohundro Institute and University of North Carolina Press, reprint edition, 1996). See also Charles L. Cohen, "The Post-Puritan Paradigm of Early American Religious History," *William and Mary Quarterly*, 3rd Series, Vol. LIV(4), October 1997, 701.

100 Roger Thompson, "State of the Art: Early Modern Migration," *Journal of American Studies*, 25 (1991), Vol. I, 62. See also Theodore Dwight Bozeman, *To*

Live Ancient Lives: The Primitivist Dimension in Puritanism (Williamsburg, VA: Institute of Early American History and Culture, 1988) and Richard T. Hughes and Crawford Leonard Allen, *Illusions of Innocence: Protestant Primitivism in America, 1630–1875* (Chicago: University of Chicago Press, 1988).

101   Ibid., 69.

102   Ann Hughes, "Anglo American Puritanisms: Introduction," *Journal of British Studies*, 39 (January 2000), 4.

103   Edmund S. Morgan, *The Puritan Family* (Boston: Harper Row, 1944), 83.

104   Quoted in Samuel Greene Arnold, *History of the State of Rhode Island and Providence Plantations*, Vol. I, 1636–1700 (New York: D. Appleton & Co., 1859), 97. Thomas Bicknell comments on Williams' failure to include Joshua Verin as among the earliest settlers, stating: "It is not easy to see how Mr. Williams could have forgotten Joshua Verin, one of the six who crossed the Seekonk to find shelter under the western slope of Moshassuck Hill. He it was, who, his next door neighbor on the north, vexed his soul to its depths, and to whom he bequeathed the title of wife whipper." Thomas Williams Bicknell, *The History of the State of Rhode Island and Providence Plantations*, Vol. 1 (New York: American Historical Society, 1920), 111.

105   Letter, Joshua Veren to Town of Providence, November 21, 1650, *Early Records of the Town of Providence*, Volume 15 (Providence: Snow & Farnham City Printers, 1892), 37, RIHS.

106   For recent biographies of Roger Williams, see John M. Barry, *Roger Williams and the Creation of the American Soul: Church, State and the Birth of Liberty* (New York: Penguin Books, 2012); Edmund S. Morgan, *Roger Williams: The Church and the State* (New York: W.W. Norton & Co., 2007). James A. Warren's *God, War and Providence: The Epic Struggle of Roger Williams and the Narragansett Indians against the Puritans of New England* (New York: Charles Scribner & Sons, 2018) focuses on Williams' relationship with the Narragansett Indians and their efforts to resist the encroachments from settlers in Massachusetts Bay and Plymouth Colony.

107   The following were in Moshassuck and Pawtuxet in the summer of 1636: William Blackstone (1634), William Arnold, Christianne Arnold, William Carpenter, Elizabeth Carpenter, Benedict Arnold, Joanna Arnold, Stephen Arnold, Thomas Hopkins, Frances Hopkins (all arriving April 20, 1636), Roger and Mary Williams with Mary and Freeborn (June 1636), Thomas Angell (June 1636), Francis Wickes (June 1636), John, Alice, John Jr. & Elizabeth Smith (June 1636), William, Susannah and Andrew Harris (June 1636), Joshua and Jane Verin (June 1636), Bicknell, *The History of the State of Rhode Island and Providence Plantations*, Vol. I, 158.

108   Ibid. Included among the men on the deed of the original proprietors of Providence (and men who were present at the time of Verin's hearing) were: Thomas Angell, William Arnold, William Harris, John Smith, Chad Brown, William Carpenter, Robert Cole, Edward Cope, Gregory Dexter, John Field, John Greene, Thomas Harris, Ezekiel Holliman, Thomas James, Thomas Olney, William Reynolds, Richard Scott, John Throckmorton, Richard Waterman, Stukely Wescott, Francis Weston, William Wickenden, Robert Williams, and Joshua Winsor.

109   Bruce H. Mann, "The Transformation of Law and Economy in Early America," in *The Cambridge History of Law in America* (Vol. I: 1580–1815), eds., Michael Grossberg and Christopher Tomlins (New York: Cambridge University Press, 2008), 367–368.

110   Ibid.

111 Letter Roger Williams to John Winthrop, summer 1636, in *antinoma* (Boston, 1863), 186, MHS.

112 *The Correspondence of Roger Williams.* Vol. I, 1629–1653, 154.

113 Quoted in Edmund J. Carpenter, *Roger Williams: A Study of the Life, Times, and character of a Political Pioneer* (New York: Grafton Press, 1909), 226.

114 Bicknell, *The History of the State of Rhode Island and Providence Plantations*, 177. The compact was signed by Richard Scott, Thomas Angell, William Reynolds, John Field, Chad Browne, John Warner, George Richard, Edward Cope, Thomas Harris, Francis Wickes, Benedict Arnold, Joshua Winsor, and William Wickenden.

115 Carpenter, *Roger Williams*, 226.

116 Edward Cope, William Reynolds, John Throckmorton, Francis Wickes, and John Winsor.

117 According to Bicknell's *The History of the state of Rhode Island and Providence Plantations*, "A singular act" followed the creation of the Proprietary, which consisted of Stukeley Westcott, William Arnold, Thomas James, Robert Cole, John Greene, John Throckmorton, William Harris, William Carpenter, Thomas Olney, Francis Weston, Richard Waterman, Ezekiel Holyman and Roger Williams, thirteen in all. On the eighth day of October, 1636, the 13 proprietors made a division of the lands described in the "Initial Deed," into two parts, known in the records as "The Grand Purchase of Providence," and "The Pawtuxet Purchase." "The Providence Purchase" remained as a Proprietary, although it was usually called a "Town." "The Pawtuxet Purchase" was divided equally between the thirteen proprietors, each agreeing to pay to Mr. Williams an equal proportion of 20 pounds for the lands in that division, 163.

118 Kimball, *Providence in Colonial Times*, 22.

119 Ibid.

120 Ibid., 23.

121 Bicknell, *The History of the State of Rhode Island and Providence Plantations*, V.1, 177.

122 Bicknell, *The history of the state of Rhode Island and Providence Plantations*, V.1, 172.

123 James Savage, *Genealogical Dictionary of the First Settlers of New England* (Boston: Little, Brown & Co., 1860), Vol. I, 57.

124 "William Arnold," in Great Migration 1635–35, A-B (Online database New England Ancestors.org, New England Historic Genealogical Society, 2008. See also, U.S. and International Marriage Records, 1560–1899, available at Ancestry. co.uk, http://trees.ancestry.co.uk/pt/person.aspx?tid=6967749&pg=39.

125 Ibid.

126 *Providence Town Records*, Vol. 5, 306–309. Roger Williams prepared the deed on October 8, 1638, RIHS.

127 Winthrop, *History*, Vol. I, 340–341.

128 Ibid.

129 Ibid.

130 Ibid.

131 Chapin, *Documentary History of Rhode Island*, Vol. I, 73.

132 Ibid.

133 See A Map of the Providence Home Lots showing Owners and Houses Erected 1636–1650. NOTE: Ezekiel Holliman also moved to Pawtuxet, but not until 1640, PPL.

134 Quoted in "William Arnold," *The Great Migration Begins*, 90.

135 Ibid., 88.

136 Source number: *1110.000*, Yates Publishing. *U.S. and International Marriage Records, 1560–1900* [databaseon-line]. Provo, UT, USA: Ancestry.com Operations Inc, 2004). See also E.S. Arnold, *The Arnold Memorial, William Arnold of Providence and Pawtuxet 1587–1675, And a Genealogy of His Descendants* (Rutland, Vermont: The Tuttle Publishing Co., Inc. From the Quintin Publications Collection, 1935).

137 Ibid.

138 Source number: *1353.000*, Yates Publishing. *U.S. and International Marriage Records, 1560–1900* [database on-line]. Provo, UT, USA: Ancestry.com Operations Inc, 2004.

139 Savage, *Genealogical Dictionary of the First Settlers of New England*, Vol. I, 338.

140 He arrived on the *Friendship* as part of the Winthrop fleet. Nathaniel B. Shurtleff, ed., *Records of the Governor and Company of the Massachusetts Bay in New England*, 1628–1686, 5 volumes in 6 (Boston: William White, 1853), Vol. I, 90.

141 Cited in "Robert Coles" in *The Great Migration Begins*. See also *Records of Church of Roxbury*, 74.

142 Robert Coles, in *Genealogical Dictionary of the First Settlers of New England*, Vol. II, 302.

143 "Robert Cole," in The Great Migration Begins: Immigrants to New England 1620–1633, Vols. I–III (Online database: New England Ancestors.org, New England Historic Genealogical Society, 2002 (Orig. Pub. New England Historic Genealogical Society. Robert Charles Anderson, *The Great Migration Begins: Immigrants to New England 1620–1633*, Vols. I–III, 1995).

144 Ibid.

145 Savage, *Genealogical Dictionary of the First Settlers of New England*, Vol. I, 429.

146 Ibid.

147 Savage, *Genealogical Dictionary of the First Settlers of New England* (Boston: Little, Brown & Co., 1860), Vol. II, 302.

148 Ibid.

149 Ibid.

150 Letter dated November 17, 1677, Roger Williams to "Assembly of Commissioners," quoted in its entirety in Edmund J. Carpenter, *Roger Williams: A Study of the Life, Times and Character of a Political Pioneer* (Boston: The Grafton Press, 1909), 225.

151 Ibid., 226.

152 Kimball, *Providence in Colonial Times*, 22.

153 Joan Olsson,"The Descendants of Thomas Olney and Marie Ashton of Providence, Rhode Island," Roots Web World Connect Project; accessed April 27, 2010, http://worldconnect.rootsweb.ancestry.com.

154 Savage, *Genealogical Dictionary of the First Settlers of New England*, Vol. II, 365.

155 Quoted in Anne Keary, "Retelling the History of the Settlement of Providence: Speech, Writing, and Cultural Interaction on Narragansett Bay," *The New England Quarterly*, 69(2), 279.

156 Ibid., 280–281.

157 Roger Williams to John Whipple, Jr., August 24, 1669, *Correspondence of Roger Williams*, Glenn W. La Fantasie, ed. (Providence, RI: The Rhode Island Historical Society, 1988), Vol. 2, June 1996, 597.

158 Ibid. See also Anne Keary, "Retelling the History of the Settlement of Providence," 250–286.

159 Elaine Forman Crane uses several microhistories to illustrate the ways in which ordinary people' s experiences were "saturated" with legal implications, and she argues that legal issues and daily life were knotted together. She traces early American legal procedures when they were still embryonic. See *Witches, Wife beaters & Whores: Common Law and Common Folk in Early America* (Ithaca, NY: Cornell University Press, 2011).

160 Roger Williams, Letter to The Court of Commissioners of the United Colonies, October 18, 1677, John Russell Bartlett, ed., *Letters of Roger Williams, 1632–1682, Now First Collected* (Providence: The Narragansett Club, 1874), 387. In the same letter, Williams blames the likes of Harris, with his unreasonable expectations of unfairly taking lands from the Narragansets, for having contributed to King Phillip's War, 393–394.

161 Ibid., 388.

162 The response by Roger Williams to William Harris's declaration against the town of Providence is quoted in its entirety in Edmund J. Carpenter, *Roger Williams*, 224.

163 Ibid.

164 Ibid.

165 Mary Sarah Bilder, "Salamanders and Sons of God: The Culture of Appeal in Early New England." In *The Many Legalities of Early America*, eds., Christopher L. Tomlins and Bruce H. Mann (Chapel Hill, NC: University of North Carolina Press, 2001), 62. See also Elaine Forman Crane, *Witches, Wife-Beaters, and Whores*.

166 Savage, *Genealogical Dictionary of the First Settlers of New England*, Vol. II, 363–364.

167 Ibid., 448.

168 Ibid.

169 Savage, *Genealogical Dictionary of the First Settlers of New England*, Vol. IV, 238.

170 See Winthrop, *Journal* I, 162 and 168, and Felt, *Annals of Salem* II, 573 and 576.

171 "Thomas James" in The Great Migration Begins: Immigrants to New England 1620–1633, Vols. I–III (Online database: New England Ancestors.org, New England Historic Genealogical Society, 2002 (Orig. Pub. New England Historic Genealogical Society. Robert Charles Anderson, *The Great Migration Begins: Immigrants to New England 1620–1633*, Vols. I–III, 1995).

172 Ibid.

173 Ibid.

174 *Winthrop's Journal*, 1: 51 and 1:217.

175 See the March 11, 1635/6 entry *Winthrop's Journal*, Vol. I, 217.

176 Savage, *Genealogical Dictionary of the First Settlers of New England*, Vol. II, 537.

177 See Providence Town Records, Vol. 1, 4 and 108 and Vol. 3, 90. The records also include Thomas James as one of the original "13 proprietors of Pautuxet" (4:73).

178 Quoted in "Thomas James" in The Great Migration Begins: Immigrants to New England 1620–1633, Vols. I–III (Online database: New England Ancestors.org, New England Historic Genealogical Society, 2002).

179 *The Great Migration Begins* cites both the Winthrop Papers and Bradford's *History of New England* to support this claim.

180 Savage, *Genealogical Dictionary of the First Settlers of New England*, Vol. II, 537.

181 Ibid. See also Winthrop, *History*, Vol. I, 268.

182 M. Tepper, *Passengers to America: Founders of New England*, 16–17. See also Savage, *Genealogical Dictionary of the First Settlers of New England*, Vol. III, 313, and James H. Olney, *A Genealogy of the Descendants of Thomas Olney: An Original Proprietor of Providence, RI Who Came from England in 1635* (Providence: Press of E.L. Freeman, 1889).

183 Ibid.

184 Felt, *Annals of Salem*, Vol. II, 576. Savage's entry in the *Genealogical Dictionary* cites both Hutchinson and Felt's histories of the colony in support of this, pointing out that both Olney and his wife were excommunicated, although they did not appear on the list of church members.

185 Joan Olsson, "The Descendants of Thomas Olney and Marie Ashton of Providence, Rhode Island."

186 "Henry Ainsworth," *Dictionary of National Biography, 1885–1900*, Vol. I (London: Smith, Elder & Co, 1885), 191–194.

187 Savage, *Genealogical Dictionary of the First Settlers of New England*, Vol. 4, 432. See also Austin's *Genealogical Dictionary of Rhode Island*, 408.

188 For analyses of the Antinomian Crisis, see David W. Hall, ed., *The Antinomian Controversy, 1636–1638: A Documentary History*, 2nd ed. (Durham, NC: Duke University Press, 1990); Michael P. Winship, *Making Heretics: Militant Protestantism and Free Grace in Massachusetts, 1636–1641* (Princeton, NJ: Princeton University Press, 2002); Nicholas McDowell, *The English Radical Imagination: Culture, Religion, and Revolution, 1630–1660* (Oxford: Clarendon Press, 2003); Theodore Dwight Bozeman, *The Precisionist Strain: Disciplinary Religion and Antinomian Backlash in Puritanism to 1638* (Chapel Hill: University of North Carolina Press, 2004); and David R. Como, *Blown by the Spirit: Puritanism and the Emergence of an Antinomian Underground in Pre-Civil War England* (Stanford, CA: Stanford University Press, 2004).

189 For recent biographies of Anne Hutchinson, see Eve La Plante, *American Jezebel: The Uncommon Life of Anne Hutchinson, the Woman who Defied the Puritans* (New York: Harper One, Reprint edition, 2005) and Michael P. Winship, *The Times and Trials of Anne Hutchinson: Puritans Divided* (Landmark Law Cases and American Society) (Lawrence, KS: University Press of Kansas, 2005).

190 "Antinomian." Merriam-Webster.com.

191 David W. Hall, ed., *The Antinomian Controversy, 1636–1638*, 205–208. See also Bruce Traister, *Female Piety and the Invention of American Puritanism* (Columbus, OH: The Ohio State University Press, 2016).

192 Ibid.

193 Charles L. Cohen, "The Post-Puritan Paradigm of Early American Religious History," *William and Mary Quarterly*, 3rd. Series, Vol. LIV(4), October 1997, 701. Cohen argues that by 1660, women regularly composed two-thirds of church membership, a figure that held steady throughout the eighteenth century, 719. He agrees with Bonomi and Treckel that American religion had been "feminized" by the mid-seventeenth century, a fact that enabled women to "institutionalize a broader definition of church membership that enabled Puritan theology to continue functioning as the dominating ideology of New England's social order," 720.

194 Carol Berkin, *First Generations: Women in Colonial America* (New York: Hill and Wang, 1996), 37–40. See also Eve La Plante, *American Jezebel*, 39.

195 *Records of the Colony of Rhode Island and Providence Plantation in New England*, Vol. I, 52.

196 Letter, Roger Williams to John Winthrop, May 22, 1638, in *Winthrop Papers*, Vol. I, 209.

197 *Town Records of Providence*, Vol. 15, 37.
198 Ibid.
199 *Town Records of Providence*, Vol. 15, 145.
200 Ibid.
201 *Town Records of Providence*, Vol. 4, 18. Arnold was allowed to charge a share of the meadow, and Power was to receive sixty acres of land and five areas of "low land."
202 Ibid.
203 *Town Records of Providence*, Vol. 4, 34. The men who signed the official protest were: Thomas Harris Sr., Thomas Olney Jr., William Hawkins, Sr., Samuel Bennet, Thomas Roberts, Valentin Whittman, Thomas Field, Andrew Harris, John Whipple, Sr., Nathaniel Waterman, Thomas Olney, Sr., Epenetus Olney, and Joseph Jenckes.
204 Town meeting of May 24, 1675, *Town Records of Providence*, Vol. 4, 43.
205 For example, a list of lands that were divided on the western side of the seven-mile line include Joshua Verin, as possessor of original rights to the fifth lot. See List made March 17, 1683/4, appearing on 64–65 in vol. 4 of the *Town Records of Providence*.
206 *Town Records of Salem, Massachusetts*, Vol. I, 1634–1659, Essex Institute, Historical Collections, Second Series, Vol. I, Part I (Salem: Essex Institute, 1868). (PIL) Town records indicate that Verin received a two-acre house lot on February 6, 1635, 9. On August 29, 1638, he was granted a 10-acre lot (73) and on November 21, 1638, he received a 40-acre land grant (97). See also Felt, *Annals of Salem*, Vol. I, 2nd Edition (Boston: W.&S.B. Ives, 1845), 170.
207 *The Records of the First Church in Salem*, 144. PIL.
208 John Noble, supervisor, *Records of the Court of Assistants of the Colony of Massachusetts Bay 1630–1692* (Boston: County of Suffolk, 1904). Quarter Court held at Boston on October 4, 1638, 79, MHS.
209 *Records of Quarterly Court*, Essex County, Vol. I, 10, PIL.
210 Richard D. Pierce, ed., *The Records of the First Church in Salem, 1629–1736*, 10, PIL.
211 William Duke, *Memoirs of the first Settlement of the Island of Barbados and other the [sic] Caribbee Islands, with the Succession of the Governors and Commanders in chief of Barbados to the year 1742* (Extracted from the ancient records, papers, and accounts, taken from Mr. William Arnold, Mr. Samuel Bulkly and Mr. John Summers (London: E. Owen & W. Meadows, 1743), 3. Boston Athenaeum, Boston, MA. See also Robert H. Schomburgk, *The History of Barbados Comprising a Geographical and Statistical Description of the Island; A sketch of the Historical Events Since the Settlement, and an Account of Its Geology and Natural Productions* (London: Longman, Brown, and Longmans, 1848).
212 By the time Governor-General Ligonde parted from Barbados in 1650, the number of whites numbered 50,000. Schomburgk, *The History of Barbados*, 79.
213 Ibid., 287.
214 Ibid., 92.
215 Survey of Barbados in 1683–1684, Schomburgk, *The History of Barbados*, 82.
216 He appears on the list of *English Settlers in Barbados, 1637–1800*, http://search.ancestry.com/cgi-bin/sse.dll?db=barbadossettlers_ga&h=57272&ti=0&indiv=try&gss=pt().
217 Records of the First Church of Salem indicate Jane Verin was removed on May 2, 1640. *The Records of the First Church in Salem*, 9, PIL.

218 Between 1660 and 1663, Joshua's brother Philip and his wife Joanna (Jane) were presented many times for nonattendance at public worship and Philip was set by the heels in stocks in November 1663 for denying the country's power to force any to come to the public worship.
219 Hughes, "Anglo American Puritanisms," 2.
220 Ibid.

2 "Piety tempers patriarchy"

Women of conscience in the English Atlantic world

In Luke 12, Christians are warned that obeying God's will be no easy task. In passages 49–53, Christ promises not peace, but division:

> Do you think that I have come to give peace on earth? No, I tell you, but rather division. For from now on in one house there will be five divided, three against two and two against three. They will be divided, father against son and son against father, mother against daughter and daughter against mother, mother-in-law against her daughter-in-law and daughter-in-law against mother-in-law.[1]

This was an injunction that seventeenth-century English puritans took seriously, risking life and property in acting on their conscience, as they challenged the hierarchy of the Church of England and one another to live out their faith. The warning was especially significant as some separatist women found themselves challenging the authority of their ministers and sometimes their own husbands, bringing strife to the commonweal as they answered the dictates of their conscience. Female piety, especially in the form of a "persistent spiritual extremism," was clearly perceived to be a threat to gendered relations in the seventeenth-century English Atlantic world; lay and clerical authorities took actions to contain the threat.[2]

At first glance, the violence Joshua Verin directed against his wife, a devout and pious woman, appears to be a seventeenth century example of a domineering husband controlling an unruly wife, not atypical of a patriarchal English marriage in the pre-modern era. Like many others, Jane Verin was a woman "much afflicted with conscience."[3] Their marriage sheds light both on the agency of puritan women in early New England and the tensions they experienced as they struggled with ranking obedience to their conscience, obedience to their spouses, obedience to the established church, and, as in the case of Jane Verin, obedience to a dissenting minister. They found themselves challenging patriarchy, without questioning their place within that system.[4] So, a woman like Jane Verin, who defied her husband by obeying her minister, could still accept her husband's authority over her as exemplified by the rope around her body.

As in many other English communities, the Verins' neighbors were uncertain about how much family discord they would tolerate without resorting to traditional disciplinary means. The differences among the residents of Providence on how best to respond to Joshua Verin's behaviour also reflect deep schisms among English puritans regarding domestic violence or "turbulent carriage," as it was sometimes called. An examination of ministerial and prescriptive literature and legal codes shows that the civil and ecclesiastical leaders were divided on the extent to which a husband could use physical violence in exercising governorship over an unruly wife, just as the Joshua Verin's neighbors in Rhode Island were divided on how to respond to his behavior. The puritans engaged in a rich pamphlet culture. These included sermons, theological examinations, self-help manuals, marriage manuals, and a variety of other printed materials. All agreed on the vital importance of safeguarding marriage and family as the most stable foundation for an orderly society and government. All reflect a world view that is hierarchical. They also reveal deep divisions among puritans in the English Atlantic world when it came to devout puritan women who, feeling compelled to act on the dictates of their conscience, came into conflict with male leaders, both civil and ecclesiastical, in their communities, their churches, and in their marriages.

Women and puritanism

Historians of gender and morality in Anglo-American culture have concluded that reform Protestantism was generally empowering for women, partially because of the stress on the priesthood of all believers, but also because of the insistence on literacy to give every individual access to the Scripture.[5] Many women, despite repeated exhortations to be submissive and accept their place in a male-dominated puritan order, underwent deeply emotional faith experiences that inspired them with a sense of spiritual or moral authority. The confidence stemming from that sense of God's personal salvation empowered them to act on their faith, even if it meant approbation from ministers, magistrates, or their spouses. One historian has concluded that "Puritanism in its practical effects quietly undermined its own patriarchal assumptions, allowing women a latitude of behavior and de facto personal authority that they would not have possessed without the psychological and social structures of Puritan life."[6] Another way to examine this issue is to consider the ways in which the lived experience of women deviated from commonly held norms, as exemplified by both law and prescriptive literature.[7]

The puritan churches used censure, admonition, and excommunication as tools to keep their members in line, because the bonds of family, such as those between husbands and wives or parents and children, were the "bonds of society itself. If they snapped, neither church nor state could survive."[8] Amanda Porterfield has concluded that the puritans succeeded in organizing a society based on their view of marriage and family life as the proper context of religious life, noting, "images of female sanctity and divine espousal coalesced with domestic feelings and behaviors. This coalescence shaped both social order and religious experience."[9] Paradoxically, Laurel Thatcher Ulrich has shown that although puritan ministerial literature focused on women's roles as wives and mothers, puritan "goodwives" also played an important role in the economies of their households. Further, husbands entrusted them with a wide range of practical responsibilities, so that they in effect often functioned as "deputy husbands."[10] Elaine Forman Crane has argued that "women were actively, albeit indirectly, involved in church governance.[11] In addition, one examination of the diversity of legal cultures in early America concludes that there was a Calvinist brand of patriarchy, characterized by the magistrates' attempts to prosecute all immorality."[12] One can see this dynamic at work in both Massachusetts Bay and Rhode Island—all persons, male or female—were held accountable for sinful behavior. This does not mean, however, that either puritan ministers or magistrates would accept women who did not know their place in the puritan social hierarchy. In Rhode Island, this distinction would explain why men like William Arnold, who had fled Massachusetts Bay for conscience sake, would not endorse Jane Verin's challenge to her husband's authority, even if it too were for the sake of her conscience.

In *A Brief History of the Church of Christ of Dedham, 1638*, the Reverend John Allin describes the process by which 30 families met regularly to read Scripture passages, to pray, to address questions raised at previous meetings and so to be "further acquainted with the (spiritual) tempers and gifts of one another."[13] Each member of this small community, formed at nearly the same time as that of Providence, watched over one another, "admonishing and exhorting one another, etc. in love, wisdom and piety and for the better settling of a body newly gathered ..."[14] Eventually, the families made a collective decision regarding the acceptance of individuals into church membership that would form their congregation. This was the basis of the so-called "gathered church." Of the original 18 members, six were women, all of whom participated in a public profession of their faith and the entering into a solemn covenant with the Lord.[15] While most churches in New England had separate seating for men and women and for adults and children and servants, Providence did not have a formal "gathered" church.[16] The residents met in Williams' home or at that of their neighbors for prayer or to consider civil matters. Women would have been present, whether or not they had a formal vote in the proceedings.

Answering Christ's call

All puritans believed in the "testimony of the Holy Spirit," that is, the faith experience was central to religious life in community. While for some, that personal faith experience manifested itself by action in attempting to live a godly life, for others, the conversion resulted from a feeling of God's grace that led them to live in conformity with God's laws. Theologians have distinguished a third more mystical kind of faith experience, one accompanied by an "immediate light, joy unspeakable, transcendent, glorious, and intuitive."[17] David D. Hall emphasizes the important role that "right preaching," especially powerful sermons, played in the formation of these new godly communities. He notes that it was common to travel to hear Sunday afternoon sermons, a practice called "gadding."[18] In 1678, friends and followers of the much beloved, late minister, Mr. Thomas Allen, former teacher at the Church of Christ in Charlestown, printed one of his sermons, entitled, "The call of Christ unto thirsty sinners, to come to him and drink of the waters of life." In the preface to the pamphlet, John Higginson notes that those who had heard the late Mr. Allen preach were "much affected with it," and they hoped it might encourage and be of use to others who were "Thirsty Souls in their coming to Jesus Christ."[19] Allen begins his sermon with an analysis of John 7:37, in which Christ calls out to any man who thirsts and invites him to "come onto me and Drink." According to Allen, this invitation issued by Christ during his sermon in the Temple has two parts: it is a gracious invitation to all that thirst, and it is a gracious promise that those who come, shall drink.[20] He describes this as a spiritual thirst, a deep sense of wanting and longing. Allen anticipates his congregation's question: How may the soul come to drink? He quotes Paul, who said "Ye received the Spirit by having the Gospel Preached." Allen calls on his congregation to answer Christ's call by "enclining the Ear"—finding Christ in his ordinances.[21] In other words, listening to scripture readings and sermons would, if one listened with an open heart, lead one closer to God. Allen reassures those who worry they have not the strength to do all that the scripture requires, stating "but it is our Duty to be doing what lies in us to the performance, and wait upon the Lord for His coming in with Power to enable us to perform." He comments on the fullness of spiritual blessings, the fullness of the Spirit, and a "Fullness of Righteousness & Satisfaction in Jesus Christ, so as to make a poor sinner to be accepted as Righteous before God, and discharge it of all Sins."[22] This sense of fullness is empowering and consoling—connecting Christ the Vine to his people, the branches of the tree. The call to salvation is like an unquenchable thirst and one that, according to Allen is *open to all*: "Be it known unto you Men and Women that are capable of knowledge, Know it, that Jesus Christ doth invite every one of you that stands before him in this Ordinance, to come unto Him and draw water out of this Well of Salvation."[23] In his sermon, Allen continues both to call and to reassure his congregation, noting that once a person has heard and answered the call, they receive an invitation from Christ that "perswades [sic] the Soul of the truth and reality of it, it is perswaded [sic] to trust in it, to rely upon it, and to expect an accomplishment and performance of it."[24] In other words, those who hear this call (or answer the thirst) assent of their own free will to answer the call. At the end of his sermon, Allen reiterates the call of Christ includes both old men and women, young men and maids, even old sinners, to come and drink and hence achieve salvation of their soul.

A study of puritan conversion narratives by Charles Cohen focuses on the intense emotional transformation, particularly the transition from a complete sense of debility and terror to one of joyful regeneration, a rebirth that changed "helpless unregenerates into puissant Saints."[25] The conversion narratives of William and Elizabeth Adams of Ipswich illustrate Cohen's analysis; they indicate that sermons preached by their ministers were instrumental as these congregants struggled with their faith and their fears, particularly the hope that despite their sinful natures, "God might yet have mercy upon me."[26] William Adams was born of godly parents who brought him up to fear God, yet he confesses, "my heart was very corrupt & sinful."[27] William Adams cites the preaching of Mr. Rogers regarding the mystical marriage of Christ and his church and the divorcing of the soul from sin. According to Adams, "This did much affect my heart & gave be greater Encouragm[ent] than Ever I had before & Caused me more Earnestly to be Seeking after Xt.(Christ)."[28] Adams particularly worried that his everlasting soul depended on obeying God's commands; he considered himself in great Sin and saw himself in "great Strait, Seeing yet if I did miscarry, I was Undone for Ever."[29] Thus, he recognized his peril; but although he had heard many sermons and read many tracts on faith, he still could not be satisfied that he was on the right track. At this point, he read a little book entitled, *Comforts to Strengthen the Weak in Faith*, a pamphlet that answered the many questions of those seeking salvation and provided encouragement to such souls. In effect, it was a how-to manual for puritans, one that Adams describes as having been a great help to him in that he was so far as to "assent to ye truth of God's promise." He professed his belief and earnestly asked God to work faith.[30]

Sixteenth-century Englishmen approached printed materials with "reverence." According to an analysis of early New England print culture, including descriptions of spiritual life, psalm books, and religious verse—all elements of devotional practice—readers not only reverenced, but they "returned to such texts many times over, whether in public ceremonies or in reading silently."[31] Some of these devotional manuals were issued in multiple editions in a relatively short period of time. For example, between 1601 and 1640, a book entitled *The Plaine Mans Pathway to Heaven* by Arthur Dent appeared in 25 editions.[32] Generally speaking, readers of this devotional literature tended to read slowly, but with unusual intensity.[33] Both William and Elizabeth Adams attest to this in their conversion narratives. When Adams declared his condition to his elders; that is, when he made a profession of his faith experience, his confession was filled with such a sense of sweetness and comfort that his heart was "often breathing out in thankfulness & admiration."[34] However, he continued to struggle with temptations, even after his conversion experience, sometimes feeling overcome and oppressed by the difficulty of living his life in a way that answered the call. Adams cites the positive influence of his new wife, the continuing counsel of the ministers, and his persistent reading of the scriptures as aids to reviving his faith.[35] In fact, when his wife fell ill, Adams believed it was a sign of a God provoked by his sinfulness. When his wife improved, Adams interpreted it as a sign of God's favor.

Similarly, Elizabeth (Stacey) Adams, who died at the age of 31 in 1655, describes her struggles, especially her fears that she was a sinner who would not be among the elect. Her reading of the scriptures was of great comfort, particularly the passage in Romans 9:18 which states "God hath mercy on whom he will have mercy." She discussed this passage with her minister, especially when her father sickened and died. She feared that he had been taken from her solely because of her sins. She also questioned whether she was earnest enough in seeking out God. Again, it was a sermon preached by Mr. Rogers that encouraged her to be patient and to wait. She struggled especially with the sin of lust and feared that she may die and go to hell as an unredeemed soul.[36] When Elizabeth confided in Mr. Rogers, she shared her fear that her heart was so "vile" that she was beyond salvation. Rogers urged her not to give way to the temptations of such fears and reassured her that all things were possible for God. Nevertheless, Elizabeth was filled with doubts, and the feeling of being under God's curse and judgement much affected her heart. She describes her predicament: "I then feared to Stand out any Longer, yet I knew not how to believe."[37] Elizabeth Adams' conversion narrative, her "tale of grace," demonstrates the real struggle that puritan women confronted in fighting what they viewed as their sinful natures and following their conscience on the path to both hearing and answering the call of Christ. At the end of her narrative, she notes her heart was much taken with admiration of God's mercy; she found that the "many Doubtings & Questionings in my heart" were in some measure answered by the word of God.[38] Both conversion narratives also reveal in emotion-laden language the fear devout puritans felt should they fail to obey God's laws. Their conversions resulted from intense self-examination over a prolonged period of time, punctuated by periods of self-doubt and fear.[39] The community of believers, their ministers, and a faithful reading of the scriptures enabled both William and Elizabeth Adams ultimately to profess their belief that God had called them to salvation. Puritan sympathy or "fellow feeling" is exemplified in the way the Allens prayed with and for one another; and the "sympathie," that is the warm relationship with their minister and other members of the congregation, that led to their ultimate realization, is one that filled them with joy and thankfulness.[40] Like the promises made to the Reverend Allen's congregation in Charlestown, the Adams had been "perswaded" by God's grace, resulting in their professions of conversion.

Jane Verin, like Elizabeth Adams, would have undergone a similar experience. Her willingness to continue with her defiance of her husband's will and to endure the repeated physical beatings testify to the strength of her ardor. In her case, she followed the guidance of her minister, Roger Williams. Similar to Elizabeth Adams, who frequently consulted and prayed with her minister, Jane Verin attended frequent prayer meetings and sought to act in a way that conformed with the dictates of her conscience. And, both in Salem and in Providence, she followed Roger Williams' guidance in challenging the legitimacy of the churches of Massachusetts and in challenging the authority of her husband when it came to spiritual matters. Her mother appears to have supported her in these endeavors. Given the experiences of both William and Elizabeth Adams as they struggled to answer God's call, one can only imagine the anguish Jane Verin experienced when her conscience inspired her to disobey her husband. Puritan women were socialized to be modest, submissive and obedient; and husbands were expected to conform to prescribed social norms as well. The sermon at the wedding of William and Elizabeth Adams was based on an analysis of Colossians 3.18,19 that admonished wives to "submit yourselves to your Husbands, as it is fit in the Lord."[41] At the same time, husbands were instructed to "love your Wives and be not bitter onto them."[42] The Reverend Hardy, who presided at their wedding, urged them to "ravish each other with love."[43] While Hardy instructed Elizabeth Adams to "reverence her husband," he also noted that love should temper William Adams' discipline, so that he would exercise his power "sparingly, mildly, and affectionately." He warned that "without love, that authority will degenerate into tyranny."[44] It seems this had happened with the Verins, given the fierceness of Joshua Verin's carriage. Remember that Roger Williams characterized Jane Verin as gracious and modest; and yet, she still disobeyed her husband. In addition to the brutality of Joshua Verin's beatings, one can assume she was also wracked by guilt or fear that she might be disobeying God's laws by disregarding her husband's will. She must have been torn by these conflicting imperatives. It is clear, that like Elizabeth Adams, Jane Verin frequently consulted with Roger Williams and prayed with him and others to find the righteous way forward. Either way, she risked displeasing either God or male authorities to whom she owed allegiance and obedience.

In addition to women's religious activism, prophesying, an emotional and authoritative form of speech also became a point of dispute for puritan ministers in New England. While all puritans believed that God lead people to salvation through the Word rightly preached, many also believed in the "possibility of a mystical, ecstatic union with God."[45] Anne Hutchinson, for example, is quoted as saying, "It is said, I will pour my spirit upon you Daughters, and they shall prophesy, & if God give me a gift of

Prophecy, I may use it."[46] Here she was quoting Daniel. John Winthrop later commented that the people "grew into so reverent an esteem of her godliness, and spiritual gifts, as they looked at her as a Prophetess, raised up of God for some great work now at hand."[47] In sixteenth and seventeenth century England, both Catholics and Protestants believed that devotion to God's will superseded obedience to a husband's authority. In fact, women were allowed to join churches separate from their husbands' place of worship.[48] Indeed, "If God commanded a Protestant woman to prophesy, she was required to do so, 'yea though the Husband should forbid her.'"[49] In Massachusetts, in contrast, women were punished for prophesying. For example, Sarah Keayne was found guilty in 1646 of "irregular prophesying in mixed assembly," while Joan Hogg was convicted in 1655 of "disorderly singing and idleness and for saying she [was] commanded by Christ to do so."[50] There is no evidence to support the idea that Jane Verin was called to prophesy; but certainly, the facts support the contention that she was willing to challenge both the ministry in Massachusetts Bay and her husband's authority in following her religious conscience. In a fascinating twist, Winthrop's journal notes that some of the Providence residents who voted to disenfranchise Joshua Verin believed that "if Verin would not suffer his wife to have her liberty, the church should dispose her to some other man who would use her better."[51]

Roger Williams' letter to Winthrop asserts that Jane was willing "to stay and live with him or else where [sic], where she may not offend, etc."[52] What is significant about this exchange is that Jane Verin obviously was given a choice. She *could have chosen* to separate from a husband who had beaten her savagely when she had challenged his authority within the marriage. As subsequent events demonstrate, she was evidently ready to continue to submit to his authority, *except* in the case of her religious conscience. Williams urged Winthrop *not* to countenance Joshua Verin in any way.[70] Interestingly, a few years later in 1656, a similar situation occurred in Massachusetts Bay. In response to a petition by Joanne Halsey, the General Court ruled that she had the "libertie to goe to the publicke meetings on the Lords & lecture days, or at other times ... without interruption or disturbances from George Halsey."[53] In fact, the court went one step further, adding that if Halsey or any acting on his behalf tried to "seaze on her, vex, molest, or any way disturbe her," he would be committed to prison until he could give "bond for his good behavior."[54] As in the Verin case, a woman's right to attend prayer services was once again upheld, despite the opposition of her husband.

Puritan ministerial literature

New Englanders were most likely familiar with the works of William Perkins, a leading English puritan divine. William Bradford and Roger Williams both quoted him frequently. Born in 1558, Perkins matriculated at

Christ's College, Cambridge. In his younger days, he was noted "for reck-lessness and profanity, and addicted to drunkenness."[55] He reformed his life, often preaching to the prisoners. He was known as much for his clear and persuasive sermons as for his outspoken resistance to vestiges of Roman Catholic worship, such as kneeling during communion.[56] He taught at Christ's College until 1594, having tutored John Robinson, a puritan divine who would become one of the most frequently quoted pur-itan theologians in New England. Perkins considered faith the result of God's effectual call rather than of sinful man's "free will." He published *The Golden Chain, Or the Causes of Salvation and Damnation* in 1591. This is basically a how-to manual designed for ignorant people that desire to be instructed. It is a no-nonsense guide. As he states it,

> And for a help in this your ignorance, to bring you to a true know-ledge, unfeigned faith, and sound repentance: here I have set down the principal point of Christian religion, in fixed plain and easier rules, even such as the simplest may easily learn; and hereunto is adjoined an exposition of them word by word.[57]

In his introduction, he rejects the typical excuses that his contemporaries might have offered to justify their sinful nature, reminding them

> it is not sufficient to say all these [the Creed, Lord's prayer, and Ten Commandments] unless you can understand the meaning of the words and be able to make right use of the Commandments, of the Creed, of the Lord's prayer, by applying them inwardly to your hearts and con-sciences, and outwardly, to your lives and conversations.[58]

It was not enough to practice the outward forms of faith; the meaning of these (inspired by faith) had to be at the heart of religious practice. Perkins reaffirms the basic Calvinist creed of predestination whereby, God (before the founding of the world) "hath ordained certain men to salvation." The order of salvation to damnation, according to Perkins, is that God fore-knew, predestined, called, justified, and glorified. Perkins cites Romans 8:28–30 as his source to argue that this order represents an unbreakable golden chain. In his pamphlet, "*Christian Economy: Or a Short Survey of the Right Manner of Erecting and Ordering a Family, According to the Scriptures*," Perkins reaffirms God's will and intent as they relate to the institution of marriage, stating, "marriage was made and appointed by God himself to be the fountain and the seminary of all other sorts and kinds of life, in the Common-wealth and in the Church."[59]

A student of Perkins, William Ames was among the most influential of the divines in Puritan New England. Born in 1576, Ames completed his theological studies at Christ's College, Cambridge under Perkins' tutelage. After refusing to wear a surplice to chapel and then preaching a sermon that attacked card-playing, he left Cambridge and tried to settle with a congregation at Colchester.[60] He was forbidden to preach by the Bishop of London. He ultimately gained the backing of wealthy merchants who financed his move to Leyden, Holland. The view of his English peers is a good indicator of how uncompromising Ames was in his puritan beliefs; he was deemed "no obedient son of the church, being a rebel against her authority."[61] Once in Frieland, Ames took a theological chair at the University of Franeker, where he was named rector ten years later. Ames was a champion of Calvinist doctrine and a staunch opponent of Arminianism, particularly the tenet that human will played an important role in salvation and the assertion that Christ died for all men, not just the elect. Like other puritans, Ames rejected these beliefs as heretical. His *Medulla Theologia* ("Marrow of Theology") was reprinted numerous times and used as a text during the first 50 years of Harvard College. Ames developed his theology within the framework established by Augustine, emphasizing man's sinful nature and absolute powerlessness to effect his own salvation.

In the classic 1939 monograph, *The New England Mind: The Seventeenth Century*, Perry Ellis succinctly summarizes the central tenets of the Puritan approach to understanding revelation:

> When God created the world, He formed a plan or scheme of it in His mind, of which the universe is the embodiment; in His mind the plan is single, but in the universe it is reflected through concrete objects and so seems diverse to the eye of human reason; these apparently diverse and temporal segments of the single and timeless divine order are the various arts; the principles of them are gathered from things by men through the use of their inherent capacities, their natural powers; once assembled, the principles are arranged into series of axiomatical propositions according to sequences determined by the laws of method. It must be obvious to begin with that God sent forth His wisdom to an end, and so each of the arts, being a part of that wisdom, tends toward the end; God created the arts by the method of genesis, combining arguments into the patterns of His intention, but man must find the principles of the arts by the method of analysis, discriminating the particulars within the synthesis; however, once man has formulated the rules of the arts, he should imitate God by using them, according to the method of genesis, to achieve the results for which they were predestined.[62]

Puritans believed, in effect, that God created the universe that functions according to natural laws, that man can then ascertain with his reason. That wisdom is also part of God's plan, in that according to the Divine Will, man should use his God-given reason to understand God and God's creation. This emphasis on both reason and faith are evident in the writings of other puritan divines. For example, William Ames' *Medulla* provides the reader with another methodology for understanding religious principles. His preface stresses care for "method and logical form." In other words, Ames attempted to apply human reason to revelation and to understand the ways in which the mind worked in order to make reason, choice and action possible.[63] Among his other works, his *de Conscientia, ejus Jure et Casibus* (published posthumously in 1634) is noteworthy for attempting to apply general principles of Christian understanding that work with one another in the development of moral thought.

> The will, in keeping with the divinely created goodness that remains even in a fallen creature, seeks to obtain good and wants to distinguish the greatest good from a variety of competing goods. In so desiring the ability to make this distinction, the will "commands" the understanding to undertake what is appropriate for the rational faculty: the search for truth.[64]

In this analysis, God's will, individual conscience and the public good are all connected through the individual exercise of reason. Thus, morality and ethics are based directly on the Bible, *not* on nature or reason. Under Ames's influence, New England Puritans eagerly undertook to extract hidden meanings from the Bible in absolute certainty that the method was infallible. "Wisdom lies in the *Rational Application* of general Rules of Scripture to ourselves and our own conditions, and in the *induction of particulars*, and due Reasoning from it."[65] Reason, the preachers frequently declared, is "the fore-horse in the team," and as it turns, so the will must follow; it is the "governor and captain of the soul" and "the will dependeth of it." William Ames wrote this doctrine deep into the New England tradition and founded the whole ethical system upon it: he defined faith as an act both of the understanding, which yields assent, and of the will, which embraces the assent; but reason's act must come before the act of will; "The Will ... cannot will or nil anything unless reason have first judged it to be willed or nilled; neither can it choose but follow the last practical judgement, and do that which reason doth dictate to be done."[66] Preachers in New England repeated this doctrine throughout the century. According to one biographer, Ames was quoted more often than Luther and Calvin combined.[67] Ames died in 1633. On May 11, 1637, his widow and children received a permit to emigrate, arriving in New England on the *Marr Ann*. Ames' family received a land grant from the General Court on September 15, 1637, made out to "The Widow of Doctor Ames, of famous memory, who is deceased."[68] His books established the foundation for the library at Harvard University.

But where did women fit into this paradigm? Edmund Morgan's *The Puritan Family* is a hallmark in the study of the Puritan family and the relationship between husband and wife. Puritans, according to Morgan, tended to view women as the "weaker vessel in both body and mind." A husband was not to expect too much from her. Puritan wives who attempted to use their reason to solve problems of theology by themselves could take warning from the wife of Governor Hopkins of Connecticut. Mistress Hopkins went insane; and according to Governor Winthrop, the reason was that she spent too much time in reading and writing:

> Her husband, being very loving and tender of her, was loath to grieve her; but he saw his error, when it was too late. For if she had attended her household affairs, and such things as belong to women, and not gone out of her way and calling to meddle in such things as are proper for men, whose minds are stronger, etc., she had kept her wits, and might have improved usefully and honorably in the place God had set her.[69]

Winthrop is saying that if only Mrs. Hopkins had known her place and occupied herself with women's work in the home, instead of trespassing in the world of men, she might have avoided losing her mind.

Historians of the early modern period have been fascinated by the tensions inherent in the activism of Puritan women. It was possible for Puritan women to use their piety to temper patriarchy. Many women, despite repeated exhortations to be submissive and accept their place in a male-dominated Puritan order, underwent deeply emotional faith experiences. The confidence stemming from that sense of God's personal salvation empowered them to act on their faith, even if it meant approbation from ministers, magistrates, or their mates. A recent study focuses on the central role female piety played in seventeenth-century puritanism.[70] Another historian has concluded that "Puritanism in its practical effects quietly undermined its own patriarchal assumptions, allowing women a latitude of behavior and de facto personal authority that they would not have possessed without the psychological and social structures of Puritan life."[71] David R. Como examines the case of one English Puritan woman, Anne Fenwick, and he finds that much like Anne Hutchinson in New England, women on both sides of the Atlantic claimed the right to prophesy and carved out a place for "enthusiastic" modes of worship. In a world where puritans rejected the forms of worship within the Church of England, the private meetings (also called "godly conferences" or informal gatherings of "Saints") were extra-institutional church assemblies where women were expected to participate. Further, in the "subterranean milieu" of the conventicles, "effusive, powerful, and emotive outpourings of the spirit were not merely tolerated but in fact highly prized."[72] Clearly, the issue of women's roles in puritanism must be understood in a transatlantic context. In a volume examining the diversity of legal cultures in early America, historian Cornelia Hughes Dayton asks an intriguing question: Was there a Calvinist type of patriarchy?[73] Dayton attempts to answer this question by examining legal encounters in Geneva during the time of Calvin's tenure as a pastor and as head of the bench of clerics who sat on the Consistory, the main body for disciplining sinners and miscreants within the city. Dayton then compares these with the attempts to enforce moral laws nearly a century later by Theophilus Eaton, governor and chief magistrate in New Haven. Dayton has found that almost eighty five per cent of defendants admitted their guilt before conviction, a fact she argues attests to the remarkable degree of consensus among the early settlers of New Haven "about their God-given mission to lead morally upright lives."[74] Dayton concludes that there was a Calvinist brand of patriarchy, characterized by the magistrates' attempts to prosecute all immorality (thereby attacking the double standard) and by "reconfiguring the regulation of marriage such that domestic violence was taken seriously, husbands were held accountable for irresponsibility, and full divorce was made available on adultery and desertion grounds."[75] In effect, Dayton concludes, the lay-pleading and simplified procedures established in the puritan legal system, "invited and encouraged" women's testimonies "in ways that clashed with English legal traditions."[76] One can see this dynamic at work in both Massachusetts Bay and Rhode Island where all persons had to account for their sinful behavior. This does not mean, however, that either ministers or magistrates would accept women who did not know their place in the puritan social hierarchy. Dayton points out, for example, that although Governor Eaton and the Reverend Davenport attacked all moral transgressions, they nonetheless did not sanction female insubordination. Reverend Davenport, for example, supported the proceedings against Anne Hutchinson in 1637; Governor Eaton acceded to the excommunication of his wife, Anne Yale Eaton, for her unorthodox opinions.[77] In Rhode Island, this distinction would explain why men like William Arnold, who had fled Massachusetts Bay for conscience sake, would not endorse Jane Verin's challenge to her husband's authority, even if she too were acting for the sake of her conscience.

Given the violence of the Joshua Verin's discipline of his wife, why did the people of Providence charge Joshua Verin with violating his wife's liberty of conscience? Why not charge him with putting his wife in "danger of life"? The dynamics of the controversy clearly raised issues of religion and authority within the Puritan patriarchy and within the institution of marriage. Despite the fact that Roger Williams' acted in support of Jane Verin's liberty of conscience, he believed in a woman's inferiority. He accepted an essentially subordinate role for women as one consigned by the Bible, arguing that even

> though the Holy Scripture were silent, yet Reason and Experience tell us, that the Woman is the weaker Vessel, that she is more fitted to keep and order the House and Children, & ... that the Lord hath given a covering of longer Hair to Women as a sign or teacher of covering Modesty and Bashfulness, Silence, and Retiredness; and therefore, [women are] not fitted for Manly Actions and Employments.[78]

Clearly, he valued humility and modesty as female qualities, and as the above quotation attests, believed women should be confined to their domestic and maternal roles. He was equally staunch in his opposition to female prophesying, arguing that any woman who preached in public assemblies represented "open violence" to God's way, a "business sober and modest Humanity abhor to think of."[79]

The antinomian crisis continued

Remember that all were responsible for maintaining the covenant with God; therefore, unrepentant sinners and those who challenged the authority of civil and religious authorities charged with enforcing God's laws would be either disciplined or evicted. It is for this reason that both Roger Williams and Anne Hutchinson were expelled from Massachusetts Bay for "new and dangerous opinions," which, according to Governor John Winthrop, "were adjudged by all the magistracy and ministers ... to be erroneous and very dangerous, and the calling of him to office at the time was judged a great contempt of authority."[80] Jane Verin, a devout and devoted follower of Roger Williams, would rather reject the authority of the Church of Salem, which in her view had not separated itself adequately from the Church of England by failing to cut ties with the other churches of Massachusetts (and hence been rendered corrupt), rather than violating the terms of the new covenant. Williams attracted many men and women with his uncompromising stand regarding the true churches in the colonies. In his *History of Plymouth Plantations*, William Bradford writes that Williams was beloved among his congregation in Salem precisely for this reason noting, "He was friendly entertained according to their poor ability and exercised his gifts among them .... his teaching well approved, for the benefit whereof I still blessed God."[81] In his account, Bradford also expresses his thanks to Williams, "even for his sharpest admonitions and reproofs, so far as they agree with truth."[82] This partially explains why so many, especially women, became followers of his.

The congregation of the First Church of Boston was reconciled after the breach caused by the Antinomian Crisis in Massachusetts Bay, "and the church was saved from ruin beyond all expectation."[83] By 1639, religious enthusiasm had grown to the point that Winthrop and other civil leaders feared that it might endanger the public welfare. Winthrop writes,

> There were so many lectures now in the country, and many poor persons would usually resort to two to three in the week, to the great neglect of their affairs, and the damage of the public. The assemblies also were (in divers churches) held till night, and sometimes within the night, so as such as dwelt far off could not get home in due seasons, and many weak bodies could not endure so long, in the extremity of the heat or cold, without great trouble, and hazard of their health.[84]

Apparently, the situation was so dire, that the general court ordered the church elders to meet with the magistrates and deputies to discuss the length and frequency of church assemblies. Many of the magistracy took umbrage at this, expressing their dislike in no uncertain terms. Winthrop makes a sardonic note in his journal. He points out that the elders challenged the edict from the general court

> alleging their tenderness of the church's liberties, (as if such a precedent might enthrall them to the civil power, and as if it would cast a blemish upon the elders, which would remain to posterity), that they should need to be regulated by the civil magistrate, and also raise an ill savor of the people's coldness.[85]

What is interesting to note about this entry is the ways in which the civil and religious leaders worked together to ensure the common good, while simultaneously emphasizing the safeguarding of liberty. In this instance, it is the liberty of the churches to conduct their affairs without interference from the general court. Winthrop and the other deputies hastened to explain that this was a recommendation, rather than an order. The civil authorities also recognized that if they were to push this matter, it might

> make some breach or disturbance at least, for the elders had great power in the peoples' hearts, which was needful to be upheld, lest the people should break their bonds through abuse of liberty, which divers, having surfeited of, were very forward to incite others to raise mutinies' and foment dangers and groundless jealousies of the magistrates, etc.[86]

Mollified, the elders agreed to the proposition put forward by the magistrates to break off their meetings in a timely way to enable their congregants to reach home by daylight.[87] Note that, at the same time, these measures also were intended to keep the peace. If religious enthusiasm can be measured in terms of church attendance, these events certainly are a testament to the level of religious fervor among ordinary citizens in Boston, even after the Antinomian crisis had passed.

The women of Providence

None of the women who followed Williams into the wilderness in 1636 left personal written records but examining their personal histories does shed light on their lives. The biographical sketches that follow might also answer questions about what influence, if any, the women in Providence had on the male heads of household who made the ultimate decision regarding Joshua and Jane Verin. Although only male property-owners who were heads of household could be admitted into the "fellowship of vote," women very much played a decisive role in the outcome. In addition to Jane Verin and her mother, the Widow Reeves, who were the other women of Providence? What experiences shaped their world view, and how did these influence their response to Verin's brutal assault on his wife? The men who made the ultimate decision shared not only experiences, but convictions, with their wives. These would at the least predispose them to be sympathetic to the plight of a woman like Jane Verin, a woman who acted out of religious conviction and devotion. Indeed, Jane Verin shared with many of the men and women who founded Providence a willingness to defy authority in following her conscience. As the following biographical sketches will attest, some of these women constituted a kind of "spirit group," a community of like-minded individuals that supported defiance of male authority when matters of conscience were involved. Many women in the colony, given their previous experiences in defiance of authority in defense of individual conscience, might through their spouses and male relatives, exert both a tacit and an indirect influence on male decision makers that could result in the community condemning Joshua Verin for his disrespect of Jane Verin.

Alice Daniell(s) was born ca 1597 in Dorset, England.[88] She was married sometime before 1630 to Richard Beggarly.[89] The couple apparently had severe difficulties because she immigrated to New England without him. In fact, John Winthrop reports that the Court had considered "the cause between Richard Beggarly and his wife, who had been here six years, and he in England."[90] Alice sued for divorce, but the Court decided it had insufficient evidence to grant her request. Instead, the Court granted her 20 shillings to send to England for further proof.[91] Alice was a well-educated woman of stature in the community. In 1634, Alice Daniel Beggarly was granted controlling interest in the estate of the Reverend Samuel Skelton. Subsequent court records indicate that she was actively involved in the disposition of his properties. It is interesting to note that the Reverend Skelton was chosen to be pastor of the first Salem church organized on July 20, 1629. Samuel Skelton was described as "a friend to the utmost equality of privileges in Church and State."[92] Roger Williams was co-pastor with the Reverend Skelton of the Salem church from 1633 until Skelton's death. This was the first church organized by the English emigrants to Massachusetts Bay, a church that acted "on principles of perfect and entire independence of every other ecclesiastical body."[93] Interestingly, the church at Salem also allowed women the opportunity to make a public confession of faith, but not on Sundays, only "upon the week days."[94] John Winthrop noted that the Rev. Skelton had criticized regular meetings by the ministers of the Bay, "fearing 'it might grow in time to a presbytery or superintendency, to the prejudice of the churches' liberties.'"[95] In 1636, Alice was admitted to the Salem Church. Subsequently, she received several land grants not only in Massachusetts Bay, but also in the new settlement of Providence. She appears in two lists of Providence landowners as early as 1638; she became John Greene's second wife on December 14.[96]

It should be noted that John Greene had a long association with the Verin family. Prior to his departure from England, John Greene was a surgeon in Salisbury; he married Joanne Tattershall in 1619 at St. Thomas Parish, the same church where the Verin family worshipped. His first wife died in 1635—the year he left for New England. Greene and his six children had arrived to Salem on the same ship as the Verins; and Greene and Joshua Verin accompanied Roger Williams to Providence. Greene was one of original twelve to whom Roger Williams deeded land in 1638 (after he brought it from Miantonomoh); he bought house lot number 15 on Main Street. Alice was a landowner even before she married John Greene (according to a petition by her step-son, John Greene, who in 1682/1683 petitioned the town of Providence to demand the "right of commonage & undivided lands which appertained to that lot which was granted and laid out to my mother-in-law before my father Mr. John Greene Sr. married her who was at that time called Mrs. Alise Daniell."[97] Although she could not vote in town matters, certainly her opinion must have influenced some of the decision-makers. An educated, responsible landowner who had exercised independence of judgement and action by leaving her husband and emigrating to New England, she was clearly associated with a puritan minister who carefully guarded the religious liberties against any potential usurpations. These factors might have influenced Alice Beggarly Greene to be sympathetic to a woman like Jane Verin who had followed her conscience and disobeyed her husband in the process.

According to John Endicott, Alice also had considerable medical knowledge. Additionally, her husband John was referred to as one of "two local surgeons" in Goodwin's *Pilgrim Republic*, noting that "the people of Providence relied solely upon him for surgical aid long before his removal to 1643."[98] Is it not conceivable in the event of grievous bodily injury, *both* Alice and John Greene might have been called in to tend to Jane Verin after her husband's assault? There are no official records attesting to the fact, but in a close-knit, small community such as Providence, it is probable that the Greenes would have been involved when Jane Verin became the victim of her husband's brutal carriage, *especially since the Greenes lived only two house lots from the Verins.*[99] It appears that the bonds of community, which might have influenced John Greene to support his Wiltshire countryman, were trumped by the bonds of mutual affection and experience between John and Alice Greene, as well as their roles as healers. If this is the case, it is likely the Greenes would have been willing to condemn Joshua Verin's behaviour by supporting the decision to disenfranchise him. Alice Greene died on January 12, 1643.[100]

Born Margaret King about 1570, Margaret Weston was the daughter of Francis King, in Great Baddow, Essexshire, England. She married Robert Pease (b. 1565 in Great Baddow) in 1586.[101] Their son, Robert, was born on June 10, 1604 and their son, John, was born November 20, 1608 in Great Baddow. Her husband Robert died at the age of 58 on April 16,

1623. Sometime between that time and 1630, she married Francis Weston and had a daughter Lucy, because the three of them appear on the passenger list of the *Mary and John*, part of the Winthrop fleet that arrived in Plymouth in 1630.[102] Her sons, Robert and John Pease (ages 26 and 27), both arrived in Boston on the *Francis* which departed Ipswich on April 30, 1634 and arrived in November of that year.[103] The Weston family moved to Salem by 1633, as indicated by the fact that her husband was admitted to Salem church prior to November 5, 1633 (implied by the granting of his status as a freeman).[104] Her husband took on Joshua Harris as an apprentice for 5 years. On November 3, 1635, it was ordered that "John Pease shall be whipped, & bound to his good behavior, for striking his mother, Mrs. Weston, & deriding of her, & for diverse other misdemeanors, & other evil carriages."[105] The exact reason for John Pease's abuse of his mother is unknown. What is significant here is that Margaret Weston, like Jane Verin, was a victim of family violence. It is also apparent that, like Jane Verin, Margaret Weston also had a history of challenging the authorities of Massachusetts Bay.

Francis Weston was chosen by the town of Salem to serve as a representative in the newly formed House of Representatives on May 14, 1634.[106] Despite this vote of confidence, by March 12, 1637/1638, Francis Weston was included in a list of eight men (four, including Weston, from Salem) who were licensed to leave Massachusetts Bay—all Salem men who later joined Roger Williams in Providence.[107] Clearly his wife was also willing to challenge local authorities, for Essex Quarterly Court records indicate that on December 26, 1637, "Margret Weston challenged three of the jurymen of Salem, Jeffrey Massie, Edm. Batter, and Anth. Dike."[108] Later that year, at a Quarter Court held at Cambridge on June 5, 1638, "Francis Weston's wife was censured to be set 2 hours in the bilboes here, & 2 hours at Salem, upon a lecture day."[109] They moved to Providence in 1638 prior to that punishment being carried out. They appeared as a proprietor of jointly owned meadow ground at Pawtuxet and Warwick 1642.[110] At some point after the Verin decision, they returned to Salem and apparently continued their defiance of religious authority, because on October 17, 1643, Francis Weston and several other men were confined to various towns, including Dorchester, "to be set on work, & to wear such bolts or irons as may hinder his escape" and not to "either by speech or writing publish, declare, or maintain any of the blasphemous or abominable heresies wherewith he hath been charged by the General Court."[111] Her son Robert died on October 27, 1644; Francis Weston died in Dorchester before June 5, 1645 when the Massachusetts Bay General Court sent a warrant "to the executors of Francis Weston ... to take notice of an attachment against the lands of Francis Weston."[112] What is significant, however, is that both Margaret and Francis Weston also continued to challenge authority after the Verin decision. He was a wanted man in the last few years of his life. Ultimately, records indicate that Margaret Pease died on New Year's Day, 1645 in Salem at age 75. There are multiple reasons to believe that Margaret (Pease) Weston would have been sympathetic to Jane Verin. Both women had a history of challenging male authorities when acting out of conscience. Further, both women had been victims of family violence perpetrated by a male member of their family; it would be logical to assume that Francis Weston would have agreed with the Williams faction in censuring Joshua Verin.

Christanna Peak Arnold, child of Thomas Peak, was christened on February 15, 1583/1584 in Muchelney, Somerset, England. Sometime between 1610 and 1614, she married William Arnold of Cheselbourne, in Dorset in Ilchester Parish. It was there that the Arnolds' children would be baptized: Elizabeth (b. 1611), Benedict (b. 1615), Joane (b. 1617) and Stephen (b. 1622). William and Christanna Arnold sailed from Dartmouth, England on May 1, 1635 with their four children, together with a group of relatives and neighbors from Ilchester. They arrived in America on June 24, 1635—on William Arnold's 48th birthday. They settled in Hingham, Massachusetts until April 20, 1636, when William moved the family to Providence, Rhode Island.[113]

William Arnold was one of the original thirteen proprietors of Providence. Their extended household included son Benedict (and later his wife), and their daughter Elizabeth and her husband, William Carpenter. In addition, William Arnold's niece and nephew, Thomas and Frances Hopkins, lived with them. William Arnold opposed Roger Williams in the matter of Verin. After the Verin decision, in 1638, the Arnolds moved again, this time about five miles south of Providence on the Pawtuxet River to a new settlement in Pawtuxet, Rhode Island. Here William died in 1675 during King Phillip's War, seven years after Christanna's death. The Arnolds and the Carpenters were among the wealthiest and most influential of Rhode Island families. Benedict Arnold would later serve as governor of the colony in 1663. Despite the fact that Christanna prayed regularly with the other members of the community in Providence, it is unclear whether her sympathy for Jane Verin would have trumped her obedience to her husband.

The parish records of St. Albans Abbey in Hertfordshire show that Mary Ashton, daughter of James and Alice Ashton, was baptized on August 25, 1605 and married in the Abbey to Thomas Olney on September 16, 1629.[114] Thomas was a shoemaker from Hertford. The couple left London on *The Planter*, arriving in Boston in 1635.[115] In 1637/1638, the couple was censured by the Church of Salem for refusing to hear the word and for rejecting the church as a true church.[116] The Olneys joined the community in Providence in 1638. Mary Olney and Alice Angell were sisters. The Baptist Church at Providence was organized in March 1638/1639. Roger Williams baptized Thomas Olney, who appears on the list as one of the founding members. Shortly after their arrival, Thomas was named treasurer of the colony. In 1649, he was elected Assistant. Mary

Ashton Olney had seven children, Thomas (b. 1632 in Hertford, lived in Providence), Epenetus (b. 1634), Nabadiah (baptized 1637 at Salem), Stephen, Mary, James and Lydia. Thomas died in 1682.[117] Given their friendship and their activism, along with Jane Verin and the Widow Reeves, one can confidently argue that *both* Mary Olney and her husband would have both supported the decision to disenfranchise Joshua Verin for the violence of his carriage against his wife.

Mary Sweet Holliman was born Mary Periam in 1581. She married John Sweet of Modbury, Devon in 1619.[118] Their sons John and James were born in 1620 and 1622. The family arrived in Salem in 1632, where they settled next door to the Rev. Samuel Skelton and his family. After Mr. Skelton's death, Alice Beggarly Daniels was the executrix for Mr. Skelton's estate. Given what has been described as the dense network of social interactions in Salem, it is highly likely that Mary Sweet knew Alice Daniels. They would be reunited in Providence where the Greenes and Hollimans were neighbours. John Sweet died at age 67 sometime between June 1637 and Christmas Day, 1637, when his widow received a grant of meadow and swamp and ¾ acre for a household of four.[119] She married Ezekiel Holliman, one of the original proprietors of Providence, in 1638. Her husband was called by some, the "leader of the followers of Roger Williams," and had been summoned to appear before the general court on March 12, 1637–1638 "because hee did not frequent the publike assemblyes, & for seduceing many."[120]

Clearly Mary Sweet Holliman agreed with her new husband's radical views, because she and Jane Verin's mother, the Widow Reeves, are two women listed in Hugh Peter's letter as persons who had "wholly" refused to hear the word at the Church of Salem. Like Jane Verin and her mother, the Widow Reeves, both Margery and her husband Ezekiel challenged the ecclesiastical authorities while acting on their faith. Later, Holliman would baptize Roger Williams and be a founding member of the First Baptist Church of Providence, another indication of their likely support for censuring Joshua Verin. In 1640, the couple moved to Portsmouth, Rhode Island where Ezekiel Holliman operated a mill. She died in 1681.

There is no information available about Elizabeth James's surname, origins, or early years. Based on her year of marriage, one can estimate that she was born around 1610. She married Thomas James of Lincolnshire between 1627 and 1631 in England. As noted in the discussion of the first proprietors of Providence, Elizabeth and Thomas James left their congregation in Charlestown after a rancorous disagreement and by June of 1637, the couple had relocated to Providence where they joined Roger Williams and his community of people "distressed of conscience."[121] They were neighbours of John Greene and William Arnold. They became among the founding members of the First Baptist Church in Providence but, by 1639, James sold all of his lands, rights, and privileges in Providence. He relocated Elizabeth and his family to New Haven, Connecticut where their son Nathaniel was born in 1641. Thomas and Elizabeth returned to England, while their sons chose to remain in the colonies. In his will, dated February 5, 1682/1683, Thomas James bequeathed to his son, Thomas of Long Island, New York (in the event that he was still living), all of his books and household goods. Elizabeth must have predeceased her.

Susan (or Susannah) Harris was born in England around 1614. She married William Harris. He and his brother Thomas had arrived in New England on the *Lyon* in 1631. William Harris is listed as one of the Salem church members who followed Roger Williams to Providence in 1636. In the land deeds by which Williams conveyed Providence territory in October of 1638, William Harris is one of the nine men from Salem who would be admitted "into the same fellowship of vote with us."[122] According to ancestral files, William and Susannah had several children, including a son, Andrew (b. 1635) who would have been a very young child upon their arrival to Providence. The family joined with William Arnold in opposing Roger Williams on the Verin case and moved to Pawtuxet shortly thereafter. In the ensuing years, their family grew when their daughters, Howlong, Susannah, and Toleration, were born between 1642 and 1648. William Harris went to England to confer with government officials on land questions in 1679. He was taken prisoner by an Algerian corsair on January 24, 1679 and sold in Barbary. He spent a year in slavery before he was redeemed. He returned to London where he died before he could return to Rhode Island; his death was recorded on February 22, 1682. Susanna is listed as his widow; she died sometime later in the year.[123]

Mary Bernard Williams was the daughter of a minister, the Reverend Richard Bernard. She was baptized at Worksop, Nottinghamshire on September 24, 1607. She married Roger Williams, the chaplain to Sir William Masham of Otes in High Laver, Essex on December 15, 1629.[124] The couple departed for the colonies in 1631 on the *Lyon*, settling first in Plymouth and then in 1633 in Salem, where Roger Williams was teacher and then pastor of the First Church of Salem. Roger and his wife had several children: a daughter Mary, born at Plymouth in August 1633, a daughter, Freeborn, born at Salem in October 1635, and a son, Providence, born in Providence in September 1638, just a few months following the Verins' return to Salem.[125] Two other children, Mercy and Daniel, were born in Providence, in 1640 and 1641/1642, respectively. Given how bitterly Roger Williams condemned Verin's brutal actions, it is highly likely Mary Bernard Williams too would have agreed on the town's decision.

Julia (Julianne) Marchant was the daughter of John Marchant and the granddaughter of John and Eva (Corminge) Marchant, an old and established family in Yeovil, Somerset. She was born on August 8, 1591. She married Stukely Wescott of Ilminster on October 5, 1619. The marriage is recorded in the parish register of the ancient St. John the Baptist Church at Yeovil, as is the baptism of their two oldest children, a daughter Damaris, baptized in 1621 and son Samuel baptized in 1623. They had four more sons and a daughter, none of whom appear on the register. They arrived in Massachusetts Bay on June 24, 1635. Stukely was made a freeman in 1636 and received a one-acre land grant on December 25, 1637. However, their religious views began to cause them trouble. Within a few short months, the General Court granted them permission, in March 12, 1638, to leave Salem. They quickly packed up their young family and followed Roger Williams to Rhode Island. Both Julia and her husband were devout separatists as evidenced by the fact that they were included with the Verins in the letter of the Reverend Hugh Peter (in 1639), as those who "disobey the truth." The couple was also censured by the Church of Salem for having denied that the church was a true church. In Providence, Stukely Westcott was rebaptized by Roger Williams and became one of the founding members of the First Baptist Church. Given these facts, it is reasonable to assume that Julia and Stukely Westcott would have sided with the Williams faction in the Verin decision. On August 8, 1638, a few weeks after Joshua and Jane Verin returned to Salem, Roger Williams "freely admitted twelve loving friends and neighbors" into equal ownership with himself of lands he had first purchased from the Indians in 1636. Stukely Westcott is included on that list, making him one of the original proprietors of Providence. Their daughter, Damaris, married Benedict Arnold on December 17, 1640; he succeeded as governor when Roger Williams left Rhode Island in 1644. By that time, Julia and Stukely had relocated to Warwick, Rhode Island where they lived until their deaths in 1670 and 1677, respectively.

Making sense of women's experiences

The biographical sketches of the women who helped found Providence reveals several interesting points. While Anne Hutchinson and Mary Dyer are well-known dissenting women who were punished for their defiance of church authorities in New England, it is clear there were many more lesser known women who engaged in similar behavior. Like Jane Verin, women like her mother, Margery Reeves, Margaret Weston, Alice Daniels, Julia Marchant Wescott, and Mary Sweet Holliman, had histories both in Old and New England of challenging the authority of the Church of England and of the ecclesiastical authority in New England. All had been admitted into membership into a congregation of "Visible Saints." Often, this meant they had testified either in public or in private to a faith experience. As is evident from their subsequent actions, they tried to lead sanctified lives, living out their faith in ways that lead them into conflict with their ministers or their husbands, males who had authority over them within the puritan patriarchy. In Providence, they formed a spirit group—attending prayer services together and supporting one another as they most likely would in a small, newly established community. They were bound together by fellow-feelings and mutual affections, that is, puritan sympathy. Evidence also seems to suggest that their husbands supported their activism and would most likely have welcomed their counsel when it came to decide how best to respond to Joshua Verin's violent discipline of his wife. Speaking out according to a biblically-informed conscience was central to puritanism but paradoxically, it could also be a threat to it. Women like Jane Verin and Anne Hutchinson were not feminists. They did not challenge their God-given roles within the social order or within their marriages. But their conscience drove them to actions which challenged male authority in puritan society. Amanda Porterfield has concluded that although women lived constrained lives as a result of seventeenth-century puritan patriarchy, that belief and social system nonetheless depended on women for its continued survival. Within that belief system, then, women exercised considerable authority in their roles as wives and parishioners, and sometimes as preachers and prophesyers. She notes the paradox: "In all these roles, the Puritan reverence for Christ-like humility and devotion to patriarchal authority limited the range of women's authority but also enabled them to exercise indirect influence of others as wives and church members, and direct authority as mothers."[126] It seems evident that the women of Providence exercised this indirect influence on at least a majority of the original founders when it came to the matter of the Verins.

On marriage: puritan prescriptive literature

In attempting to reform marital relations and put them on a godlier track, puritan ministers frequently wrote guides and manuals. These formed a rich prescriptive literature that was widely read by the devout in both Old and New England. Examining the roles ascribed to men and women provides a context for understanding the dysfunctions in the Verin marriage and why the Providence community was so divided on how best to respond to the outbreak of violence within the Verin household.

The puritan Divine William Gouge published *Of Domesticall Duties* in 1622. This collection of eight treatises, the frontispiece of which is pictured below, provides the reader with a remarkable opportunity to understand the Puritan world view, particularly the place of marriage in a civil and religious society. The first treatise analyzes the Scriptures as the source of authority on marital structure and responsibilities. Gouge begins with an exposition of Ephesians 5:21: *Submit yourselves one to another in the fear of God,* in which he distinguishes between general and particular duties. General duties are those to which God calls every person, including faith, obedience, repentance, love, mercy, truth, justice, etc. In contrast, particular duties are those which are required by God of individuals, according to their place in the "Commonwealth, Church, or family." Divine providence accords everyone a place in God's earthly kingdom, regardless of their sex, state, degree or condition. The focus on the common good is pervasive. Gouge states explicitly that *it is the duty of Christians as to set forth the praise of God, so to be serviceable one to another*.[127] The world Gouge describes is hierarchical, one based on deference and submission. Just as all men and women must submit to the will of God, the highest authority, so, too, must men and women recognize the authority over them and submit themselves to it. While a husband is the head of the family, to whom the wife and children must submit, the father is himself subject to the magistrates and ministers, who are in turn subject to God.

Gouge reiterates that the purpose of this social structure, ordained by God, is to promote the common good "because every one is set in his place by God, not so much for himself, as for the good of others."[128] Describing the family as a "seminary of the Church and the Commonwealth," Gouge argues that "a conscionable performance of domesticall and household duties, tend to the good ordering of Church and Commonwealth, as being means to fit and prepare men thereunto."[129] Preserving the family, it follows, contributes to the good of both the religious and civil order. The husband and the wife are the governors of all of the rest of the household, although wives are inferior to, and therefore subject to, the authority of their husbands. Gouge exhorts both husbands and wives to do their duty and to honor one another. Put more precisely, Gouge instructs a wife to submit herself voluntarily to the authority of her husband. However, this must be a "subjection of reverence."[130] Gouge also exhorts both men and women to love one another, as Christ loved his Church. In fact, he makes a direct connection between the duty of husbands and wives to love one another and the commonweal when he states, "a loving and mutual affection must pass betwixt husband and wife, or else no duty will be well performed: this is the ground of all the rest."[131] Abram C. Van Engen argues that spiritual love and the power of familial affections meant that regenerate Christians belonged, in effect, to two families: one bound by blood and one tied together by their common faith experiences.[132] This is another way of understanding why the majority in Providence supported Jane Verin's liberty of conscience—the spirit group in Providence was bound together by their common faith experiences and this small fledgling community in the wilderness acted as a surrogate family.

While women are enjoined by the Scripture to obey their husbands, Gouge does, however, note the limitations on a wife's duty to obey. Namely, "they may not be subject in anything to their husbands, that cannot stand with their subjection to the Lord." In other words, God's authority takes precedence over that of the husband. Paradoxically, "wives in refusing to be subject to their husbands, refuse to be subject to the Lord."[133] To a devout woman like Jane Verin, obeying her husband's wishes when they contradicted what her God (and her conscience) dictated would be the equivalent of disobeying God. But disobeying her husband's wishes also risked offending God. This would explain why Jane Verin expressed her willingness to stay with Joshua Verin and therefore submit

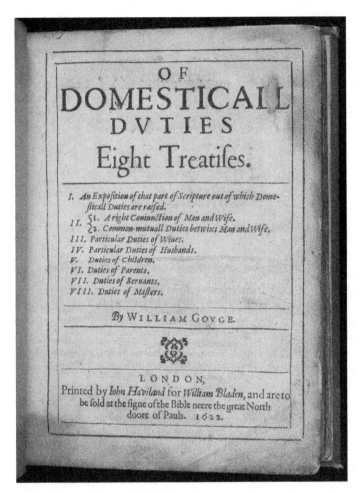

Figure 2.1 Frontispiece, *Of Domesticall Duties*, 1622
©The British Library Board, BLL01001474473

herself to the authority of her husband, despite his foul and brutish carriage. Her submission, however, was limited by her unwillingness to
accede to her husband's judgements regarding religious matters. On this
issue, she adamantly followed her conscience and continued to disobey her
husband.

Gouge also makes recommendations on how husbands should exercise
their governorship of their wives, families, servants, and others in their
household. He likens a husband's authority to that of Christ and his
Church. He advises that the head "ruleth the body not as a cruel lord and
tyrant, rigorously, inhumanely, basely, and slavishly, but meekly, gently,

with great compassion, and fellow-feeling." Another paradox emerges in this treatise. While Gouge calls for a loving and mutual affection between husbands and wives, he at the same time points out that Christ may "have a golden scepter of grace and favor to hold out to his Church ... yet he hath also a *rod of iron to break* the men of this world ...."[134] Later in *Domesticall Duties*, Gouge uses the following analogies to describe the duties of husbands and wives to one another: "*Love* as sugar to sweeten the duties of authority, which appertain to an husband. *Fear* as salt to season all the duties of subjections which appertain to a wife."[135] Perhaps, some violence (or threat of it) was allowable after all.

Another seventeenth-century Puritan marriage manual, *A Godly Form of Household Government*, written by Robert Cleaver, posits that every household should correspond to what he calls "a godly form." That is, godly families are those who operate "according to the direction of God's word," and which are ordered according to "wisdom, discretion and counsel do prosper in inward and outward goods."[136] Every member in such a household has a place. He divides these into two main categories, "the Governors" and "those that must be ruled."[137] The "governors" derive their authority from God; they are the father and mother, the master and mistress. Cleaver, too, makes a direct connection between good governance in the family and the larger civil society, claiming "... it is not possible for a man to understand how to govern the Common-wealth, that doth not know to rule his own house."[138] A man who governs his household with wisdom and righteousness glorifies God. Later, Cleaver does point out that although the status of the governors is unequal (the husband is "chief governor" and the wife is "fellow-helper"), they both owe duties to their family and to one another.[139]

If the analogy of Christ as the head of the Church and the husband as the head of the family is accurate, then a loving husband might need to resort to discipline, potentially violent, to maintain his authority. Clearly, Joshua Verin's actions indicate he believed this to be true. Gouge likens the relationship between Christ and his Church as a marital union, stating "Christ and the Church are to one another as husband and wife," a union that is as indissoluble as that of the marriage covenant.[140] In this mystical marriage between Christ and the Church, all are joined with Christ in one body. As a result, all the members of the Church, the Saints, are equal. All are one in Christ (Galatians 3:18). While the transgressions of a wife against her husband are heinous, so too are the transgressions of a Church against Christ. This provided a rationale to separatist puritans who wished to purify their churches from what they considered the defilement and pollution of the Church of England. In line with Gouge's reasoning, *not* to separate their church from the Church of England would have represented an offense in the eyes of God. So, Jane Verin's insistent rejection of the authority of Massachusetts churches in essence was in complete accord with her understanding of the dictates of her faith.

Barren in Zion

There is an additional factor that needs to be examined when considering Joshua Verin's violent carriage toward his wife. There are no birth or baptismal certificates either in Salisbury, Salem, or Providence to indicate that Joshua and Jane Verin ever had any children. Neither do any of the records make any mention of Jane Verin having either miscarried or experienced any other problems with a pregnancy. It is impossible to determine whether she ever conceived a child or if she was barren, nor is there any evidence to determine whether Joshua Verin was infertile. The glaring absence of any children among a devout married couple who would have been exhorted to "be fruitful and multiply" provides another element in their complicated relationship. Most authors note the importance of childbearing in the early New England colonies. Children were not just "a matter of personal happiness; fertility meant survival."[141] A recent study examines the contradictory expectations puritans in New England had about their religious identity and reproduction as it related to sexuality. "These New English settlers used notions of 'generation' and 'regeneration' to create a surprising, multifaceted discourse about sexuality that ultimately created a revised sense of group identity and continuity."[142] Puritan theologians stressed the obligation to care for the regeneration of the community, particularly through the "seed" and lines of descent. As one minister noted, "God casts the line of election in the loins of godly parents."[143]

Fertility rates were far higher in the colonies than in England; New England women gave birth to an average of eight children, usually beginning during the first year after marriage and then every two years. It was not unusual for a woman to be bearing her last child at the time her eldest daughter might be bearing her first child. Households also functioned as economic units of production and it was not uncommon for children as young as five or six to begin working on the family farm. In a study of infertility in America, historian Elaine Tyler May discusses the case of Ann Bradstreet, an English-born puritan woman who in 1642 prayed to God to forgive her sinful ways and end her barrenness. Believing that her inability to conceive was God's punishment for her "vanity and the follies of youth," Bradstreet saw her barrenness as a test of her faith. Ultimately, her prayers were answered: "It pleased God to keep me a long time without a child, which was a great grief to me, and cost me many prayers and tears before I obtained one, and after him gave me many more, of whom I now take the care."[144] Later in the century, Cotton Mather, the great puritan minister and sermonizer, warned female congregants that their faith and their ability to bear children were connected. He preached a sermon in which he emphasized, "Without your faith in Christ … no good fruit is to be expected from you."[145] For a devout woman like Jane Verin, being without child would have been difficult to bear. Puritan ministers frequently idealized motherhood; even more frequently these ministers relied on mother's milk and breast-feeding as a metaphor for divine love. Religious imagery frequently focused on God's love represented through the act of breast feeding.

> Ministers' equation of God and good mothers, both full of care and concern for their offspring, both providing the necessities of life—even eternal life—with selfless devotion, demonstrates the power of motherhood to evoke feelings of devotion and gratitude.[146]

The social role of puritan women as wives and mothers prepared them for sainthood. Suffering and redemption were often connected. Cotton Mather specifically linked the qualities of female submissiveness, suffering in childbirth, and women's capacity for piety. "Women's [c]urse in the difficulties of subjection & Childbirth ... has been turned into a blessing."[147] May's study of infertility shows that most ministers in the seventeenth and early eighteenth centuries tended to view childlessness as a call to puritan woman to redouble their efforts to lead a pious and godly life. Women were exhorted not to complain but rather to accept their fate, and "be more fruitful in all the good Works of Piety and Charity ... And she will consider with herself What Service of God, and His people, and my own Soul have I now a Leisure for." Jane Verin was by no means a unique case; almost one in twelve New England women was barren.[148]

At the least, her lack of children seems a plausible reason to understand her determination to live in a godly way, despite her husband's efforts to interfere. Barrenness may also be the key to understanding her as a woman of stubborn conscience. Children were seen as a gift from God; sometimes, God chose to withhold that blessing. Although some puritans viewed childlessness as a sign of God's disfavor, most historians point to the many opportunities that childless couples would have had in the seventeenth century to act as surrogate parents and to nurture a child. Despite the relatively healthy climate in New England, the childbirth and infant mortality rates were high. John Demos has estimated that in Plymouth Colony, as many as one in five mothers might have died due to complications during and immediately after childbirth.[149] Historians Margaret Marsh and Wanda Ronner examine the many ways in which childless couples would have been able, their infertility notwithstanding, to care for children. They conclude that in a society where the boundaries between private life and public life and between the family and the community were permeable, "adoptive practices, guardianship, and being on the receiving end of the putting-out system served the community by creating households and providing for children and childless couples by enabling them to enjoy some of the benefits of parenthood."[150] The records provide no evidence that Joshua and Jane took advantage of any of these options.

For Joshua and Jane Verin, barrenness would have been a particularly bitter pill to swallow. Their extended family seems to have been especially afflicted. Genealogical records indicate that of his five siblings, three died without marrying. His older brother Robert had married Joanna (Cash) on July 15, 1626. Their son, Edward, was christened in 1632. His brother Philip, a shoemaker, married Joanna in 1640, years after Joshua and Jane returned from Providence.[151] In subsequent years, Philip and Joanna had three children who survived infancy. His brother Hilliard (b. 1623) got married late in life in 1670 to Hannah Price, who was 25 years his junior.[152] The Verins would have stood out in Providence, precisely because they had no children. Their next-door neighbors, Roger and Mary Williams already had two children, Mary (born in 1633 in Plymouth Colony) and Freeborn (born on August 4, 1635 in Salem). At the time of the Verin controversy, Mary Williams was about five-months pregnant with their third child, Providence, who was born in September 1638. One can only speculate at Joshua Verin's feelings. Roger Williams, the man whose spiritual influence over his wife seems to have superseded his own also appeared to be enjoying gifts from God in the form of a fertile and fecund wife. Perhaps, the perception that he had been cursed with a defiant *and* barren wife (in contrast to the blessings Roger Williams seemed to be enjoying) is what pushed Joshua Verin beyond the limits of socially tolerated behavior. Unfortunately, the gap in the evidence precludes a definitive statement about whether the inability of the Verins to have a child played any role in the escalation of their marital dispute that resulted in brutal beatings. Given the context of seventeenth century family life and the great emphasis that Puritans placed on procreation, it is hard to believe that the failure to produce an heir wouldn't have been at least an indirect source of their rupture.

In women's voices

Female-authored works from the seventeenth century are much rarer, but they *do* exist. Documents such as *The Mothers Counsell or, Liue within Compasse, Being the last Will and Testament to her dearest Daughter*, an example of mothers' advice books, and female-authored petitions in colonial records provide an indication of what women believed to be important and what they expected from the men in their lives. *The Mothers Counsell* is a treatise authored by M.R. and published in London in 1630. She dedicates the book to her "dearest daughter" and "all the Women in the World."[153] The cover is illustrated with a sketch of a compass, representing all of the qualities of righteous living for Christian readers, including temperance, chastity, beauty, humility, and at the center of the compass, modesty. For the author, to "live within the compass" meant an individual was required to live a life in which a woman, first and foremost, kept a "narrow watch" over her heart and made sure she did not idle away her time. M.R. introduces the text with 12 counsels, including frequent private prayer and meditation so that the family may be "instructed, watched over, & Christianly governed."[154] M.R. moves between a life lived within the compass and without it. A woman's lot is to obey "the heft of mans well ruling hand" and to understand that a virtuous woman is "borne to Humilitie."[155] Clearly, the author would have had little sympathy for Jane Verin, arguing rather, that it was her lot to be governed by her husband's "ruling hand." One can anticipate that she would have counselled Jane Verin to submit to her husband's authority. Later in the tract, M.R. repeats the assertion that "Happy is the woman whose calling is great, and her spirit humble." Repeatedly, M.R. admonishes her daughter (and her female readers) to examine themselves to prevent themselves from falling outside of the moral compass. Essentially, it is a conservative tract, reinforcing traditional Christian values and patriarchal beliefs about appropriate female behavior.[156] Given the close relationship between the Widow Reeves and her daughter, Jane Verin, one can easily imagine her counsel as Jane Verin challenged her husband's authority, while she tried to remain pious, devote, and gracious. Like M.R., Reeves and Verin were both devout Christians concerned with living "godly" lives, but they apparently disagreed with M.R. when disobedience to a husband was inspired by religious conscience.

Female-authored petitions, particularly those of married English women, are another important source for understanding women's expectations. A study by Lindsay Moore of female petitioners in Common Law Courts between 1674 and 1697 in the English Atlantic world has estimated that thirty six per cent of petitioners in the Middlesex Quarter Sessions, England were women, while 21.6 per cent of the Massachusetts General Court petitioners and 17.5 per cent of Maryland Provincial Court petitioners were female.[157] Among these petitions were women who were petitioning independently of their husbands or sometimes against their husbands; these included petitions for marital separation and divorce, requests for financial maintenance from husbands, especially from husbands who had been negligent or deserted them, and petitions related to their ability to control their property.[158] Moore argues that women who remained in England also had access to ecclesiastical courts in which the number of female litigants was far greater than in any other legal jurisdiction in the English Atlantic world. These courts, while not available to colonial women, dealt with issues relating to morality, specifically, fornication, bastardy, and adultery; another area of jurisdiction concerned the settlement of estates, legacies, and the division of moveable property—all issues of concern to English women.[159]

Family violence in early New England

Paradoxically, Puritan families and communities were patriarchal and hierarchical, but Puritan marriages stressed reciprocity and partnership.[160] At times, however, living out their faith led devout women into conflict with their ministers or their husbands, males who had authority over them within the Puritan patriarchy. This activism of English puritan women dates back to the earliest days of the Protestant Reformation in England. Puritan writers, who envisaged a natural order in which the family was central, sought to increase a husband's power. Devout women who acted on their conscience inherently threatened this vision.

Puritans were a covenantal people; among the most important covenants governing their lives was marriage. However, despite couverture, a woman's standing in church could be claimed with or without a husband. "In Puritan New England, women, in particular, were justified by faith alone."[161] A study of New Haven colony court cases involving married couples between 1638 and 1670 finds that, aside from violence directed against Indians, "most violence in New England was probably one variant or another of family violence within English-led households, and most of it was probably directed against wives, children, servants, and slaves."[162] A study of seventeenth-century Rhode Island court records indicates only a handful of prosecutions for wife beating after 1641. At the same time, between 1640 and 1680, Puritans in Massachusetts Bay would enact the first laws anywhere in the world against "domestic tyranny," especially spousal and child abuse. Puritans used both church and civil courts to intervene in cases of family violence, particularly because the family was the foundation upon which the religious commonwealth would be constructed. Family violence was "'wicked carriage'—assaultive and sinful behavior—that threatened the individual and community's standing before God."[163] David Little has argued that the Massachusetts Body of Liberties went well beyond incorporating elements drawn from English statutes and precedents; instead, he concludes the new code "redefined and restructured the traditional rights of English subjects in the light of Puritan Christianity, adding modified portions of biblical law."[164] He notes that the document refers to rights that "humanity, civility, and Christianity call for as due to every man in his proportion without impeachment or infringement."[165] According to a study by Mary Beth Norton, however, relatively few men ("the small tip of a very large iceberg") were prosecuted for battering their wives, despite the proscriptions contained against it in the Body of Liberties.[166] Elaine Forman Crane speculates that local customs more so than legal guidelines defined the parameters of appropriate behavior.[167]

A fissure seemed to have developed among puritan ministers on this issue.[168] One might ask, is there a correlation between non-separatist puritans and their willingness to allow a husband to discipline his wife? Do the differences among the divines regarding discipline of women correlate to differences among the Puritans about the "True Churches"? It is interesting to note that Nathaniel Ward is both the author and compiler of the Body of Liberties in 1641 that granted women limited protection from abusive husbands, and also the author of a noted anti-religious toleration tract published only five years later. Among the most influential of the Cambridge Puritans were William Ames and William Perkins. In fact, the Reverend John Cotton trained under William Perkins. Reverend William Perkins has been called an Elizabethan "Apostle of Practical Divinity," whose sermons were widely read both in England and American in the century after his death in 1602.[169] Perkins's ministry is what Cotton considered the "one good reason why there came so many excellent preachers out of Cambridge in England, more than out of Oxford."[170]

Sectarian groups and women's religious rights: the Baptists and Quakers

The shifting religious affiliation of the original proprietors of Providence and their wives yields some interesting lines of inquiry and provide further context for understanding the Verin case. Sometime during the early years of his residency in Providence, Roger Williams became interested in the theological tenets of the Baptists (known as Anabaptists by their detractors). Many of his followers raised serious questions regarding the validity of infant baptism. Instrumental among the residents in Williams' thinking were Ezekiel Holliman and Katherine Scott (Anne Hutchinson's sister). According to Governor Winthrop,

> At Providence things grew still worse; for a sister of Mrs. Hutchinson, the wife of one Scott, being infected with Anabaptistry and going last year to live at Providence, Mr. Williams was taken (or rather emboldened) by her to make open profession thereof, and accordingly was rebaptised [sic] by one Holyman, a poor man, late of Salem. Then Mr. Williams rebaptised him and some ten more. They also denied the baptizing of infants and would have no magistrates.[171]

Anabaptists were radical Protestant dissenters who believed that the only true church community was one based on voluntary membership. They rejected infant baptism, arguing that only adults could understand and assent to God's saving grace and then attest to their faith experience. As is evident in the quotation above, the Anabaptists also rejected any ecclesiastical hierarchy, stressing instead the "priesthood of all believers." As early as 1611, English Baptists had issued a "Confession of Faith," in which they argued against the use of civil power in spiritual affairs. The Confession argues that "the Magistrate is not to meddle with religion or matters of conscience, not to compel men to this or that form of religion; because Christ is the King and Lawgiver of the church and conscience."[172] They also attempted to remove the church from state authority. This, particularly, would have resonated with Roger Williams, who had been arguing much the same, although he did not go so far as the Anabaptists and other radical groups who rejected *all* civil authority. Although Williams believed the practice of adult baptism was closer to the practices of the early Christian church, he worried that it was not officially sanctioned by the Scripture. In November 1649, he wrote to John Winthrop, indicating that many in Providence agreed with his friend John Clarke "about the point of a new Baptism and the manner by dipping." He concurs that "their practice comes nearer the first practice of our great Founder Christ Jesus, than other practices of our religion do," but adds that "yet I have not satisfaction, neither in the authority by which it is done, nor in the manner."[173] It is interesting to note that puritan ministers critical of both Williams and Clarke conflated their separatism, their Baptist leanings, and their ultimate insistence on liberty of conscience. Note the last line in the preceding quotation above. In *Magnalia Christi Americana*, in another example, Cotton Mather makes these connections quite clearly in his analysis of Williams and his followers. Mather uses the pejorative term "seekers," which he defined as those who "keeping to that one principle 'that everyone should have the liberty to worship god according to the light of his own conscience'; but owning of no true churches or ordinances now in the world."

The Confession of Faith reveals the egalitarian nature of Baptist belief:[174]

That God ... is one with all believers, in their fullness, in relations, as head and members, as house and inhabitants, as husband and wife, one with Him, as light and love, and one with Him in His inheritance, and in all His Glory; and that all believers by virtue of this union and oneness with God ... heirs of Christ, co-heirs and joint heirs with Him of the inheritance of all the promises of this life, and that which is to come.[175]

The literature of the early English Baptists also reveals an active role for women as deacons. Early confessions of faith were prepared by John Smith, the pastor of the first Baptist congregation in Amsterdam in 1609, and by Thomas Helwys, among the first Baptist ministers in England. Both of these emphasized a role for women, sometimes called "widows," who served as deacons: "the church hath power to Elect, approve, & ordeyne her owne Elders, also: to elect, approve, & ordeine her own Deacons both men & women."[176] According to Smyth's confession, women deacons had the power to dispense "both the word and the sacraments, but also deacons, men and widows, who attend to the affairs of the poor and sick brethren."[177] A study of Baptist primary sources from the early 1600s concludes that the earliest Baptists accepted women deacons and that local church records in England prove the presence of women deacons, although "the more Calvinistic group, called Particular Baptists, allowed less active roles for women, in both England and America."[178] Charles DeWeese, finds, for example, no record of deaconesses in either the First Baptist

Church of Providence, formed by Roger Williams, or the First Baptist Church of Newport, founded in 1640 by Dr. John Clarke.[179] Nevertheless, several of the men who formed the first Baptist congregations in Rhode Island were most likely the same who voted to censure Joshua Verin and support Jane Verin.

Not long after the Verins returned to Salem, several of the original proprietors joined with Williams and Dr. John Clarke in establishing the First Baptist Church of Providence and (later also the First Baptist Church of Newport).[180] It is highly likely that their Baptist leanings would have influenced them to be sympathetic to the plight of Jane Verin, a woman who had followed her conscience. Some Baptists allowed women to preach to female assemblies. The founders of Providence might not have approved of her sex challenging the authority of her husband, but they certainly would have been even less approving of Joshua Verin attempting to limit his wife's exercise of that liberty of conscience that was so central to their tenets.

Several of the original founders of Providence ultimately converted to Quakerism. The Quaker emphasis on "the inner light" or the light of one's conscience would most certainly have predisposed men like Thomas Harris, Richard Scott, and Francis Weston to be sympathetic to the plight of Jane Verin. Mary Dyer, who had arrived in Rhode Island with Anne Hutchinson, was later hanged in Boston for her Quaker beliefs.[181] The Quakers insisted on the possibility of being reborn in the spirit; they did not sex differentiate that faith experience. Because the Divine Light was viewed as a continuing process toward revelation, it could be used as a guide to reinterpret the earlier revelations as laid out in the Scripture. Insofar as women were concerned, George Fox could argue:

> For man and woman were helpmeet, in the image of God and in Righteousness, and holiness, in the dominion before they fell; but, after the Fall, in the transgression, the man was to rule over his wife. But in the restoration by Christ into the image of God and His righteousness and holiness again, that they are helpmeet, man and woman, as they were before the Fall.[182]

Fox later asked, "May not the spirit of Christ speak in the Female as well as in the Male?"[183] Early Quakers rejected inequality of men and women and accepted an active role for women in lay ministry and church governance. And throughout the English Atlantic world, Quaker women consistently participated in "acts of public agitation and evangelism."[184] Roger Williams would later lament that "the weaker sex" are "too much inclin'd to Quakerism." Benedict Arnold (son of William Arnold), a future governor of Rhode Island, would leave his gray horse to Quaker women to use in their preaching. Although Williams himself was opposed to the Quakers, he nonetheless tolerated their presence in Rhode Island, among the few refuges where Quakers could follow their conscience and practice their faith free from the fear of persecution.

Women's spiritual activism in the English Atlantic world

The earliest residents of Providence had experienced first-hand the tensions that arose when pious women acted on their faith and conscience, challenging in the process some of the traditional early Christian views of women as subordinate, lacking in intellect, and being weak of spiritual strength (and therefore susceptible to temptation). In England, they had experienced the upheavals caused by puritan dissent and criticisms of the Church of England. Women played an important role in early English nonconformity. In addition to offering hospitality to dissident clergy, they often advanced the cause of non-conformists by allowing their homes to be used for Separatist religious services. For example, Elizabeth Crane "kept what was virtually a puritan salon in her London house," whereas Lady Margaret Hoby, "while in London in late 1600, welcomed the great Puritan casuist, William Perkins."[185] Women's patronage of puritan and separatist ministers was especially significant.[186]

Radical seventeenth-century English men and women often "*felt* certain kinds of knowledge."[187] When a woman described herself as a vessel of Christ, it had both a literal and figurative meaning, "for the woman's body was understood to be a potentially explosive device, the carrier of an inflammable spiritual essence."[188] The Puritan Daniel Rogers described in 1642, how this energy was transformed by the presence of God into spiritual ecstasy: "Nature hath put the fierceness into the female because of the impotency thereof ... But graces makes that natural impotency of the woman turn impotency for God."[189] Pious women frequently despaired about their salvation and these emotional pressures often led them into intimate spiritual relationships with their Protestant ministers.[190] This is clear from the relationships of Elizabeth Adams and Jane Verin with their respective ministers. Because non-conformist women were sustainers of their ministers and congregations, their ministers could act as a spiritual guide to "conduct them through the theological labyrinths and provide emotional support during periods of self-doubt engendered by predestinarian belief."[191] Ultimately, the emphasis on God's transcendence and power could become a source of encouragement. Thus, studies of New England puritan women reveal that many became devout followers of their ministers, the women sometimes braving their own husbands' displeasure in following the teachings of the puritan Divines. Jane Verin and her mother, the Widow Reeves and some of the other women of Providence seem to fall into this category of pious women.

As non-conformists, women had been actively involved in their churches in the first half of the seventeenth century. When an established church suspended or deposed sympathetic ministers, private meetings often continued. Not only was lay leadership known to English puritans, but during these years, women as well as men were frequently observed in these leadership roles. Some preachers allowed women to attend congregational meetings but have no voice; while others allowed women to speak occasionally (e.g. to witness to their own conversion or to reprove a clear fault in the congregation). Because of the persecution by the Crown, English non-conformists often met in conventicles (private meetings in the home). As members of congregations and as "Visible Saints," women signed church covenants, formed at least half of most congregations, bore either public or private witness to their faith, and sometimes preached in lay ministries.[192]

Pamphlet culture in the seventeenth-century Atlantic world

The rich pamphlet culture of the seventeenth century sheds light on devout women's activism and the way in which critics perceived their activities as threatening to the social order. For example, a pamphlet by an anonymous author entitled, *A Spirit Moving in the Women Preachers*, describes the actions of

> ... this poor ignorant sort of creatures, that puffed up with pride, divers of them have lately advanced themselves ... to preach in mixt Congregations of men and women, in an insolent way of usurping authority over men, and assuming a calling unwarranted by the word of God for women to use: yet all under colour, that *they act as the Spirit moves them.*[193]

It was in religious practice that gender roles and the social order might potentially come into conflict. As indicated by the anonymous critic in the preceding quotation, those women who claimed the right to speak out by virtue of their experience of God's presence were charged with the sins of pride, insolence and usurpation of authority. They had usurped an authority exercised as women, over men, that was unjustified by scripture. Women were expected to stay silent when it came to politics and public life; in contrast, they might make themselves heard when it came to their own private spiritual struggles. "Thus religious practice offered the individual moments of social as a well as spiritual liberation, allowing the worshiper to express a sensibility and authority that was largely inaccessible to him or her in secular life."[194] This was a potentially dangerous practice in that it could challenge the established arrangements of authority. It became the minister's task to interpret whether or not the spiritual source of a believer's vision or action was divine or diabolical.[195] In the decades prior to the English Civil War, John Foxe's *Acts and Monuments* (1563–1583) was one of the few works to address a persistent dilemma confronting Protestant theologians; namely, what to do about a wife who disobeyed her husband for religious reasons. Foxe's book provided positive examples of pious women who defied their husbands and "sharp denunciations of husbands who did not permit their wives to worship according to their consciences."[196] In the 1637 case of Anne Hutchinson, the religious leaders of the colony accused her of heresy and banished her for "being a woman not fit for our society," concluding that her spiritual power in effect threatened to undermine the social order in Massachusetts Bay. John Winthrop later documented the dangers of Antinomianism in his *A Short Story of the Rise, Reign, and Ruine of the Antinomians, Familists, and Libertines*, published in 1644. *A Short Story* explores the church's attack on John Wheelwright and his followers, Anne Hutchinson's trial, the miscarriage of Mary Dyer's "monster," and a summer of Anne Hutchinson's journal. The puritan sense of the common good is very much evident in Winthrop's analysis. During the actual examination, Winthrop claims that he cannot permit a woman to teach. Hutchinson replies, "that is meant of teaching men."[197] The court responds by asking, "If a man in distresse of conscience or of other temptation, & should come and ask your counsel in private, might you not teach him?" Hutchinson answers that she would, and the court responds that this meant teaching in public. Winthrop then accuses Hutchinson of hurting the communal good, saying:

> It is your exercise which draws them, and by occasion thereof, many families are neglected, and much time is lost, and a great damage comes to the Common-wealth thereby, which we are betrusted with, as the fathers of the Common-wealth not to suffer.[198]

A recent study of John Winthrop's treatment of Anne Hutchinson focuses on the tension between his idealized "city on a hill" as a perfectly Christian "body" and his belief that all dissent was a vile illness or deformity that threatened that body.[199] Dissenters like Hutchinson, in Winthrop's estimation, exemplified the horrors awaiting "degeneration" or society falling into anarchy and sinfulness. In sum, Winthrop believed "the taint of Antinomianism robbed women of the power to create or nurture new bodies, or even to form any sort of community, a development that might undermine his perfect body of Christians united by Christ's love."[200] If this is accurate, Winthrop had no choice but to try to excise such an illness from the body politic.

The Reverend John Cotton, too, closely affiliated Antinomianism with gender issues, characterizing it as "women's delusion,"[201] while the Reverend Hugh Peter criticized Anne Hutchinson for having "... rather been a Husband than a wife and a preacher rather than a Hearer, and a Magistrate than a Subject ..."[202] (It is Hugh Peter, who asked to speak with Jane Verin before she was excommunicated from the First Church of Salem.) In Peter's opinion, Hutchinson had openly violated her ordained place *as a woman* in Puritan society. This was such a serious challenge to Puritan conceptions of societal order that when a synod was called in

1637, the teaching elders identified and condemned more than 80 "errors" perpetrated by the Antinomians. On the last day of the assembly, the participants debated and passed a number of resolutions relating specifically to women. They agreed

1. that though women might meet (some few together) to pray and edify one another; yet such a set assembly (as was then in practice at Boston) where 60 or more did meet every week, and one woman (in a prophetical way, by resolving questions of doctrine, and expounding scripture) took upon her the whole exercise, was agreed to be disorderly, and without rule.
2. Though a private member might ask a question publicly, after sermon, for information, yet, this ought to be very wisely and sparingly done, and that with leave of the elders: but questions of reference (then in use) whereby the doctrines delivered were reproved, and the elders reproached, and that with bitterness, etc., were utterly condemned.[203]

Here, the elders condemned the deportment and behavior of women not only Anne Hutchinson, but also lesser known women such as Jane Verin and her mother, the Widow Reeves, Margaret Weston, Margery Holliman, and others. These resolutions were designed to confine women's spiritual activism to the private sphere.

A recent study labels New England Calvinists as "sympathetic puritans"; that is, puritan society rested on "fellow-feelings [and] affections."[204] It was a puritan's duty to seek a "transfer of senses and affections, an adoption of someone else's inner sorrow or joy."[205] Because non-conformist women were sustainers of their ministers and congregations, their ministers could act as a spiritual guide to "conduct them through the theological labyrinths and provide emotional support during periods of self-doubt engendered by predestinarian belief."[206] Ultimately, the emphasis on God's transcendence and power could become a source of encouragement. Studies of New England Puritan women reveal that many became devout followers of their ministers, the women sometimes braving their own husbands' displeasure in following the teachings of the Puritan Divines. Jane Verin and her mother, the Widow Reeves, seem to fall into this category of pious Puritan women. Clearly, Joshua Verin objected to the influence that Roger Williams seemed to exert. It is probable that as the patriarch of the family, he felt his governorship threatened by the close spiritual relationship between his wife and her minister.

In 1646, the Reverend Thomas Edwards, a Presbyterian minister, published in London the third edition of *The First and Second Part of Gangraena: or A Catalogue and Discovery of Many of the Errors, Heresies, Blasphemies, and Pernicious Practices of the Sectaries of this Time*. The Epistle Dedicatory indicates his purpose was to explain the increase in unrest in English churches and to investigate complaints about "all sorts of illiterate mechanick

Preachers, yea of Women and Boy Preachers."[207] Many of the errors contained in his catalog focus on women who appeared to be actively involved in their congregations, particularly reports of women who prophesied and preached, not only to female assemblies,[208] but also to "promiscuous" audiences, that is male audiences or mixed assemblies.[209] This edition of the catalog chronicles errors "within these four years last past," indicating that female religious activism had continued in England in the years following the Great Migration of puritans to the colonies. This religious activism was not confined to preaching and prophesying, but also included reports that some "honest understanding men" had accepted that "... 'tis lawfull for wives to give without their husbands consents something out of their husbands estates, for the maintenance of the Church and Ministers whereunto they belong."[210] Evidently some pious women had been providing financial support to their congregations without consulting their husbands. Years later, Thomas Parker, the Pastor of the Church of Newbury, wrote to his sister complaining about her refusal to obey either her husband or her minister by insisting on following her religious conscience. He charges that she "will not come to Ordinances, nor willingly joyn in private Prayer with your own Husband ... for you say you are above Ordinances ... living as a glorified Saint, and taught immediately by the Spirit."[211] These excerpts give clear indication that gender issues were inextricably tied in with questions of faith. Further, women's spiritual activism had the potential to challenge patriarchal assumptions regarding a husband's authority over his wife and even a minister's authority over his congregants. One study of late sixteenth-century Protestantism concludes that Elizabethan Protestant women foreshadowed the way in which devout Puritan women were able, "through lives of outstanding piety, to create a social context in which conventional gender restrictions were not enforced."[212] These female ancestors anticipated the ways which their descendants, like Jane Verin and her contemporaries, were able to use "piety to temper patriarchy" and to anticipate the tension between the status of "godly women as both vessels of the Holy Spirit and weaker vessels."[213]

Interestingly enough, women themselves participated in the pamphlet culture of seventeenth-century England, not only challenging existing authority and questioning long-standing beliefs, but also responding directly to Edwards' criticisms of nonconformism. For example, Edwards documents an instance in which a woman named Katherine Chidley confronted her minister, William Greenhill, "where she with a great deale of violence and bitternesse spake against all Ministers and people that meet in our Churches."[214] According to Edwards, Greenhill was so wearied by her "talkative and clamorous" manner, that "he was glad to goe away, and so left her."[215] In 1641, Katherine Chidley published a pamphlet entitled, *Justification of the Independent Churches of Christ*. It was a direct response to Edwards' *Reasons Against the Independent Government of Particular Congregations*, published earlier that year. One contemporary observed that Chidley's pamphlet confrontation with Edwards was in effect "a spetting in his face."[216] The Reverend Edwards obviously concurred with the anonymous author of *A Spirit Moving in the Women Preachers*; both characterized these actions as usurpations of male authority. It is clear that the gendered norms of seventeenth-century English society were being challenged by religious women in both Old and New England. A woman speaking out, even in conscience, was nonetheless perceived by puritan men, even those sympathetic to the views being expressed by radical women, as a challenge to gendered norms. In New England, women who were religious activists would be increasingly viewed as the "new Eves, threatening the social and theological order."[217] In Providence, however, the commitment to liberty of conscience was seen by at least a majority of the settlers there as taking precedence over that order.

Most of these practices continued in New England churches, although ministers disagreed on the level of female involvement in church affairs and governance.[218] Records indicate that slightly more than one-third of the one hundred and fifty persons signing the Covenant of the First Church of Boston on August 27, 1630, were women.[219] When members of the Church of Charlestown gathered on November 2, 1632, the first page of the covenant includes sixteen women among the 35 signatories.[220] The renewal of the Church covenant signed at Salem in 1637 promises that the signatories would "walke with our brethren & sisters in ... Congregation, with all watchfulness & tenderness ..." It was signed by 85 men and 79 women, including Dorcas Verin, Joshua Verin's mother.[221] Women in Salem also made public professions of their faith experience, sometimes as a condition of church membership. These recent types of female behavior would have been fresh in the minds of the heads of household who had to decide on the appropriateness of Joshua Verin's discipline of his religiously active wife. As English puritans newly arrived from England, many of the original proprietors and their families would have had experience with active female participation in Church affairs in both Old and New England. These men and women carried these memories with them as they toiled to create a new life in Rhode Island. In Providence, the small numbers of them in the early months and years of the new community mandated a kind of intimacy. The residents met about twice a month to deal with civil matters relating to the commonweal, but much more often for scripture readings, to sing psalms, to hear sermons and to pray. It would have been impossible for residents not to know what was going on in the Verin household, particularly as Jane Verin continued to attend prayer services despite her husband's vocal displeasure.

The Antinomian controversy, too, had a definite impact on the decision-makers during the Verin case. There was a direct family connection between Anne Hutchinson and Richard Scott, who was an original proprietor and married to her sister, Katherine. (Note: The Verins later sold their lot to them.)[222] Scott arrived on the same ship, *Griffin*, in 1634 as the Hutchinson family. Roger Williams personally arranged for Anne Hutchinson and her followers to obtain a land grant in Portsmouth. They arrived in late March 1638, *before* the Verin case was heard. Hutchinson and other women, including Mary Dyer, continued to prophesy and preach after their arrival in Rhode Island. One can also connect the Verins and Anne Hutchinson indirectly through Mary Oliver, a follower of Roger Williams and friend of Jane Verin. Oliver, along with Marjorie Reeves, Marjorie Holliman and Jane Verin were all excommunicated from Salem in 1638. These women appear to have fallen into the third category of conversion experience discussed earlier; that is, they represented a "radicalized, mystical, extemporaneous, and ascetic linguistic and bodily sets of religious activity ... notable for their intense commitment to a deeply religious worldview."[223] Winthrop compared Oliver to Hutchinson and found that "she was for ability or speech and appearance of zeal and devotion far before Mrs. Hutchinson, and so the fitter the instrument to have done hurt."[224] This at the least suggests that Jane Verin might have had Antinomian tendencies, although she does not appear on any official lists as such. Despite Williams' views on women's spiritual roles, Williams would nonetheless support a women's full liberty of conscience. Even prior to Hutchinson's official banishment, he arranged for her and her supporters to purchase land in what would come to be Portsmouth, RI in March of 1638.[225] He supported Jane Verin's right to liberty of conscience, even if it challenged her husband's authority in May 1638. And it is clear that women did prophesy in Rhode Island after the Verin case. Edward Johnson, a critic of female religious activism, writes,

> There were some of the female sexe who (deeming the Apostle Paul to be too strict in not permitting a room [for women] to preach in the publique Congreagation taught notwithstanding ... having their call to this office from an ardent desire of being famous ... [and Hutchinson] the grand Mistress of them all ... ordinarily prated every Sabbath day, till others, who thirsted after honour in the same way with herself, drew away her Auditors.[226]

Johnson here is not only criticizing Hutchinson and other women for their actions but for their lack of humility, noting they were motivated by their "thirst after honour." The wives of several of the original proprietors had been involved in troubles with their respective churches in Salem and Boston prior to their arrival in Providence.[227] Even if they were not Antinomians themselves, the original proprietors in Providence who had belonged to the First Church of Boston would have known William and Mary Oliver, Robert and Phillipa Harding, William and Mary Dyer, and Richard and Jane Hawkins. These families had been admonished by their churches in England and would, in 1638, come to Portsmouth, Rhode Island with the Antinomians after being banished from churches in Massachusetts Bay. In fact, John Winthrop himself linked Mrs. Oliver's heresy before the ministers and magistrates in Massachusetts Bay and the Verin case.[228]

It should also be noted that Anne Hutchinson, Mary Dyer and Phillipa Harding were puritan women who were perceived to be more radical than their husbands. William Hutchinson joined the exiles, explaining he "was more nearly tied to his wife than to the church."[229] One historian has argued, "marriage created manhood in early New England."[230] Some defended Verin for having exerted his God-given authority over his wife; perhaps this is the reason the residents of Providence did not censure Joshua Verin for his brutish carriage toward his wife. They clearly believed, however, that he had overstepped the boundaries of acceptable behaviour and were willing to take actions to restore peace and harmony in the community by taking away his civil freedoms. According to Raymond R. Irwin's study of Antinomian exiles in Rhode Island,

> the true radicals, and the ones who got the most attention from Puritan authorities, were often *women whose much less extreme husbands became guilty by association with their spouses.* More than that, these men were seen as failing to control their wives, and thereby as yielding to that weaker sex, an unacceptable state of affairs in a society where women were thought to be inclined to evil.[231]

In fact, during the Salem Witch Trials at the end of the seventeenth century, several men were condemned as witches for their "unmanly" behavior; in particular, they resorted to abuse, anger, and combativeness, rather than the service to community, self-control and carrying out of familial duties that was expected of "godly men."[232] A recent study documents the cases of four men, all of whom beat their wives savagely. They were labelled as infamous, barbarous, and acting as the "devil's tool," largely for defying masculine norms of comportment.[233]

The Verins left Salem before the Antinomian Crisis reached its climax in Massachusetts Bay. But certainly, one can see some similarities in their experiences. Jane Verin and her mother were among women who challenged the church in Salem. They appear in the records as those who had walked out of the church. There is no evidence to indicate that Joshua Verin challenged the authorities at all. In fact, upon their return, Joshua Verin remained a constant and active member of the church while Jane continued to challenge it. When Jane disobeyed her husband in Rhode Island, Joshua Verin clearly attempted to restore his authority over his wife. When she disobeyed him, he chastised her severely. The fact that he led her back to Salem, literally with a rope around her, indicates at least his desire to reassert his control over her. Such was the case with Anne Hutchinson.

> By the time of her church trial, issues of female insubordination were so closely tied to what the Puritan authorities saw as a dangerous and

heretical threat to their beliefs, their identity, and their God-given mission that any other woman who stepped out of her place would also be condemned.[234]

In short, the radical behaviour of these women challenged Puritan assumptions about gender, masculinity and the entire social order.

As noted earlier, the residents of Providence were not unanimous in their condemnation of Joshua Verin. This disagreement is connected to their beliefs about the best way in which to maintain order. Unlike their puritan counterparts in Plymouth or Massachusetts Bay, Roger Williams and his supporters endorsed complete liberty of conscience and separation of church and state as the best means of ensuring law and order. Williams later wrote that "libertie alone is the key to a l[a]sting civil peace."[235] There is no indication that religious conscience was conceived as anything but gender neutral. Ironically, Edward Johnson also included this in his catalog of errors. He noted that the great puritan ministers would "rise out of their graves" were they to see events that had come to pass in England. He wondered what these Puritans would think if "they should meet with such Ministers and Christians whom they judged godly and sound, now to plead for a Liberty of all consciences."[236] Clearly, the challenge that following one's conscience represented to the hierarchy had spread to England in the subsequent years.

All of the women in Providence at the time of the Verin decision had to have been, in one way or another, affected by the turmoil and upheaval in Massachusetts Bay precipitated both by the Antinomian crisis and by Roger Williams' challenges to the Christian hierarchy in the colony. In fact, several of the women and their spouses who were present in Providence at the time of the Verin decision had encountered problems in their congregations in Salem. In a letter dated May 1, 1639 from the church of Salem to the church in Dorchester, the Reverend Hugh Peter indicates that his purpose is to acquaint the congregants in Dorchester with names of "such persons as have had the great censure past upon them in this church." Included in his list are Roger Williams and his wife, John Throckmorton and his wife, Thomas Olney and his wife, Stukely Westcot and his wife, Mary Holliman, and the "Widdow Reeves." These men and women appearing on the list were all original proprietors of Providence. Peters explains that these had been censured because they "wholly refused to heare the Church." Further, all had denied that the Massachusetts Bay churches were true churches.[237] To avoid the censure of the general court, Francis Weston, Richard Waterman, Thomas Olney and Stukely Wescott obtained a license from the general court on March 12, 1637/1638 to remove themselves from Massachusetts Bay. All of these men were baptized by Roger Williams and became founding members of the First Baptist Church at Providence, organized in March 1638. All of these men also appear in early town records in Providence on October 8, 1638 to whom

Roger Williams conveyed territories in order to admit them into the "fellowship of vote."[238]

It must be remembered that some of the residents of Providence clearly believed that Verin was within his rights to discipline his wife, arguing that when they consented to liberty of conscience, they never "intended that it should extend to the breach of any ordinance of God, such as the subjection of wives to their husbands."[239] To this objection, John Greene responded that "if they should restrain their wives, etc., all the women in the country would cry out of them."[240] As a more orthodox Puritan male, Joshua Verin, in the absence of a church state, had to step in and exercise his "governorship" of his unruly wife. In this, Verin was not unusual. There was a long tradition of husbands and fathers who were unwilling to let the religious convictions of the women in their households expose them to ridicule. Frequently, "domestic persecution, only slightly less severe than official persecution," could result.[241]

Present in Providence at the time of the decision regarding Joshua and Jane Verin were numerous men *and* women who had demonstrated a willingness to challenge religious authorities by acting on their conscience. Numerous sources indicate that both the men and their wives had been censured by their churches or had been brought before the General Court in Massachusetts Bay for speaking out against their ministers and other religious leaders. Remember that when the Rev. Hugh Peter listed those who had come under great censure in his church, he included *both* the men *and* their wives. Many dissenters, especially the Antinomians of Massachusetts Bay had affirmed the actions, at least in part, of women activists. For example, John Underhill, who was prosecuted for his support of the Antinomian cause, advised his male counterparts not to reject completely the advice of their spouses. He qualified this by saying, "I say not that they [men] are bound to call their wives in council, though they are bound to take their private advice (so far as they see it make for their advantage and their good.)."[242]

The lives of these women, their experiences and the influence that they both exerted and shared with their husbands, ministers and other men suggest (as others have observed) that "the private actions of ordinary individuals have affected larger social and political movements as profoundly as the deeds of great and famous men, forcing us to broaden our definition of the term 'politics.'"[243] In other words, one must understand the experiences of both the male and female founders of Providence in order to explain Rhode Island's unique contributions to liberty of conscience. Further, the very act of challenging the legitimacy of their churches in Old and New England, followed by the formation of their own independent churches, contributed to a spirit that nurtured liberty of conscience, a belief essential to the development of democracy.

Katharine Gillespie makes an interesting argument to this effect. She points out that the puritan sectarians formed independent churches through voluntary association, exercising their "liberties" and "free wills." She cites several sectarian pamphlets of the 1640s that stress the covenantal and voluntary nature of these puritan churches and concludes that "the traditional notion of the father and husband as arbiter of choice and decision was disrupted."[244] Joshua Verin himself was disturbed by his wife's spiritual independence and what it implied about his authority over his wife. "As he said—he thought it inexpedient and unwise to permit his wife to attend meeting as often as she wished, or as some asserted, as frequently as R[oger] Williams wished."[245]

What is noteworthy in reviewing the lives of the men and women who were founders of Providence and Rhode Island plantations is the level of religious activism among both the men and women. The wives of several of the original proprietors had been involved in troubles with their respective churches before leaving England, an activism that they continued in Salem and Boston prior to their arrival in Providence.[246]

Notes

1 Luke 12: 49–53, English Standard Version, The Bible.
2 Bryce Traister, *Female Piety and the Invention of American Puritanism* (Columbus, OH: The Ohio State University Press, 2016), 1. Traister argues "female piety" served as an anchor for New England puritan culture and, paradoxically, contributed to the birth of an "incipient secular liberalism" that is commonly attributed to the modern era.
3 Although the term was used by the Reverend Thomas Shepard to describe his mother in his "Life in Old and New England," it very much seems to apply to Jane Verin and other pious women. See David D. Hall, ed., *Puritans in the New World: A Critical Anthology* (Princeton, NJ: Princeton University Press, 2004), 42. See also Margaret M. Manchester, "A Family 'much afflicted with conscience': The Verins and the Puritan Order," *Journal of Family History*, 42(3) (July 2017), for an earlier version of this analysis.
4 In *What You Will: Gender, Contract, and Shakespearean Social Space*, (Philadelphia, PA: University of Pennsylvania Press, 2011), Kathryn Schwarz offers a useful framework for analyzing female agency during the early modern era. Her central argument is that women who willingly conformed to social conventions during the sixteenth and seventeenth centuries could, and did, pose a threat to those social conventions. She examines the problems posed by women who take expectations, as exemplified in prescriptive and ministerial literature, as "a mandate for purposeful acts." (2). She examines women's agency, or their ability to exercise "will" within the "livable space" of the ordinary interactions of those daily lives. Her analysis of female agency focuses on the popular stage in the Shakespearean era, where the tensions between "didactic treatises that educate women into appropriate behavior" and the reality of women's lives are played out. 9.
5 Ruth H. Bloch, *Gender and Morality in Anglo-American Culture, 1650–1800* (Berkeley and Los Angeles: University of California Press, 2003), 44–45. Coupled with the structure of many Protestant congregations, Bloch argues that "the laity, male and female, now established individual relationships with God unmediated by a male ecclesiastical hierarchy." Bloch adds that this shift is exemplified in Protestant efforts to "consolidate the marriage bond by attacking the most oppressive symptoms of sexual inequality, such as wife beating and the double

standard in sexual mores, and by elaborating on the reciprocal duties of love and companionship that attend marriage." Ibid.

6 David R. Como, "Women, Prophecy, and Authority in Early Stuart Puritanism," *Huntington Library Quarterly*, 61(2) (1998), 204.

7 See for example Elaine Forman Crane, *Ebb Tide in New England: Women, Seaports, and Social Change, 1630–1800* (Boston: Northeastern University Press, 1998). Crane argues that early American women were very much shaped by a western collective memory and that women as a group lost ground in the areas of family, religion, the economy, and law during the long seventeenth century.

8 Edmund S. Morgan, *The Puritan Family: Religion and Domestic Relations in Seventeenth Century New England* (New York: Harper & Row, 1944), 88.

9 Amanda Porterfield, *Female Piety in Puritan New England: The Emergence of Religious Humanism* (New York: Oxford University Press, 1992), 3.

10 Laurel T. Ulrich, *Good Wives: Image and Reality in the Lives of Women in Northern New England* (New York: Knopf Doubleday Publishing Group, 1982). See also Mary Beth Norton, *Founding Mothers and Fathers: Gendered Power and the Forming of American Society* (New York: Vintage, 1997).

11 Crane discusses women's roles as communicants or congregants and the ways in which women could influence decisions, absent a formal authority. See Elaine Forman Crane, *Ebb Tide in New England*, 74ff. She concludes, however, that by the eighteenth century, increasingly women throughout New England were being silenced.

12 Cornelia Dayton Hughes, "Was there a Calvinist Type of Patriarchy?: New Haven Colony Reconsidered in the Early Modern Context," in *The Many Legalities of Early America*, eds., Christopher L. Tomlins and Bruce H. Mann (Chapel Hill, NC: Omohundro Institute of Early American History and Culture and University of North Carolina Press, 2001), 342–343, 353. Dayton attempts to answer this question by examining legal encounters in Geneva during the time of Calvin's tenure as a pastor and as head of the bench of clerics who sat on the Consistory, the main body for disciplining sinners and miscreants within the city. Dayton then compares these with the attempts to enforce moral laws nearly a century later by Theophilus Eaton, governor and chief magistrate in Puritan New Haven. Dayton has found that almost 85 per cent of defendants admitted their guilt before conviction, a fact she argues attests to the remarkable degree of consensus among the early settlers of New Haven about their God-given mission to lead morally upright lives. Dayton does point out, however, that although Governor Eaton and the Reverend Davenport attacked all moral transgressions, they nonetheless did not sanction female insubordination. Reverend Davenport, for example, supported the proceedings against Anne Hutchinson in 1637; Governor Eaton acceded to the excommunication of his wife, Anne Yale Eaton, or her unorthodox opinions. 353.

13 John Allin, "Á Brief History of the Church of Christ of Dedham," 1638 in David D. Hall, *Puritans in the New World: A Critical Anthology* (Princeton, NJ: Princeton University Press, 2004), 54–57.

14 Ibid.

15 See Elaine Forman Crane, *Ebb Tide in New England: Women, Seaport, and Social Change 1630–1800* (Boston: Northeastern University Press, 1998). She concludes that despite the vagueness and often gender-neutral language used in early church records, women were "voices of authority" in the decision-making process of many churches, 69. See especially Chapter II, "The Sin of An Ungoverned Tongue."

16 Ibid., 61.

17 Van Engen, *Sympathetic Puritans*, 63.
18 David D. Hall, "The Shepard Relations and 'Local Religion,'" Paper delivered at Seminar on Early America, Providence College Department of History and Classics, November 2, 2018, 5.
19 Thomas Allen, "The call of Christ unto thirsty sinners, to come to him and drink of the waters of life. As it was preached by that holy man of God, and faithful servant of Christ." Evans Early American Imprint Collection, 1608–1673, https://quod.lib.umich.edu/e/evans/N29604.0001.001?rgn=main;view=fulltext,5 (Accessed August 13, 2018).
20 Ibid., 11.
21 Ibid., 24.
22 Ibid., 43.
23 Ibid., 69.
24 Ibid., 85.
25 Charles Lloyd Cohen, *God's Caress: The Psychology of Puritan Religious Experience* (New York: Oxford University Press, 1986), 5. A recent study by Francis Bremer examines the spiritual testimonies of New England puritans and concludes they were not widely used for admission to church membership; but rather, they were a means to demonstrate fellowship and to help others achieve salvation. See Francis J. Bremer, "'To Tell What God Hath Done for Thy Soul': Puritan Spiritual Testimonies as Admissions Tests and Means of Edification," *The New England Quarterly*, 87(4) (December 2014), 625–665.
26 Robert Strong, ed., "Two Seventeenth-Century Conversion Narratives from Ipswich, Massachusetts Bay Colony," The *New England Quarterly*, 82(1) (March 2009) Massachusetts Historical Society, Boston, MA, 148. The transcriptions of conversion narratives of both William and Elizabeth Adams are included in their entirety.
27 Ibid., 149.
28 Ibid.
29 Ibid.
30 Ibid., 152.
31 David D. Hall, *Cultures of Print: Essays in the History of the Book* (Amherst: University of Massachusetts Amherst Press, 1996), 56–57.
32 Ibid., 86.
33 Ibid., 61. See especially the chapter entitled, "The Uses of Literacy in New England," for a description of the most popular books of the era. These were "steady sellers," books that were readily available over an extended period of time, books that Hall labels "cultural artifacts." 62.
34 Strong, "Two Seventeenth-Century Conversion Narratives from Ipswich, Massachusetts Bay Colony," 154.
35 See Charles Lloyd Cohen, *God's Caress*, especially Part One, "The Call of the Preachers," for an analysis of the role of ministers and their sermons in guiding their followers toward ultimate redemption.
36 Ibid., 166.
37 Ibid., 169.
38 Ibid., 169.
39 For a detailed analysis of conversion narratives and the formation of congregations, Cohen, *God's Caress*, especially Part Two, "The Cry of the Faithful."
40 See Van Engen, *Sympathetic Puritans*, Chapter One, for an analysis of the theological origins of "puritan sympathy" or "fellow feeling."
41 Nathaniel Hardy, "Love and fear, the inseparable twins of a blest matrimony: characterized in a sermon occasioned by the late nuptialls between Mr. William Christmas and Mrs. Elizabeth Adams/preached in St. Dionis Backe-Church,"

(London: Printed for TC for National Webb and William Grantham, 1658), Box 1658, Massachusetts Historical Society.
42 Ibid.
43 Ibid.
44 Ibid.
45 David R. Como, "Women, Prophecy, and Authority in Early Stuart Puritanism," 204. See also Curtis W. Freeman, *A Company of Women Preachers: Baptists Prophetesses in Seventeenth-Century England* (Waco, TX: Baylor University Press, 2011). Freeman's edited volume chronicles several women in England who actively preached and prophesied in the decades before and after the Great Migration.
46 Como, "Women, Prophecy, and Authority in Early Stuart Puritanism," 207.
47 Ibid.
48 Cornelia Hughes Dayton, "Was there a Calvinist Type of Patriarchy?" 342–343.
49 Ibid., 353.
50 Carol Berkin, *First Generations: Women in Colonial America* (Boston: Hill & Wang, 1996), 40–41.
51 Dayton, "Was there a Calvinist Type of Patriarchy?" 346.
52 Ibid., 353.
53 Nathaniel B. Shurtleff, ed., *Records of the governor and company of the Massachusetts bay in New England* (Boston: W. White, 1853), Vol. IV, Part I: 1650–May 14, 1660, 1656 entry, 272.
54 Ibid.
55 "William Perkins," in Leslie Stephen, ed., *Dictionary of National Biography* (in 63 volumes, London: Smith, Elder & Co., 1885–1900), Vol. 48, p. 6. (Hereafter referred to as *Dictionary of National Biography*).
56 Ibid.
57 William Perkins, *The Golden Chain, Or the Description of Theology, containing the Order of the Causes of Salvation and Damnation* (Cambridge: John Legat, 1600), Dedicatory: "Ignorant People," (1591), https://archive.org/details/goldenchaineorde00perk/page/n1 (Accessed October 4, 2010).
58 Ibid.
59 William Perkins, *Christian Oeconomie: Or a Short Survey of the Right Manner of Erecting and Ordering a Family, According to the Scripture* (Kingston, 1618) quoted in Michael Banner, *Christian Ethics and Contemporary Moral Problems* (Cambridge, England: University of Cambridge Press, 1999), 246.
60 *Dictionary of National Biography,* Vol. 1, 356.
61 Ibid.
62 Perry Miller, *The New England Mind: The Seventeenth Century* (Cambridge, MA: Harvard University Press, 1954), 162.
63 Lynne Courter Boughton, "Choice and Action: William Ames's Concept of the Mind's Operation in Moral Decisions," *Church History*, 56 (1987), 188. See also, Perry Miller, *The New England Mind* for an exposition and analysis of Ames's theological principles and approach.
64 Lynne Courter Boughton, "Choice and Action," 194.
65 Perry Ellis, *The New England Mind*, 203.
66 Ibid., 248.
67 C. Matthew McMahon, "William Ames," *A Puritan's Mind*, www.apuritansmind.com/puritan-favorites/william-ames/ (Accessed August 18, 2010).
68 "William Ames," *New England Historic and Genealogical Record*, Vol. 33, 1879.
69 John Winthrop, *The History of New England*, quoted in Edmund S. Morgan, *The Puritan Family* (Boston: Harper Perennial, 1944), 10.

70 Traister, *Female Piety and the Invention of American Puritanism.*
71 David R. Como, "Women, Prophecy, and Authority in Early Stuart Puritanism," 204. See also Curtis W. Freeman, *A Company of Women Preachers: Baptists Prophetesses in Seventeenth-Century England* (Waco, TX: Baylor University Press, 2011). Freeman's edited volume chronicles several women in England who actively preached and prophesied in the decades before and after the Great Migration.
72 Como, "Women, Prophecy, and Authority in Early Stuart Puritanism," 207.
73 Christopher L. Tomlins and Bruce H. Mann, *The Many Legalities of Early America* (Chapel Hill: University of North Carolina Press, 2001).
74 Cornelia Hughes Dayton, "Was there a Calvinist Type of Patriarchy?", 342–343.
75 Ibid., 353.
76 Ibid., 346.
77 Ibid., 353.
78 Koehler, *Search for Power*, 306, and *George Fox Digg'd out of his burrowes, or, An Offer of Disputation on fourteen proposals made this last summer 1672 (so cal'd unto G. Fox, then present on Rhode-Island in New Engand* by R. Williams (Boston: John Foster, 1676), Appendix, 26, https://quod.lib.umich.edu/e/eebo/A66448.0001.001?view=toc (Accessed November 12, 2018).
79 Koehler, *Search for Power*, 306, and *George Fox Digg'd*, 12.
80 Ibid. For a different view, see Van Engen, *Sympathetic Puritans*, especially Chapter Two, in which he relates the Antinomian controversy to differences between the Winthrop cohort and the followers of Ann Hutchinson and the Reverend Wheelwright over the "mutual love of brethren." Van Engen argues Winthrop and his supporters linked puritan sympathy (love of brethren) to mutuality and reciprocity—signs of election. In contrast, Antinomians discounted such love and argued only a personal experience of Christ's saving grace could lead to election. Van Engen challenges the traditional interpretation of the Antinomian controversy as stemming from differences between the moral and the spiritual, but rather he argues division among Puritans emerged over "the meaning and value of sympathy itself—over what sorts of spiritual experiences, what kinds of love could count as evidence of salvation." 59–60.
81 William Bradford, *History of Plymouth Plantation,* Collection of Massachusetts Historical Society, Vol. III (Boston: Wright & Potter Printing Co., 1898), 310.
82 Ibid.
83 Winthrop, *History of New England*, Vol. I, 324.
84 Ibid., 390.
85 Ibid., 391.
86 Ibid.
87 Ibid., 392.
88 Record group: England-Vital Record, Film number: 1,068,527, Collection: England Baptisms 1700–1900; FamilySearch (Accessed September 18, 2008).
89 Supplement to Torrey's New England Marriages Prior to 1700, Chapter B, 22, Ancestry.com.uk.
90 Quoted in "Alice Beggarly" in *The Great Migration Begins: Immigrants to New England 1620–1633*, Vols. I–III (Online database: NewEnglandAncestors.org, New England Historic Genealogical Society, 2002 (Orig. Pub. New England Historic Genealogical Society. Robert Charles Anderson, *The Great Migration Begins: Immigrants to New England 1620–1633*, Vols. I–III, 1995). See also, *Winthrop Papers*, Vol. 3, 186.
91 John Winthrop later reported that "one Green (who hath married the wife of one Beggerly, whose husband is living, and no divorce, etc., but only it was

said, that he had lived in adultery, and had confessed it." Journal entry dated, 13 or December 14, 1638, *Winthrop Papers*, Vol. 1, 341.

92   Quoted in Cobb, *The Rise of Religious Liberty in America*, 153.

93   Quoted in John T. Christian, *A History of the Baptists, of the Unites States from the first settlement of the Country to the Year 1845*, Vol. II (Nashville, TE: Broadman Press, 1926).

94   Crane, *Ebb Tide in New England*, 67.

95   Quoted in "Samuel Skelton," *The Great Migration Begins* (Accessed September 18, 2008); see also, *Winthrop Journal*, Vol. 1, 139.

96   *Winthrop Journal*, Vol. 1, 341.

97   Quoted in "Alice Beggarly" in *The Great Migration Begins*. See also, *Providence Town Records*, Vol. 8, 122 and Vol. 17, 9.

98   John A. Goodwin, *Pilgrim Republic: An Historical Review of the Colony of New Plymouth* (Boston: Houghton, Mifflin & Co., 1888), 407.

99   See Original Home Lots of Providence in Thomas Williams Bicknell, *The History of the state of Rhode Island and Providence Plantations* (New York: American Historical Society, 1920), Vol. I, 172.

100 Benedict Arnold, in a postscript to a letter to John Winthrop reported that "Mr. Green's wife is dead, about a week since." Quoted in *The Great Migration: Immigration to New England*, 1634–1635, Vol. III, 144.

101 *History of Salem*, Vol. I, 370.

102 Gale Research. *Passenger and Immigration Lists Index, 1500s–1900s* [database online]. Provo, UT, USA: The Generations Network, Inc., 2006. Original data: Filby, P. William, ed. *Passenger and Immigration Lists Index, 1500s–1900s*. Farmington Hills, MI, USA: Gale Research, 2006.

103 Passenger list, *The Francis* 1634 England to New England, Olive Tree Genealogy, online database.

104 *The Great Migration Begins: Immigrants to New England 1620–1633*, Vols. I–III (Online database: NewEnglandAncestors.org, New England Historic Genealogical Society, 2002 (Orig. Pub. New England Historic Genealogical Society. Robert Charles Anderson, The *Great Migration Begins: Immigrants to New England 1620–1633*, Vols. I–III, 1995) (Accessed August 5, 2008).

105 John Noble, ed., *Records of the Court of Assistants of the Colony of Massachusetts Bay, 1630–1692* (Boston: County of Suffolk, 1904), Vol. 2, 59.

106 Felt, *Annals of Salem*, 65.

107 John Noble, ed., *Records of the Court of Assistants*, Vol. 2, 223.

108 "Francis Weston," in *The Great Migration Begins*.

109 John Noble, ed., *Records of the Court of Assistants*, Vol. 2, 73.

110 Francis and Margaret Weston later sold their land to Thomas Angel. Chapin, *Documentary History of Rhode Island*, Vol. 1, 257—she had sold it to her nephew Richard Harcourt after her husband's death by June 5, 1645.

111 Ibid.

112 Ibid.

113 "William Arnold," in *Great Migration 1634–1635*, A–B. (Online database. NewEnglandAncestors.org. New England Historic Genealogical Society, 2008.) Originally published as: *The Great Migration, Immigrants to New England, 1634–1635*, Vol. 1, A–B, by Robert Charles Anderson, George F. Sanborn, Jr., and Melinde Lutz Sanborn. Boston: New England Historic Genealogical Society, 1999, 90.

114 Yates Publishing, *U.S. and International Marriage Records, 1560–1900* [database online]. Provo, UT: The Generations Network, Inc., 2004.

115 Gale Research, *Passenger and Immigration Lists Index, 1500s–1900s* [database online]. Provo, UT, USA: The Generations Network, Inc., 2006. Original data:

Filby, P. William, ed., *Passenger and Immigration Lists Index, 1500s–1900s*. Farmington Hills, MI, USA: Gale Research, 2006 (Accessed October 16, 2008).

116 Sydney Perley, *The History of Salem, Massachusetts*, Vol. I, 1626–1637 (Salem, MA: S. Perley, 1924), Vol. I, 271.

117 Ibid., 270.

118 Yates Publishing, *US and International Marriage Records, 1560–1900* [online database].

119 "John Sweet," in *The Great Migration Begins*.

120 Perley, *The History of Salem*, Vol. I, 270.

121 *Providence Town Records* indicate that on June 10, 1637, grass and meadow lands were laid out to several men, including "our neighbor James." Vol. I, 4.

122 Perley, *The History of Salem, Massachusetts*, Vol. I, 269.

123 Ibid.

124 "A Genealogical Profile of Roger Williams," A collaboration between Plimoth Plantation and the New England Historic Genealogical Society, www.plimoth.org/sites/default/files/media/pdf/williams_roger.pdf (Accessed September 13, 2017).

125 Perley, *The History of Salem, Massachusetts*, Vol. 1., 269.

126 Porterfield, *Female Piety in Puritan New England*, 80.

127 William Gouge, *Of Domesticall Duties* (London: William Bladen, 1622), 1. The British Library, www.bl.uk/collection-items/of-domesticall-duties-by-william-gouge-1622 (Accessed August 10, 2010).

128 Ibid., 4.

129 Ibid., 11.

130 Gouge distinguishes between subjection of reverence, which originates in one's recognition of one's superiors, while subjection of service stems from one's willingness to do good for another, a duty common to all Christians. *Of Domesticall Duties*, 3.

131 Ibid., 160.

132 Van Engen, *Sympathetic Puritans*, 181.

133 Gouge, *Of Domesticall Duties*, 18.

134 Ibid, 72. Gouge cites Esther 5:7, Psalms 2:9, John 14:3 and Psalms 110:1 in support of this.

135 Emphasis added. Ibid., 93–94.

136 Robert Cleaver, *A Godly Forme of Household Government* (London: Thomas Creede, 1603), Early English Books Online (database), 14 (Accessed September 17, 2010).

137 Ibid., 15.

138 Ibid., 16.

139 Ibid., 19.

140 *Of Domesticall Duties*, 84. He cites John 3:29, Can 1:13, 15, 2 Cor 11:2 and Eph 5:23 to argue that Christ was the bridegroom and the Church the bride.

141 Elaine Tyler May, *Barren in the Promised Land: Childless Americans and the Pursuit of Happiness* (New York: Basic Books, Inc., 1995), 25.

142 Kathy J. Cooke, "Generations and Regeneration: 'Sexceptionalism' and Group Identity among Puritans in Colonial New England," *Journal of the History of Sexuality*, 23(3) (September 2014), 334. Cooke argues that these early colonists viewed sex as a tool for reproduction, population growth, and moral judgement, which itself contributed to their group identity as "exceptional" people. 335.

143 Ibid., 337.

144 May, *Barren in the Promised Land*, 21–22.

145 Cotton Mather, *Ornaments for the Daughters of Zion* (1692), quoted in May, *Barren in the Promised Land*, 22.

146 Marylynn Salmon, "Cultural Significance of Breast-Feeding," in *Mothers and Motherhood: Readings in American History*, eds, Rima D. Apple and Janet Golden (Columbus, OH: Ohio State University Press, 1997), 13.

147 Cotton Mather, *Ornaments for the Daughters of Zion*, (1692) quoted in Amanda Porterfield, *Mary Lyon and the Mount Holyoke Missionaries* (New York: Oxford University Press, 1997), 15. See also Cooke, "Generation and Regeneration," 342–343.

148 Elaine Tyler May, *Barren in the Promised*, 26–27.

149 John Demos, *A Little Commonwealth: Family Life in Plymouth Colony* (New York: Oxford University Press, 1971), 131.

150 Margaret Marsh and Wander Ronner, *The Empty Cradle: Infertility in America from Colonial Times to the Present* (Baltimore: Johns Hopkins University Press, 1996), 17–19.

151 Perley, *History of Salem, Massachusetts*, 117.

152 "Descendants of John Croade," The Stanley History Project, http://stanleyhistory.net/ (Accessed October 3, 2010). Perley's *History of Salem, Massachusetts* indicates that Hilliard and Hannah Price were married. Verin had two daughters, Dorcas and Sarah. 17.

153 *The Mothers Counsell or, Liuue within Compasse. Being the Last Will and Testament to her dearest Daughter*, M.R. (London: John Wright, 1630). Early English Books Online; http://gateway.proquest.com.providence.idm.oclc.org/openurl?ctx_ver=Z39.88-2003&res_id=xri:eebo&rft_id=xri:eebo:image:2065:2 (Accessed October 15, 2018).

154 Ibid, A3.

155 Ibid., 9.

156 See an analysis of the pamphlet by historian Ulrike Tancke, who concludes that the "golden meane" M.R. calls for "entails both self-curtailment and stable, coherent subjectivity—limiting thought it may be, it allows for a workable, liveable sense of self." EEBO Introductions Series.

157 Moore, "Women, Property, and the Law in the Anglo-American World, 1630–1700," 553.

158 Ibid., 554–557.

159 Moore finds that women initiated 56 per cent of the testamentary cases between 1630 and 1641 and 57 per cent between 1669 and 1687. Ibid., 559–60.

160 See John Demos, *A Little Commonwealth* and Laurel Thatcher Ulrich, *Good Wives* for an analysis of Puritan family dynamics and everyday life in the early colonial era.

161 Ann M. Little, "'Shee would bump his mouldy britch': Authority, Masculinity and the Harried Husbands of New Haven Colony, 1638–1670," in *Lethal Imagination: Violence and Brutality in American History*, ed., Michael A. Belleisles (New York: New York University Press, 1999), 44.

162 Ibid., 43.

163 See Elizabeth Pleck, *Domestic Tyranny: The Making of American Social Policy Against Family Violence from Colonial Times to the Present* (Urbana-Champaign: University of Illinois Press, 2004). In Chapter One, "Wicked Carriage," 17.

164 David Little, "Roger Williams and the Puritan Background of the Establishment Clause," in *No Establishment of Religion: America's Original Contribution to Religious Liberty*, eds., T. Jeremy Gunn and John R. Witte (New York: Oxford University Press, 2012), 105.

165 Ibid.

166 Mary Beth Norton, *Founding Mothers and Fathers: Gendered Power and the Forming of American Society* (New York: Knopf, 1997), 77–81.

167 Elaine Forman Crane, *Witches, Wife Beaters, and Whores: Common Law and Common Folk in Early America* (Ithaca, NY: Cornell University Press, 2011), 86.

168 Asmussen quotes William Heale, who in 1609 wrote *Apologie for Women*, to refute arguments made in a dispute at Oxford that a man could beat his wife, using arguments from reason and nature, morality, civil and canon law, and the law of God to demonstrate that it was never proper for a husband to use force in the correction of his wife, 72.

169 See Louis B. Wright, "William Perkins: Elizabethan Apostle of 'Practical Divinity,'" *Huntington Library Quarterly*, 3(2) (January 1940), 171–196, available at JSTOR, www.jstor.org/stable/3815898 (Accessed September 18, 2010).

170 Ibid.

171 *Journal of John Winthrop*, Vol. I, 293.

172 Quoted in Roger Williams, *The Bloudy Tenent of Persecution*, Samuel L. Caldwell, ed., published in *Publications of the Narragansett Club*, First Series, Volume III (Providence, RI, 1867), 30. Available from Google books (Accessed September 26, 2010).

173 Quoted in Edmund J. Carpenter, *Roger Williams: A Study of the Life, Times, and Character of a Political Pioneer* (New York: The Grafton Press, 1909), 165. See also Publications of the Narragansett Club, VI, 188.

174 Cotton Mather, *Magnalia Christi Americana; or The Ecclesiastical History of New-England*, Vol. II, 498.

175 The London Confession, 1644, Modern History Sourcebook: Baptist Confessions of Faith, 1644, 1655; available at www.fordham.edu/halsall/mod/1644baptists.html (Accessed July 12, 2010).

176 Charles W. DeWeese, *Women Deacons and Deaconesses: 400 Years of Baptist Service* (Macon, Georgia: Mercer University Press, 2005), 49–50.

177 Ibid.

178 Leon McBeth, *Women in Baptist Life* (Nashville: Broadman Press, 1979), quoted in Ibid., 51.

179 Ibid., 56.

180 Among the men who became members were Chad Brown, William Carpenter, Robert Cole, Gregory Dexter, John Greene, Ezekiel Holliman, Thomas James, Thomas Olney, Richard Scott, Richard Waterman, Stukely Wescott, William Wickenden, and Joshua Winsor. See Henry Melville King, *Historical Catalogue of the Members of the First Baptist Church in Providence, Rhode Island* (Providence: F.H. Townsend, 1908), RIHS.

181 See Heather E. Barry, "Naked Quakers Who Were Not So Naked: Seventeenth Century Quaker Women in the Massachusetts Bay Colony," *Historical Journal of Massachusetts*, 43(2) (Summer 2015), 116–135, for a case study of Mary Dyer.

182 George Fox, as quoted by Mary Maples Dunn, "Saints and Sisters: Congregational and Quaker Women in the Early Colonial Period," Janet Wilson James, ed., *Women in American Religion* (Philadelphia: University of Pennsylvania Press, 1980), 41.

183 Ibid.

184 Traister, *Female Piety and the Invention of American Puritanism*, 84.

185 Richard L. Greaves, "Women in Early English Nonconformity," in Richard L. Greaves, ed., *Triumph Over Silence—Women in Protestant History* (Greenwood, CT: Praeger, 1985), 78–79.

186 Ibid.

187 Phyllis Mack, *Visionary Women: Ecstatic Prophecy in Seventeenth-Century England* (Berkeley, CA: University of California Press, 1994), 23.

188 Ibid.
189 From Daniel Rogers, *Matrimoniall Honour,* (London, 1642) quoted in Mack, *Visionary Women,* 23.
190 Collinson, 275.
191 Freeman, 23.
192 Marilyn J. Westercamp, "Anne Hutchinson, Sectarian Mysticism, and the Puritan Order," *Church History* 59(4), July 2009, 482–496. Westerkamp cites Stephen Foster's study, "New England and the Challenge of Heresy, 1630–1660: The Puritan Crisis in Trans-Atlantic Perspective," in which he notes private meetings organized by the laity were common practice in England. She also notes that some of the independent congregations that were formed allowed lay preaching. Many independent congregations of London allowed all lay members, including women to debate, vote and preach. "Women were also known to have preached in Lincolnshire, Ely, Hertfordshire, Yorkshire, and Somerset. The author also notes that when George Fox established the Society of Friends, women were included in leadership and preaching roles. 486–487.
193 Quoted in Katharine Gillespie, *Domesticity and Dissent in the Seventeenth Century: English Women Writers and the Public Sphere* (Cambridge, England: Cambridge University Press, 2004), 9. See also Keith Thomas, "Women and the Civil War Sects," *Past and Present* 13(1958), 42–62; Richard Greaves, *Triumph Over Silence: Women in Protestant History* (Westport, CT: Greenwood Press, 1985); and Patricia Crawford, *Women and Religion in England* (London: Routledge, 1993).
194 Mack, *Visionary Women,* 50.
195 Ibid.
196 Freeman, 32.
197 John Winthrop, "A Short Story of the Rise, Reign, and Ruine of the Antinomians, Familist, and Libertines," in David D. Hall, *The Antinomian Controversy, 1636–1638: A Documentary History* (Middletown, CT: Wesleyan University Press, 1944), 269.
198 Ibid.
199 Jonathan Beecher Field, "The Governor's Two Bodies," *Early American Literature,* 52(1) (January 2017), 40–41.
200 Ibid., 44.
201 Lyle Koehler, "The Case of the American Jezebels: Anne Hutchinson and Female Agitation During the Years of Antinomian Turmoil, 1636–1640," *William and Mary Quarterly,* 31 (1974), 68.
202 David D. Hall, ed., *The Antinomian Controversy, 1636–1638: A Documentary History* (Middletown, CT: Wesleyan Press, 1968), 382–383.
203 *Winthrop's Journal,* 234.
204 Abram C. Van Engen, *Sympathetic Puritans: Calvinist Fellow Feeling in Early New England* (New York: Oxford University Press, 2015).
205 Ibid.
206 Freeman, 23.
207 Rev. Thomas Edwards, *The First and Second Part of Gangraena: or A Catalogue and Discovery of Many of the Errors, Heresies, Blasphemies, and Pernicious Practices of the Sectaries of this Time,* 3rd ed. (London: T.R. and E.M. for Ralph Smith, 1646), 1. Massachusetts Historical Society.
208 *Gangraena:* In Part II, Edwards details the actions of a woman in Brasteed and other neighboring towns, claiming "[she]doth meet other women, and after she hath preached, she takes the Bible and chuses[sic] a Text, some

Verses in a Chapter, and sometimes a whole chapter, and expounds and applies to her auditors," 87.

209 *Gangraena*: In the Appendix, Edwards documents the actions of a woman preacher by the name of Mrs. Attaway who was discovered preaching to "4 or 5 men." Appendix, 113–114.

210 *Gangraena, Part I*, 31–32.

211 Quoted in Katharine Gillespie, *Domesticity and Dissent in the Seventeenth Century*, 40.

212 Freeman, 33.

213 Ibid.

214 Quoted in Marcus Nevitt, *Women and the Pamphlet Culture of Revolutionary England, 1640–1660* (Aldershot, England: Ashgate Publishing, Ltd., 2006), 27.

215 Ibid.

216 Nevitt, 29. See Chapter Two, "Katherine Chidley and the Discourses of Religious Toleration," for a complete analysis of gender and agency as exemplified in Chidley's discursive battle with Edwards and other critics.

217 Ben Barker-Benfield, "Ann Hutchinson and the Puritan Attitude toward Women." *Feminist Studies* 1(2) (1972), 79.

218 Gerald F. Moran, "'Sisters in Christ: Women and the Church in Seventeenth Century New England," in *Women in American Religion*, ed., Janet Wilson James (Philadelphia: University of Pennsylvania Press, 1980), 49. Moran studied women entering New England churches between 1630 and 1639. 52 per cent of entrants in the First Church in Salem (organized 1629) and 47 per cent of entrants in the First Church in Boston (organized 1630) were women.

219 Richard D. Pierce, ed., *The Records of the First Church in Boston* (Portland, ME: The Anthoensen Press, 1961), 12–15. Massachusetts Historical Society.

220 *Records of the First Church in Boston*, Footnote 4, 15.

221 David Pulsifer, "Extracts from Records kept by the Rev. John Fiske, during his Ministry at Salem, Wenham, and Chelmsford," *Historical Collections of the Essex Institute* (Vol. I, No. 2, May 1859), Salem, 1859, 37–39.

222 Richard LeBaron Bowen, "The Arms of Richard Scott," reprinted with addition in *The New England Historical and Genealogical Register*, Vol. XCVI, No. 1 (January 1942), 9.

223 Traister, *Female Piety and the Invention of American Puritanism*, 11.

224 Selma R. Williams, *Divine Rebel: The Life of Anne Marbury Hutchinson* (New York: Henry Holt & Co., 1981), 190.

225 On February 19, 1638, two of Hutchinson's supporters, John Coggeshall and William Aspinwall wrote to Roger Williams regarding the availability of land. On March 7, 1638, 19 men would form a civil compact and departed for Portsmouth, RI before Anne Hutchinson's office banishment on March 22, 1638. Hutchinson herself left for Rhode Island six days later (March 28, 1638). *Records of Colony of Rhode Island and Providence Plantations in New England*, Providence, 1856, Vol. I, 52.

226 Koehler, *Search for Power*, 324 and Edward Johnson, *Wonder-Working Providence, 1628–1651* (New York: Charles Scribner's Sons, 1910), 186; accessed October 12, 2014, https://archive.org/details/cu31924028814452/page/n7.

227 These women were Jane Verin, the Widow Reeves (Jane's mother), Margery Holliman (2nd wife of Ezekiel Holliman, Julia Marchant (wife of Stukely Wescott) and Margaret (wife of Francis Weston).

228 See footnote in Bartlett, *Colonial Records of Rhode Island*, Vol. I, 1636–1663 (Providence: A.C. Greene & Brothers, 1856), 16.

229 Ann M. Little, "'Shee Would Bump His Moudly Britch': Authority, Masculinity, and the Harried Husbands of New Haven Colony, 1638–1670," in *Lethal Imagination: Violence and Brutality in American History*, ed., Michael A. Bellesiles (New York: NYU Press, 1999), 45. Little argues that in Puritan society, duties and privileges were assigned to people according to their gender. "Men freed themselves of their fathers' authority by assuming governorship over—and responsibility for—wives, and eventually over their children, servants, and slaves," 45.

230 Ibid.

231 Emphasis added. Raymond D. Irwin, "Cast Out from the 'City upon a Hill': Antinomian Exiles in Rhode Island, 1638–1650," *Rhode Island History* 1994 52(1), 2–19; 7.

232 Richard Godbeer, "'Your Wife Will be your Biggest Accuser': Reinforcing Codes of Manhood at New England Witch Trials." *Early American Studies, An Interdisciplinary Journal*, 15(3) (Summer 2017), 474.

233 Ibid.

234 Susan Hill Lindley, *"You Have Stept Out of Your Place": A History of Women and Religion in America* (Louisville, KY: Westminster John Knox Press, 1996), 7.

235 Quoted in Theodore Dwight Bozeman, "Religious Liberty and the Problem of Order in Early Rhode Island," *New England Quarterly*, 45(1) (March 1972), 62.

236 Edwards, *Gangraena*, Part 1, p. 145. Quoted in Hughes, "Anglo-American Puritanisms," 1.

237 The entire letter is included in Sydney Perley, *The History of Salem, Massachusetts*, Vol. I, 1626–1637 (Salem, MA: S. Perley, 1924), 271.

238 Perley, *The History of Salem, Massachusetts*, Vol. I, 269.

239 Winthrop, *History*, Vol. I, 340–341.

240 Winthrop, *History*, Vol. I, 340.

241 Freeman, 14.

242 Quoted in Lyle Koehler, *A Search for Power*, 231.

243 Phyllis Mack, *Visionary Women*, 5.

244 See Chapter 1, "'Born of the mother's seed': liberalism, feminism, and religious separatism," in Katharine Gillespie, *Domesticity and Dissent in the Seventeenth Century*, 25–61.

245 Perley, *The History of Salem, Massachusetts*, 272.

246 These women were Jane Verin, the Widow Reeves (Jane's mother), Margery Holliman (2nd wife of Ezekiel Holliman, Julia Marchant (wife of Stukely Wescott) and Margaret (wife of Francis Weston).

3 "Forced worship stinks in God's Nostrils"

Government, law and liberty of conscience in puritan New England

The puritans were not a homogenous group by any stretch of the imagination. While membership in the churches of New England was based on personal salvation, they were nonetheless divided on many issues. As Calvinists, they stressed that faith alone could save the individual who had been preordained by God for salvation or damnation. The faith experience involved the freedom of the sinner to *assent* to God's saving grace. One recent study describes this connection between true conversion and "Christian liberty" as the liberty of the individual, "through evangelism and the gift of God's grace to assent voluntarily to religious truth and convert—literally, to 'turn'—toward God."[1] This did not include the *right to dissent* when it came to matters of theology or worship. Issues that proved the most divisive included separatism, the meaning of liberty of conscience and toleration of diverse or contradictory religious views, and the best means to maintain civil order. The Calvinists who came to Massachusetts in the late 1620s and early 1630s were for the most part Congregationalists. Viewing themselves as "Godly" people and among God's "Elect," many of them favored autonomous gathered churches, a preference which inherently challenged the legitimacy of the Church of England that was still Episcopalian in its church structure. These Puritans zealously guarded their independence and autonomy; it was the congregations who elected and paid the ministers. Each congregation, like each individual, was directly responsible to God, as revealed to them in the Scripture.

The English context

It is worthwhile to review the key political developments in England in order to contextualize the experience of the first settlers in Roger Williams' Providence settlement. Charles I ruled from 1625 to 1640. During this time, he appointed William Laud to be the Archbishop of Canterbury. According to one biographer, it was Laud's attempts to bring uniformity of worship and the "beauty of holiness" into the Anglican liturgy, a liturgy that most Puritans considered corrupt and "popish," that radicalized devout Puritans and precipitated the slide into Civil War.[2] After Laud's ascension to office, official persecution increased dramatically. Puritans who criticized Laud's policies could find themselves brought before the Court of Star Chamber, a special court whose members also served on the King's Council and who circumvented judicial process and imposed severe penalties including whipping, branding and other forms of physical torture. According to one account, Roger Williams personally witnessed in 1630 a leading puritan reformer being pilloried and branded as a "Sower of Sedition."[3] This led to his decision to immigrate. Likewise, many others decided to do the same and the Puritan migration increased dramatically. In contrast to Plymouth Bay Colony, Massachusetts was settled primarily by *non-separatist* Congregationalists. Consonant with the Crown and the Church of England's attempts to restore monarchical power, in 1634, Laud also set up a Commission for Foreign Plantations to coordinate policies related to colonial settlement. Plans to reorganize the New England colonies and bring them under closer supervision followed, including the appointment of Sir Fernando Gorges as a royal governor-general. This attempt was interrupted by the outbreak of Civil War in England, and the New England colonies were left practically to themselves.

It was during this period of emigration that Providence residents signed the Town Fellowship in 1637 and decided on the Verins in the following year. Resistance to Laud's policies, particularly to his persecution of puritans, grew until 1640, when the Long Parliament convened. Shortly thereafter, the first Civil War began in 1642, about the same time that William Arnold requested that Pawtuxet submit to Massachusetts. The puritans dominated Parliament, but divisions among their ranks centering on the proper form of church government soon emerged. The two main factions were the Presbyterians who favored a church governed by Presbyters, echoing the structure of the Church of England. In contrast, the Independents supported the liberty of congregations to order their own affairs. Roger Williams would have belonged to the latter group. In response to the rising sectarianism within the Long Parliament, the Warwick Commission was constituted. It was this committee that granted the first patent to Rhode Island in 1644, although no royal seal was affixed. Archbishop Laud was executed in 1645, and the First Civil War ended. During the brief intermission in fighting in England, Rhode Islanders codified their laws and organized an Assembly. King Charles was executed in 1649, and by 1653, Oliver Cromwell established a Protectorate. In 1660, the monarchy under Charles II was restored. Parliament issued the Declaration of Breda, which is key to understanding the 1663 Charter that Rhode Islander William Clark was able to secure for the colony. The Declaration of Breda listed the principles by which Charles II hoped to be restored to the monarchy. Included among them was:

> And because the passion and uncharitableness of the times have produced several opinions in religion, by which men are engaged in parties

and animosities against each other (which, when they shall hereafter unite in a freedom of conversation, will be composed or better understood), we do declare a liberty to tender consciences, and that no man shall be disquieted or called in question for differences of opinion in matter of religion, which do not disturb the peace of the kingdom; and that we shall be ready to consent to such an Act of Parliament, as, upon mature deliberation, shall be offered to us, for the full granting that indulgence.[4]

Clearly, the long years of sectarian violence brought about by differences over religious conviction convinced the authorities to seek greater toleration in hopes of restoring peace in the land. Charles II had, in effect, released Rhode Islanders from the laws requiring conformity with the Church of England, but securing royal support in England for the notion of liberty of conscience for Rhode Island has not been an easy task.[5] The controversy continued to rage in New England.

Puritan women and English law

The puritans attempted to replace English common law with one based on the Scripture. The parallels between the two are striking, particularly when one considers the views of social and familial organization reflected in each. One of the most important treatises on English law was Sir Edward Coke's *Institutes of the Laws of England*. In a long career, the Lord Coke (1552–1634) served is a number of capacities, including speaker of the House of Commons during Elizabeth's reign. He kept careful notes of cases he had heard argued; these were published in what would become a thirteen-volume "Reports." These included not only the arguments and the reasons for the judgement in a particular case, but also general propositions of law that could be derived from each case. The reports cover a period of almost forty years and "... represent a fairly complete account of English law in the time of Elizabeth and James."[6] One recent study of domestic law as developed in Coke's *Institutes* argues that the concept of *femme couvert* was conceived very narrowly, relating almost solely to the selling of freehold property that had no other restraints on it. Legal historian Holly Brewer also concludes the "common laws did not have a fully developed conception of domestic power except with respect to servants and that the tripartite array of master/husband/father was not in place, at least when it came to criminal matters."[7] In fact, one of the most widely used guides for justices of the peace in seventeenth-century New England was Dalton's *Countrey Justice*, another manual which did not have a well-defined vision of domestic law. In colonies established far from the centers of judicial power, lawmakers had to take heed not to pass local laws that were "contrary" to English laws. A recent analysis of women, property and law in the English Atlantic world concluded that the seventeenth-century English

legal system provided women with a variety of robust methods to circum-
vent the restrictions of couverture.[8]

When it came to a woman challenging her husband's authority within
the household, Roger Williams and his supporters in this controversy,
while they expected Puritan wives to be submissive and obedient, also
expected these same women to obey God. In his May 22, 1638, letter to
John Winthrop, Williams describes Jane Verin as a "gracious & modest
woman," qualities that were deemed most desirable in a woman. Williams
also states that Verin tried to draw his wife "to the same ungodliness with
him." The wording of Williams' description of the events leading up to
Verin's censure seems to indicate more than one physical admonishment:
"he hath trodden her under foot tyrannically & brutishly: *which she and
we long bearing* ..." [my emphasis]. Clearly, it was not the fact of the
beating, but rather the severity of the beating that finally propelled Williams and the others to act. He states, "though with his furious blows she
went in danger of life, *at the last* [my emphasis] the major vote of us discard him from our civill freedome, or disfranchize, etc."[9]

In seventeenth-century England, the status of married women was determined by *The Lawes and Resolutions of Womens Rights* which put forward the doctrine of *femme couverte*, that is, that "after marriage, all will
of the wife in judgment of the law is subject to the will of the husband."[10]
The law, however, was unclear about the extent to which the will of the
husband prevailed in the event of the wife's challenge to his authority. The
editor of the seventeenth-century *The Lawes Resolution of Women's
Rights* argued that under English law, "castigation" was permissible, but
he was uncertain as to the limits beyond which a husband's reasonable
right to correct his wife became unlawful and unreasonable.[11] The author,
"T.E.," was probably Thomas Edgar, a seventeenth-century puritan
lawyer. It is likely that Edgar was influenced by puritan prescriptive literature, particularly the religious advice manual, *Domesticall Duties*, published ten years earlier by the Puritan Divine William Gouge.[12]

Controlling insubordinate wives

Historians also disagree on the extent to which domestic violence against
wives was tolerated by seventeenth century Puritans. For example, an influential legal guide published by William Lambarde in 1599, *Eirenarcha: Or
of the Office of the Justices of the Peace*, details "allowable battery."
These included the rights of those who exercised civil power or authority
over others, e.g., a master over a servant, a parent over a child "within
age" or a schoolmaster over a scholar, to correct and chastise them for
their offenses. In this guide, a husband is not allowed to beat his wife.
Indeed, scholars point out that physical beating could be the grounds for
separation suits in the ecclesiastical courts, or the basis for alimony or
"separate maintenance."[13] Section VII of the *Laws Resolution of Women's*

Rights allows that "The baron may beat his wife."[14] Such action is "dispunishable, because by the Law Common these persons can have no action." Despite this clear statement, the document itself is ambiguous as to the extent of the right of a husband to beat his wife. There are certain limitations. For example,

> ... she may sue out of chancery to compel him to find surety of honest behavior toward her, and that he shall neither do nor procure to be done to her (mark, I pray you), any bodily damage, otherwise than appertains to the office of a husband for lawful and reasonable correction.[15]

In addition, *The Lawes* is equally unclear about the extent of a husband's right to discipline his life, stating, "How far that extendeth I cannot tell."[16] The key variable seems to be the level of community intervention. John Demos' landmark study of Puritan families, *A Little Commonwealth*, describes a very dense network of community relations, in which neighbors, ministers, and civil authorities might intervene to "admonish" those who violated the rules or in some other way threatened to undermine the peace and order of the community. So, in the event of marital discord, neighbors, ministers and magistrates might at different times attempt to intervene in order to restore harmony. Admonishment and prayer were the favored ways by which peace might be reinstated. Both Anglican ministers and puritan divines were divided on this issue. "An Homily of the State of Matrimony" (1563) appeared in a collection of sermons to be read by all parsons, vicars and curates during the reign of Elizabeth I.[17] The homilist points out how "few matrimonies there be without chidings, brawlings, tauntings, repentings, bitter cursings, and fightings."[18] The source of all of these challenges to the peace of the household is attributed to the work of the devil, "the ghostly enemy." He cites Peter as the authority when husbands are exhorted to "deal with your wives according to knowledge, giving honor to the wife, as unto the weaker vessel, and as unto them that are heirs also of the grace of life, that your prayers be not hindered."[19] Here the tension between the egalitarian and the patriarchal impulses is quite clear. Women too can be saved, and this fact must inform the actions of husbands when they govern over their wives. Later in the sermon, women are advised to patiently suffer anything their husbands do, but that husbands should under no circumstances beat their wives—this being the "greatest shame that can be ... to him that doeth the deed."[20] Stressing woman's weaker nature and constitution, husbands are further urged to spare their wives harsh punishments. "By this means," it is argued, "thou shalt not only nourish concord, but shalt have her heart in the power and will; for honest natures will sooner be retained to do their duty rather by gentle words than by stripes."[21] Puritan divines such as William Gouge argued that a husband should correct his wife only verbally, since to beat her would be like beating himself. In contrast, William Whately argued that in extreme cases, physical punishment might be necessary, although he cautioned against it being undertaken in anger in that "it seemeth too impious in him to do it and too servile in her to suffer it."[22] *In The Mutual Duties of Husbands and Wives Towards Each Other*, Richard Baxter (1615–1691) warns married couples to love one another, care for each other's souls, and to avoid contention, stating, "If different religious understandings come between you, be sure that you manage it with holiness, humility, love, and peace, and not with carnality, pride, uncharitableness, or contention."[23] Like puritan sermonizers before him, Baxter draws parallels between the loving relationship between husband and wife and that between Christ and his church.

As mentioned earlier, Protestant wives were expected to defer to the authority of their husbands. The Elizabethan minister, Richard Greenham, explained that regardless of the virtues a wife might have, "yet not being subject to her husband they are nothing ... if she be not obedient she cannot be saved."[24] Women could, and did, inherit land, if there were no other male heirs. Widows received for the rest of their lives, a "widow's dower," that at least allowed them to live out their lives without fear of losing their homes. At the same time, both common law and statutes made it possible for wives and daughters to retain control of their land and personal possessions. For example, fathers or first husbands could create encumbrances on estates that preserved the property of their daughters and their progeny for posterity. A legal historian has found that although English women were at a significant legal disadvantage during the early modern period, they nevertheless enjoyed relatively greater authority within marriage than they would in later times, suggesting that "... both within and outside the household, legal disadvantage was modulated sharply by status."[25] Numerous other studies have demonstrated that there was a gap between the ideal role of women as identified in ministerial and prescriptive literature and the reality of women's lives in Old and New England in the early modern era.[26]

When Joshua Verin began beating his wife, his neighbors gathered together to decide how best to intervene. Williams and his neighbors had not had time to set up any kind of judiciary, nor had a formal legal code been adopted—the colony was not quite three years old. The first circuit quarter courts were not established until 1640, after the union of the towns of Portsmouth and Newport; these met alternately in the two towns. Rhode Islanders adopted the Code of Laws in 1647 and consequently the Colony Court of Trials was established. This new court was also a circuit court, meeting first semi-annually and then on a quarterly basis.[27] There were very few cases of domestic abuse heard before the newly established courts in seventeenth-century Rhode Island. Shortly after the Aquidneck Quarterly Court was established, in 1644, John Hicks appeared before the court accused of beating his wife, Harwood.

He was ordered to continue his bonds till the next court meeting when his wife was summoned to give evidence concerning the case.[28] A few years later, Elizabeth Stevens asked for "reliefe" from the court, claiming she was "in fear of her life of sayd Husband Henry Stevens." He was required to post a bond of 20 pounds.[29] Ann Warner petitioned the General Assembly for a divorce on June 26, 1683. According to her petition, her husband, John Warner, had violated the marriage covenant and abused her "by laying violent hands on her." The Court heard their allegations, examined the evidence, and chose not to grant an absolute final divorce, until it had been tried at the Court of Trials. Notwithstanding this, the Court did see cause for separation and ordered John Warner to provide maintain for his wife and children.[30] In October 1685, the General Assembly considered what to do about petitions that had been made by several women "concerning their husbands deserting them, and so absenting themselves, not only to neglect providing for them," but also for long periods of time without having been heard from. In response, the Assembly ordered that if either a husband or wife deserted, after five years' time, the husband or wife would be free of their spouse. The Assembly reasoned that a "negative cannot otherwise be made to appear," thus depriving their spouse of their ability to seek relief. As a result, if a husband or wife absented themselves for a period of five years, the absent party would be deemed as dead.[31] Clearly, women did try to take advantage of whatever recourse was available to them to petition for relief when they were abused, neglected or deserted.

Domestic violence, broadly interpreted to include violence between or against any member of the household, including servants, took many forms in Plymouth, the earliest of the Puritan settlements in New England. Laws regulating behavior called for a Grand Enquest and appearance before Court to answer for "all such misdemeanors or any person or persons as tend to the hurt & detriment of society civility peace & neighborhood." Officers of the Court would have wide latitude to punish violators "according to the nature of the offence as God shall direct them."[32] Of the ten instances found in court records of violence toward a spouse that did not result in murder, eight of the cases involved charges against the husband, while the wife was charged in the remaining two cases. Punishments ranged from imposing fines on the offender to whipping or sitting in stocks. The Court seemed ready to intervene when married couples demonstrated "turbulent carriages" within the home.[33]

Roger Thompson analyzes the court records of seventeenth-century Middlesex County for sexually related crimes in his study, *Sex in Middlesex: Popular Mores in a Massachusetts County, 1649–1699*. Thompson's findings challenge the traditional view of puritan family relations that argues that marital relations were based on the assertion of an oppressive patriarchalism. Thompson found only seven cases of wife-beating in the Middlesex records for the period, of which five occurred in between 1649 and 1663. He points out that wife-beating was a punishable offense, except in the case of self-defense; this diverged from English law, "even though there was strong and widespread condemnation of husbandly violence in the old country, especially among puritans."[34] Thompson concludes that most puritans exhibited "tolerance, mutual regard, affection, and prudent common sense" in their marital relations.[35] Perhaps that is why Joshua Verin's tyranny over his wife is so noteworthy.

On liberty of conscience and forced conformity

Liberty was inherent in Puritan efforts to construct both an ecclesiastical and a civil order in New England. They believed that those elect among them, that is, those who could demonstrate evidence of God's saving grace, could, and should, create churches and civil societies that conformed to their interpretation of Scripture. Looking to the Bible, John Winthrop and his confreres set up a Christian Commonwealth, in which the body politic consisted of male church members, and a civil authority, the General Court, whose members were "bound by law to serve both God and the Gospel."[36] The General Court regularly enforced the Scripture, and Puritan ministers regularly upheld civil law. "Among the fundamentals of Puritan jurisprudence were the integrated and determined use of legal and ecclesiastical institutions to foster a godly community."[37] Each person contributed to the welfare of the whole. "Taking love of neighbor to be a sign of salvation, Puritans put group above individual and used scripture to shape legal definitions of the public good."[38] A communitarian ethic evolved and fused with liberty in the sense that individuals were expected to exercise their freedom to conform their lives to the teachings of God. "As late as the 1740s, judges charged juries 'to use law to create a civil and Christian state' so as to eliminate 'vice, profaneness, and immorality' and reform mankind 'with a Due Regard to God.'"[39]

It was this attempt to use the law to serve religion that so distressed Roger Williams, and this fundamental disagreement on civil and ecclesiastical authority ultimately led to his banishment from Massachusetts Bay. He argued that the use of civil force to enforce religious authority, even if emanating from the Scripture, violated that fundamental freedom that individuals exercised when they followed their conscience. More than ten years later, Rhode Island enacted its first code of laws, which while based on Scripture, nevertheless, relied much more heavily on English law than the Bible.[40] One can surmise that Roger Williams' years of service as personal secretary to Sir Edward Coke, one of the most influential compliers of English common law, had a direct impact on Rhode Island's legal development. According to one analysis, the earliest Providence settlers relied on equality, not religion to foster community. The Verin case, it is argued, resulted from a contest over the very meaning of religious liberty. According to McGarvie and Mensch, the town refused to sanction Joshua Verin's beating, which he considered his religious duty to administer. They argue, in essence, that Rhode Islanders refused to recognize Joshua Verin's freedom to perform his religious duty when they made the decision to disenfranchise him.[41]

Few issues were more contentious the question of religious liberty and toleration. The General Court of Massachusetts Bay passed an act in 1634 that entreated church elders to "consult and advise of one uniform order of discipline in the churches ... and to consider how far the magistrates were bound to interpose for the preservation of that uniformity and peace of the churches."[42] It was partially in response to this that Roger Williams published in 1644 his famous tract, the *Bloudy Tenent*, in which he began to lay out his ideas on separatism, separation of church and state, and the absolute right to liberty of conscience.[43] Citing numerous passages from the New Testament, Williams argues that persecution for sake of conscience violates the teachings of Jesus Christ. Williams, whose statue is pictured below, argues that the "souls of all men, [who are] forced to the religion and worship which every civil state or commonweal agrees on ... [results in] a dissembled uniformity."[44] In other words, forced orthodoxy results in hypocrisy. Further, the joint actions of church and civil government had thrown "all the world into combustion" and fuelled sectarian violence and enmity.[45] He endorsed evangelism but rejected proselytism.[46]

Perhaps one of the most famous Puritan tracts in defense of *intolerance* was the Reverend Nathanial Ward's, *The Simple Cobbler of Aggawam in America*, first published in England in 1646. Ward believes God to be "shaking the heavens over his head and the earth under his feet" while Satan must be feeling "his passions approaching, he loves to fish in roiled waters."[47] In part, Ward was responding to "unfriendly reports" of New Englanders who have been "reputed a colluvies [hodge-podge] of wild opionists, swarmed into a remote wilderness to find elbow room for our fanatic doctrines and practices."[48] While Massachusetts had been nearly torn asunder by the Antinomian Crisis, for Ward, it was a simple matter. He very clearly reaffirms his beliefs: First, "I dare aver that God does nowhere in His word tolerate Christian states to give toleration to such adversaries of His truth, if they have power in their hands to suppress them."[49] Second, he states that all challengers to puritan orthodoxy (he includes Familists, Antinomians, Anabaptists, and other enthusiasts among these) have the liberty to leave and the sooner the better. (The Familists were a sect in England and Holland who had professed love for all human beings, including those who were not among the "elect;" orthodox puritans regarded both the Familists and Anabaptists with horror.)[50] Ward holds "liberty of conscience to be nothing but a freedom from Sin, and Error." He believed toleration would be the ruin of true religion. Even earlier, Section 95 of the Body of Liberties, also penned by Ward, had reaffirmed liberty to practice religion according to one's conscience, *but only if* these practices or beliefs were "orthodox in judgment" and if the church

officers were "able, pious, and orthodox."[51] According to Ward's interpretation of the scripture,

> every conscience [must] contend earnestly for the truth; to preserve
> unity of spirit, faith, and ordinances; to be all likeminded, of one
> accord, every man to take his brother into his Christian care, to stand
> fast with one spirit, with one mind, striving tougher for the faith of
> the Gospel; and by no means to permit heresies or erroneous
> opinions.[52]

Directly challenging Roger Williams' analysis that state-enforced uniformity is the source of civil unrest, Ward calls for all Christian states to dis-
avow all such errors. After passing such statutes, he avers, citizens in time
would know "fully the mind of the State, [and] might not delude themselves with vain hopes of unsufferable [sic] Liberties."[53] He argues very
strongly for punitive measures, including severe penalties, stating, "Persecution hath ever spread Truth, Prosecution scattered Error."[54] The Reverend John Cotton, too, believed that Williams' "corrupt doctrines ... tend
to the disturbance both of civil and holy peace."[55]

   John Cotton (1585–1652) was educated at Cambridge where he was especially known for persuasive and well-formulated sermons. He became a
vicar at Boston in Lincolnshire and kept that position for more than 20
years before coming into conflict with Laud. Later he reflected on his
reasons for emigrating to New England. In a letter addressed to clergy in
England dated December 3, 1634, Cotton writes about the options available
to him, "To choose rather to bear witness to the truth by imprisonment
rather than banishment is indeed sometimes God's way."[56] Cotton con-
ferred with his congregation and other ministers who persuaded him to flee,
"thinking it better for themselves and for me, and for the church of God, to
withdraw myself from the present storm, and to minister in this country to
such of their town as they had sent before thither."[57] He responded to the
arguments against persecution for cause of conscience that Roger Williams
had made in the *Bloudy Tenent*, arguing that while none should be constrained either to believe or to profess the "true religion till he be convinced
in judgment of the truth of it," at the same time, that same person should be
constrained from "blaspheming the truth, and from seducing any unto pernicious errors."[58] In his response, Cotton points out that for those famous
princes Williams had posited as exemplars of religious toleration, he could
name scores who had not tolerated "Heretics and Schismatics, notwithstanding their pretense of conscience."[59] He notes that excommunicating a
heretic is allowable, because that person is not an innocent, but rather "a
culpable and damnable person" who is not being punished for conscience,
"but for persisting in error against the light of conscience."[60] Williams concluded that Cotton's doctrine undermined the "spirit of Love, Holines, and
Meeknes by kindling fiery Spirits of false zeale and Furie."[61]

William Bradford, in his history of Plymouth colony, labels the beliefs of Rhode Islanders as harmful and infectious. He points out that the "chiefest of them" are gone from Plymouth and Massachusetts Bay because of their offenses "either to churches, or commonwealth, or both." The actions that had separated the "Islanders at Acquidneck" included "public defiance against magistracy, ministry, churches, and church covenants." Bradford suspects that these defiant neighbours were "secretly also sowing the seeds of Famililism, and Anabaptistry, to the infection of some, and danger of others." The danger was so great, according to Bradford, that the leadership of Plymouth Bay was not willing to join with the Rhode Islanders in any kind of league or confederacy. Instead, they sought advice how they

Figure 3.1 Statue of Roger Williams, photograph courtesy of Christopher Judge

"may avoid them and keep ours from being infected by them."[62] Winthrop also echoed, in his journal entry, the fear that Providence might be the source "from when the infection would easily spread to these churches."[63]

The commitment to complete liberty of conscience in Rhode Island is widely attributed to Roger Williams and John Clarke.[64] Williams, pictured above, states quite clearly that his purpose in establishing a new community at Providence was to create a shelter for persons "distressed of Conscience."[65] He believed that "enforced uniformity is the greatest occasion of civil War ... of the hypocrisy and destruction of millions of souls. The permission of other consciences and worships than the state professeth, only can ... procure a firm and lasting peace."[66] Included in his definition of persecution for cause of conscience were both belief and practice. In *The Bloudy Tenent*, he clearly rejects the Massachusetts Bay notion of enforced orthodoxy, calling persecution for the cause of conscience a "bloody tenent," that was "lamentably contrary to the doctrine of Christ Jesus the Prince of Peace."[67] He had come to believe that "Forced Worship stinks in God's Nostrils."[68] Williams asserts that "Faith is that *gift* which proceeds alone from the Father of Lights."[69] He uses the term "soul liberty" to describe the natural right of every person to freedom of religion, a freedom he extends to Christians, Jews, Muslims and Pagans alike. Toleration and liberty of conscience go hand in hand with the separation of ecclesiastical and civil functions in Williams' reasoning. He uses the terms "Garden of Christ" and "Wilderness of the World" in *The Bloudy Tenent* to illustrate the distinction between the two types of authority. The authority of the civil state, instituted by men (in accordance with God's laws), is reflected in the actions of Fathers, Masters and Magistrates who are to "judge and accordingly to punish such sinners as transgress against the good and peace of their civil state." He does point out, however, that those who wield civil power are bound by the teachings of Christ to

> suffer opposition to their doctrine with meekness and gentleness, and to be so far from striving to subdue their opposites with the civil sword, that they are bound with patience and meekness to wait if God ... will please to grant repentance unto their opposites.[70]

Here he explicitly rejects any attempts by magistrates to use the law to put down dissidents. At the same time, Williams also affirms his believe that the "sovereign, original, and foundation of civil power, lies in the people" who decide what form of government "seems to them most meet for their civil condition." Williams adds that these governments constituted by the people "have no more power, nor for longer, than the civil power, or people consenting and agreeing, shall betrust [sic] them with."[71] In contrast, the Scripture is the source of authority for punishing those whose offenses are "spiritual and of a Soule-nature" in the Garden of Christ.[72] Williams relies on his belief in the Final Judgement to reassure those who are opposed to tolerating those whose views they see as sinful, heretical, or wrong, pointing out that "an arm of flesh and sword of steel cannot reach to cut the darkness of the mind, the hardness and unbelief of the heart, and kindly operate upon the soul's affections."[73] In other words, civil coercion, whatever its form, cannot change what people believe or how they feel. As such, he calls for a "wall of separation" between the two types of power: civil and ecclesiastical, temporal and spiritual, the wilderness and Christ's garden.

For Williams, separation of the New England churches from the Church of England went hand in hand with the separation of civil and ecclesiastical authority. Cotton Mather published an ecclesiastical history of New England entitled, *Magnalia Christi Americana*, in which he asserts that Roger Williams was so intent on this separation that he refused "... to *communicate* with the church of Boston, because they would not make a public and solemn declaration of repentance for their communicating with the church of England, while they were in the realm of England."[74] According to Mather's analysis, Williams was "violent" in his insistence that the civil magistrate might not punish breaches of the first table in the laws of the Ten Commandments.[75] Again, for Williams, separatism included both official separation of the churches of New England from those of the Church of England *and* a separation of the civil and ecclesiastical functions among their governors.

John Clarke, too, shared these beliefs. He arrived in Boston in 1637 and immediately became embroiled in the Antinomian controversy. For "peace sake," he moved to Aquidneck with the help of Roger Williams "who for matter of conscience had not long before been exiled from the former jurisdiction."[76] In *Ill Newes from New-England*, John Clarke challenges the magistracy in Massachusetts Bay Colony, particularly the way in which the colony attempted to enforce religious orthodoxy by persecuting persons of conscience. He describes his arrest and persecution by Massachusetts Bay magistrates, noting that "the spirit by which they are led, would order the whole world."[77] He also lists laws from the Bay colony, which according to Clark, prove "that the Authority there established cannot permit men ... freely to enjoy their understandings and consciences, nor yet to live ... unless they can do as they do, or say as they say ... or else say nothing."[78] Echoing Williams' language, Clarke too challenges "the use of the civil sword" to enforce a religious order, arguing that it leads only to hypocrisy. The Massachusetts Bay colony had sentenced Baptists to banishment. Further, Baptist beliefs, particularly about visible baptism were considered blasphemous, a capital transgression punishable by death. He concludes by reiterating his opposition to religious intolerance:

But by outward force to seek to constrain, or restrain another's conscience in the worship of God, & doth presuppose one man to have dominion over another man's conscience, and is but to force servants, and worshippers upon the Lord ... and is the ready way to make men dissemblers and hypocrites ... [79]

While in the Verin Case, Williams and the other proprietors of Providence had upheld a woman's right to liberty of conscience, the 1663 Charter of Rhode Island formally extends that liberty to all persons. In a letter to the town of Warwick on New Year's Day, 1665, Williams reflects on the success of John Clarke's mission to England to secure a charter from the King Charles II. He notes that the royal grant and charter bestows upon Rhode Islanders, "inestimable Jewels," primary among them being peace and liberty.[80] The Charter includes the provision that "no person within the said colony ... shall be any wise molested, punished, disquieted, or called in question for any differences in opinion in matters of religion." As long as citizens behaved in a peaceable and orderly fashion, they could "freely and fully have and enjoy his and their own judgments and consciences."[81] Given Williams' willingness to support Jane Verin's liberty of conscience in 1638, it is no accident that the Charter of 1663 uses gender neutral language in codifying that liberty for all Rhode Islanders to enjoy. In the letter, Williams acknowledges with gratitude John Clarke's respect for the peace and liberty of others as having been a determining factor in the royal decision to grant the charter, but he also goes on to express his belief that the "weight which turned the scale with him was the truth of God ... a just Liberty to all Men's Spirits in Spiritual matters together with the peace and prosperity of the whole Colony."[82]

In *Fierce Communion: Family and Community in Early America*, Helena Wall concludes that "Colonial society began by deferring to the needs of the community and ended by deferring to the rights of the individual."[83] In the case of Rhode Island and the problem of liberty of conscience, this is clearly true. Since neither the legal code nor the court system had been established at the time of the Verin case, it is not surprising that an examination of the legal history of Rhode Island reveals no cases that cited the Verin decision as the legal precedent for upholding any person's liberty of conscience. Nor did the Verin case set any precedent for subsequent cases involving women's rights in Rhode Island. This might lead one to conclude that the case had no subsequent impact and is therefore of negligible import. However, examining the case within the full context of events in the English Atlantic world results in very different conclusions. Very early in its development, the Verins forced Williams and other residents to confront the very issues which were perceived to be undermining the quiet and calm of England and the colonies of New England, namely, the right to dissent with the Church of England, the issue of liberty of conscience, the differing positions within puritanism on the issue of domestic violence, the place of women in puritan social and religious life, and the role of civil government in responding to these developments. Jane Verin's challenge to her husband's authority and his response to her *forced the residents to clarify their beliefs*. Issues of faith and gender were clearly intertwined in a complicated situation. At the foundation of their decision was the question: What shall take precedence—a husband's authority over his wife or a wife's authority in matters of her own conscience? The male property owners who were heads of households had a clear choice. This choice forced them to rank their priorities. Their response was by no means unanimous; but the majority of them voted to uphold Jane Verin's liberty of conscience. Their response to this question was specific to that particular time and place. In Massachusetts Bay, the answer would have been quite different, favoring the authority of Joshua Verin as taking precedence over the authority of Jane Verin's conscience. This is a logical assumption, given the response to Anne Hutchinson and the Antinomians in Massachusetts Bay.

All of the proprietors who decided to disenfranchise Joshua Verin were recent arrivals to New England. Given their earlier experiences in New England, there was a predisposition to be sympathetic to a person's liberty of conscience. Roger Williams himself escaped to Rhode Island before he could be imprisoned for his challenges to both the civil and ecclesiastical authorities in Massachusetts Bay; eight of the other heads of household were admonished, excommunicated or banished by their respective New England churches prior to their arrival in Providence. Thus, they had firsthand experience of religious intolerance. In his *Documentary History of Rhode Island*, Howard M. Chapin argues that the town permitted Verin full liberty to worship as he chose and took no action until his actions came under civil censure for civil disturbance and for violating the covenant of religious toleration. He concludes, "Verin persecuted his wife for her religious practices. The town did not persecute Verin for his religious practices, but punished him for his religious intolerance of others, particularly of his wife."[84] Ultimately, this view was written into the most fundamental law of the colony. The language and substance of the Charter of 1663 embeds this principle as the foundation of the colony's very identity.

Massachusetts body of liberties

All patents issued by the Crown authorizing the establishment of colonies in the English Atlantic world specified that no laws could be enacted that were repugnant to English law. At the beginning of the seventeenth century, English law was comprised of common law (unwritten laws based upon custom that had been recognized or enforced by courts), legislation passed by Parliament, and pronouncements by the Crown and the judiciary.

The General Court of Massachusetts administered the civil authority of the colony. A law enacted in 1634, in essence, prohibited any new congregations from forming without the approval of the General Court and the already established churches in the Commonwealth. Further, any member of a church which had not been approved by these would be denied the franchise.[85] The law was being used to reinforce the religious establishment. The intent of the new law is clear, namely, to prevent the spread of religious heterodoxy. According to John Winthrop, Rhode Island exemplified the deadly impact of the lack of religious establishment. In describing the settlement of Rhode Island by Williams and his followers, Winthrop emphasizes the "great strife and contention" of the colony.[86] Rhode Island was often cited by more conservative puritans as "proof that toleration of schismatics would always lead to civil chaos."[87] J. Stanley Lemons reconsiders the opprobrium attached to Williams, as exemplified by the label "Seeker" or a heretical troublemaker, that was used to describe him by his puritan critics. He argues that Williams himself preferred the term a "witness in sackcloth," a term that encompassed the suffering he had endured in both England and New England as a result of his rigid separatism.[88]

In 1636, the General Court asked the Reverend John Cotton and several other ministers to assist the magistrates in compiling a body of fundamental laws. Cotton drew up an "Abstract of Laws" that was based on the "model of Moses his judicial, compiled in an exact method." Although the General Court considered these, they were never adopted.[89] In 1641, the Rev. National Ward, who later published *The Simple Cobler of Aggawam*, compiled a another version of the code of laws that was eventually adopted by the legislature and named the *Body of Liberties*, the court being compelled to this action by "the murmurs of the people, who had become impatient of a situation which left all penalty to the discretion, and sometimes whimsical caprice, of the courts."[90] The public wanted to be judged by clear standards visible and understandable to all. In his journal, Winthrop notes the discontent that some in the colony had expressed about the arbitrariness of the General Court:

> There fell out at this court another occasion of further trouble. The deputy governor having formerly, and from time to time, opposed the deputies' claim of judicial authority, and the prescribing of set penalties in cases which may admit variable degrees of guilt, which occasioned them to suspect, that he, and some others of the magistrates, did affect an arbitrary government, he now wrote a small treatise about these points, showing what arbitrary government was, and that our government (in the state it now stood) was not arbitrary, neither in the ground and foundation of it, nor in the exercise and administration thereof. And because it is of public, and (for the most part) of general concernment, and being a subject not formerly handled by any that I have met with, so as it may be of use to stir up some of more experience and more able parts to bestow their pains herein, I have therefore made bold to set down the whole discourse, with the proceedings which happened about it, in a treatise by itself, with some small alterations and additions (not in the substance of the matter) for clearer evidence of the question.[91]

Winthrop's journal entries of 1639 provide some sense of the process that resulted in the new body of laws. Both the Reverend Cotton's and Nathaniel

Ward's models were presented to the General Court and reviewed by the governor and some of the deputies. According to Winthrop, most of the magistrates and some of the elders were not "very forward in this matter," partly out of a lack of experience "of the nature and disposition of the people, considered with the condition of the country and other circumstances, which made them conceive, that such laws would be fittest for us."[92] Many apparently worried that by calling some of the fundamental laws of England "customs or consuetudines," Massachusetts Bay risked transgressing the limits of the charter that provides that no laws repugnant to the laws of England would be instituted. Winthrop defended Bay colony practice, arguing:

> But to raise up laws by practice and custom had been no transgression; as in our church discipline, and in matters of marriage, to make a law, that marriages should not be solemnized by ministers, is repugnant to the laws of England; but to bring it to a custom by practice for the magistrates to perform it, is no law made repugnant.[93]

Ultimately, Winthrop and other magistrates bowed to public pressure:

> At length (to satisfy the people) it proceeded, and the two models were digested with divers alterations and additions, and abbreviated and sent to every town, (12) to be considered of first by the magistrates and elders, and then to be published by the constables to all the people, that if any man should think fit, that anything herein ought to be altered, he may acquaint some of the deputies therewith against the next court.[94]

This process, involving the civil and ecclesiastical leaders *and* the public, resulted in formal ratification of Nathaniel Ward's code of laws in 1641. John Winthrop later wrote that this provided "for the officers of this body politic ... a rule to walk by in all their administrations, which Rule is the Word of God, and such conclusions and deductions as are or shall be regularly drawn from thence."[95] Among the decrees relating to the liberties of women is the following prohibition: "Every married woman shall be free from bodily correction or stripes by her husband, unless it be in his own defense upon her assault."[96] The language is clear and unambiguous: wife-beating was prohibited.

Many biographies of Roger Williams connect his love of liberty and his willingness to defy authority with his mentor, the legal scholar Sir Edward Coke. Coke is revered for his commitment to upholding English common law against encroachments by the Crown.[97] Coke became famous in his own lifetime for his detailed and careful notes of cases which he heard argued. He began publishing these in what would become a 13-volume series known as *The Reports*. In these reports, Coke summarized the arguments that were offered in each case, as well the reasons for the judgements; these were in the form of general propositions of law. His other great contribution is the *Institutes*, a four-part series on the history of English law from the Magna Charta to the time of James I. This spirit is reflected in the Charter of 1663. Its section on religious matters reads,

> No person within the said colony, at any time hereafter, shall be any wise molested, punished, disqualified, or called in question for any difference of opinion in matters of religion: every person may at all times freely and fully enjoy his own judgment and Conscience in matters of religious concernments.[98]

Although all laws passed by the legislature must be "agreeable to the laws of England," this was qualified by a "reference to the constitution of the pace and the nature of the people."[99] In 1664, the year after the charter was granted, the Rhode Island legislature renewed its declaration, asserting that "liberty to all persons as to the worship of God had been a principle maintained in the colony from the very beginning thereof; and it was much in their hearts to preserve the same liberty forever."[100]

In stark contrast to Massachusetts Bay's efforts to use law based on the Old Testament to serve the interests of the religious establishment, the first Rhode Island Code of Law, enacted just a few years after the *Body of Liberties*, "looked to scriptural authority for their recourse to English law by basing organization of the Code on 1 Timothy 9–10." In this biblical passage, Paul notes that law is for the sinful. A comparative analysis of Massachusetts and Rhode Island criminal law shows that Massachusetts based its penal law almost equally on both English law and the scripture, while Rhode Island law used Dalton's *Manual for Justices of the Peace* as inspiration; some 85 per cent of criminal law in Rhode Island was based on English law.[101] The study concludes that despite the perception of anarchy brought on by the lack of a state-sanctioned church in Rhode Island, within a century, the colony, "by moving from radical church/state separation to legally protected denominationalism ... in fact achieved a high level of stability by the mid-1700s."[102]

The issues in transatlantic context

The debates over the best means to maintain civil order, by means of enforced orthodoxy or by means of toleration, were not just local disputes; but rather they were discussions that took place within a trans-Atlantic context. New Englanders frequently returned to England to visit families, to conduct business, or to resettle after a sojourn in the wilderness. Roger Williams had extended stays in London in the 1640s and again during the 1660s, when he attempted to secure a charter for the colony. Although not quite routine, English puritan ministers were invited to serve as Elders in

New England congregations for stays of varying durations. The Atlantic served as a vast highway for the exchange of people, goods and ideas, travelling in both directions. In his analysis of cultures of print, David Hall concludes that one can find a recognizable group of writers and booksellers earning their livelihoods in seventeenth-century England, although he concedes that readers of devotional literature, written primarily by ordained ministers, were quite different from readers of other popular forms of literature.[103]

Roger Williams and John Cotton exemplify the transatlantic nature of this debate. As has been mentioned, both Williams and Cotton were devout Calvinists, but they were at odds in Massachusetts Bay over Williams' insistence on the absolute separation of the New England churches from the Church of England. They also disagreed vehemently (although civilly) about separation of church and state and liberty of conscience. Inherent in these disagreements was their differing view on the best means to maintain civil order. They engaged in an exchange of correspondence where they attempted to refute the other's arguments, point by point. So, for example, Roger Williams published two works in 1644: *Mr. Cotton's Letter lately Printed, Examined, and Answered* and *The Bloudy Tenent of Persecution for Cause of Conscience*. The Reverend Cotton responded to Williams' criticism of forced orthodoxy in *A Reply to Mr. Williams: his Examination*. In addition, he published a pamphlet, *The Controversy concerning Liberty of Conscience in Matters of Religion*, in 1646. The pamphlet war heated up with Williams' rebuttal in the form of *The Bloody Tenent yet more Bloody: by Mr. Cotton's Endeavor to wash it while in the Blood of the Lamb; of whose precious Blood, spilt in the Blood of his Servants; and of the Blood of Millions spilt in former and later Wars for Conscience sake, that most Bloody Tenent of Persecution for Cause of Conscience, upon, a second Tryal is found more apparently and more notoriously guilty, etc.* (1652). These were published in London and widely discussed within puritan circles on both sides of the Atlantic.

In addition to the political divisiveness that originated in these theological and political disputes, the New England colonies also had to confront growing resistance from Native Americans that ultimately spilled over into the Pequot War during the 1630s. A recent analysis of "evangelical toleration," that is, the idea that toleration is a "necessary precondition for individuals to preach and propagate the Gospel and so convert others to it," persuasively argues that Roger Williams' approach to toleration was inspired in part by his relations with the Narragansett Indians, whom he wished to convert.[104] The Charter of 1663 commends Williams, for example, for attempting to convert the "poor ignorant Indian natives" to Christian faith and practice.[105]

Mid-century England, too, roiled with disputes over liberty of conscience and religious freedom which spilled over into the political arena as puritans led the resistance to efforts by the Crown to use royal power to enforce religious conformity. The Presbyterians in Parliament, for example, publicly burned *The Bloudy Tenent*, a clear indication that there was no more consensus in England as in New England on the issue of toleration and the separation of church and state.[106] The turmoil of this period was also marked by an increased activism by religious women, particularly with the emergence of the Quakers during the 1650s. One historian has shown there "was a great overturning, questioning, revaluing of everything in England; a question of old institutions, beliefs, values."[107] The radical sects tended to reject any type of established church—favoring the congregational model of church organization. The sects were all egalitarian in the sense that they believed Christ made no distinction between men and women, and that God should be obeyed before men. "Although the practical implications [of these beliefs] varied from congregation to congregation—and certainly no one argued that spiritual equality had civil dimensions—women's participation in the sects was evidence of female assertiveness, frequently resisted or resented by men."[108]

One of the most radical groups to emerge during this period of the Civil War and Interregnum were the Quakers, especially because of the major role that female Quakers played during this period of intense persecution of them. The two core beliefs of Quakers, as they were articulated by leaders like George Fox, were: one, that everyone has an innate inner capacity to hear and understand the word of God (often called the "inner light") and express themselves in spiritual matters; and two, each individual, male or female, has direct access to God—ministers and churches are therefore unnecessary. Following the inner light (the call of God) would lead the individual toward spiritual perfection and ultimate union with God. A group of Quaker women had taken a petition with more than 7,000 signatures urging Parliament to abolish tithes, which they believed supported the ministry. In addition, driven by their belief that the spirit guided them, these women preached, engaged in theological debates with men, and invaded the public sphere, a traditional bastion of male authority, to urge political reforms.[109] Parliament received a request to take "repressive action" against Quaker women who were speaking in public, prophesying and protesting against the collection of tithes.[110] These debates took place within the larger context of decades of tensions that resulted in civil war, regicide and ultimately to the Revolution of 1689, when William of Orange and his wife Mary, daughter of King James II, accepted the limitations on royal prerogatives in the form of the An Act Declaring the Rights and Liberties of the Subject and Settling the Succession of the Crown, effectively instituting a constitutional monarchy. The philosophical justification for these developments would bring together all of the threads of a discussion that had been troubling Puritans for decades, in England proper as well as the colonies of New England. A recent study focuses on the experiences of Elizabeth Hooton, a Quaker prophetess who travelled within England and between England and its colonies in the English

Atlantic world, including the West Indies, Virginia and New England.[111] Labeled a "Godly Woman" by George Fox, Hooton exemplifies in multiple ways the political agency of religious minorities and the ways in which the "lived history of toleration" modifies the traditional narrative of intolerance, as exemplified by the Mary Dyer story, concluding that "the lived politics of toleration in Massachusetts included a restrictive judicial framework and an all-too-human willingness to use the gallows and the whip to punish dissenters."[112]

On John Locke

Almost 50 years after Roger Williams published *The Bloody Tenent*, Locke was reaching the same conclusions. Where in *The Bloody Tenent* Williams had argued that, "The permission of other consciences and worships than the state professeth, *only* [my emphasis] can ... procure a firm and lasting peace," Locke would make the same arguments in a number of works published between 1689 and 1692. John Locke was born in 1632 in Somerset, England.[113] His father, a devout puritan, served in Cromwell's army during the civil war of the 1640s. He attended Christ Church College at Oxford University and later earned a degree in medicine. During the 1660s, he joined the staff of Lord Anthony Ashley Cooper, the first Earl of Shaftesbury, one of the founders of the Whig movement. Locke personally witnessed these great upheavals in seventeenth-century England. In fact, he was forced to flee to the Netherlands in 1683, because of his political associations. Many of his political and philosophical writings were completed during this time. Ultimately, Locke returned to England after the Revolution of 1689, where he subsequently published *A Letter Concerning Toleration* in 1689 and the *Second Treatise on Government* in 1690. Additionally, he published *Some Thoughts Concerning Education* in 1692. In these tracts, Locke answers the same questions that the residents of Providence had grappled with at the time of the Verin decision. Most significantly, he provides a rationale that renders the actions of the decision-makers in Providence both logical and comprehensible, uncannily echoing the thoughts and reasoning of Roger Williams. A recent analysis comparing Williams and Locke stresses both were concerned with evangelism, but focuses on Williams' polemical, as opposed to Locke's irenical, motivations in promoting toleration. In other words, Williams' evangelical toleration was directed at creating a community out of many disparate and contentious voices, noting that liberty of conscience was essential to "provide a bond of mutual charity by which all may be brought together in one body."[114] In contrast, Locke, while writing in exile in the Netherlands during a period of civil war, endorsed toleration as a means to a peaceful development of a "spirit of genuine inclusiveness in wanting to bring as many outsiders *in*—to the Commonwealth or to the Church of England— as possible."[115]

In *A Letter Concerning Toleration*, Locke posits that "toleration ... [is] the chief characteristic mark of the true Church"; he argues that toleration of those that differ in matters of religion is "so agreeable to the Gospel of Jesus Christ, and to the genuine reason of mankind, that it seems monstrous for men not to perceive the necessity and advantage of it in so clear a light."[116] Here he is citing both the Scripture and natural law as the source of authority. He distinguishes between a civil and an ecclesiastical sphere. Civil society, or the commonwealth, is constituted by men only for the protection of life, liberty and property. The sole end of government is to protect and secure those rights for individuals who have voluntarily given up some of their *natural* liberties (those enjoyed by men living as free and equal individuals in a state of nature) in order to enjoy *civil* liberties (men consenting to be governed in a voluntary association whose purpose is to protect those same freedoms). Locke argues that the "whole jurisdiction of the magistrate reaches only to these civil concernments," and the power of that magistrate therefore cannot be "in any manner to be extended to the salvation of souls."[117] The residents of Providence had independently reached this same conclusion when they voluntarily joined together in 1637 to form a civil compact. The wording of the compact is clear: "in an orderly way, by the major consent of the inhabitants, masters of families, incorporated together into a town fellowship, and such others whom they shall admit unto them *only in civil things* [my emphasis]."[118]

Locke points out that the care of souls is not the responsibility of the civil magistrate, nor that of any other man. He adds that "no man can so far abandon the care of his own salvation as blindly to leave to the choice of any other ... to prescribe to him what faith or worship he shall embrace." His reasoning is based on the Calvinist reconciliation of two seemingly contradictory truths: that man is born with free will and that God preordains who will be among the saved. Protestants stress the individual's freedom to assent, that is, the individual can choose to believe or not to believe, to heed or to ignore God's call to salvation. As Locke puts it, "All the life and power of true religion consist in the inward and full persuasion of the mind; and faith is not faith without believing." Locke distinguishes between outward force and inward persuasion, in arguing for the separation of civil and ecclesiastical authority.

Locke next develops his argument for toleration by drawing parallels between the process by which governments and churches are formed. Chief among the characteristics of these is that they are voluntary associations of men, stating, "... everyone joins himself voluntarily to that society in which he believes he has found that profession and worship which is truly acceptable to God." (In the case of the Verins, Jane Verin had clearly found that society in the community established by Roger Williams, while Joshua Verin had not.) When men consent to form government, they surrender some of their natural liberties, but *not* their rights to their life, liberty or property. These cannot be alienated from the individual. Similarly, when individuals form a church, it remains a free and voluntary society and church members retain for themselves their individual right of assent and the freedom to act on that conscience. Later in the letter, Locke uses clear and unambiguous language to assert that, when it comes to matters of conscience, every man has the "supreme and absolute authority of judging for himself." Locke rejects any rationale for the use of force in matters of conscience, stating unequivocally that all force and compulsion are unacceptable: "Nobody is obliged in that matter to yield obedience unto the admonitions or injunctions of another, further than he himself is persuaded." Once again, Locke seems to have arrived at the same conclusion that Roger Williams and his supporters had reached decades earlier. They rejected Joshua Verin's attempts to use force to compel his wife to obey his commands, rather than obeying the dictates of her conscience. Like Williams before him, Locke lays the blame for all of the religious wars that have upset the peace of Europe for more than a century "*not* [my emphasis] on the diversity of opinions (which cannot be avoided) but the refusal of toleration to those that are of different opinions (which might have been granted)." He agrees with Williams that forced conformity would only lead to hypocrisy when he says, "It is in vain for an unbeliever to take up the outward show of another man's profession." Forcing someone to act against their judgement (their conscience in the case of religious judgement) is in effect "to command them to offend God, which considering that the end of all religion is to please him, and that liberty is essentially necessary to that end." Locke cites both natural law and revelation to argue for the separation of church and state and a divide between religious and civil authority.

A recent analysis of the origins of liberty of conscience in the First Amendment points out that contemporary notions of freedom of conscience tend to be secular in orientation. However, the Dutch philosopher Anders Schinkel situates the origins of these ideas in the debates over toleration during the seventeenth century, some of which have been analyzed in this work. He states that "an important part of its evocative power as a symbol" rests in the "radical religious conscience of English Puritans," which Schinkel argues empowered them as a "revolutionary conscience." He quotes the puritan John Reeve as an example:

Whosoever hath the divine light of faith in him, that man hath no need of man's law to be his rule, but he is a lower unto himself, and lives above all laws of mortal men, yet obedient to all laws.[119]

When it came to marriage and marital relations, John Locke would also question the absolute authority of the father in the household and of the husband over his wife. In Chapter VI, "Of Paternal Power," of the *Second Treatise on Government*, Locke tries to deflect criticism of his "impertinent criticism."[120] Calling it mistaken, Locke challenges the popular understanding of parental power as resting exclusively in the father. He argues that this assumption is contrary to both reason and revelation, asserting that when it comes to the responsibility of parents over their children, "she [the mother] hath an equal title." In Section 54, Locke once again asserts that all men by nature are equal and free, that is, that every man has an equal right "to his natural freedom, without being subjected to the will or authority of any other man." In his analysis of family rule, Locke points out that "the end of law is not to abolish or restrain, but to preserve and enlarge freedom." While the natural freedom of a child or minor may be restrained by parental power, it is only a *temporary* authority, until he or she is able to exercise their reason to govern himself. Locke concludes that "It is one thing to owe honour[sic], respect, gratitude and assistance; another to require an absolute obedience and submission."[121]

In Chapter VII of the *Second Treatise*, Locke analyzes marriage, arguing that the "first society was between man and wife."[122] He uses the term "conjugal society" for marriage and applies the idea of covenant to the relationship between husband and wife, calling it a "voluntary compact between man and woman" (Section 78). Locke recognizes that husbands and wives may have different understandings and different wills. Aside from their common interest and property, Locke nonetheless stresses that the wife "in the full and free possession of what by contract is her peculiar right and gives the husband no more power over her life than she has over his."[123] By definition, these would be those natural rights which the individual cannot alienate from himself or herself. Although John Locke probably never even heard of Jane Verin, it can be argued that he would have absolutely upheld her liberty of conscience independent of her husband's. In Section 86, Locke uses the same language as William Gouge to describe the family: a "commonwealth." Just as he rejects the absolute power of the monarchy as contrary to reason and natural law, he also rejects the absolute authority of the master of the family. He asserts, "the master of the family has a very distinct and differently limited power ... he has no legislative over of life and death over any of them, and none too but what a mistress of a family may have as well as he. *And he certainly can have no absolute power over the whole family, who has but a very limited one over every individual in it*" [my emphasis].[124]

Where Massachusetts Bay and Rhode Island puritans had responded differently to the issues and controversies relating to liberty of conscience, the place of women within their society, and the best means of maintaining civil order, in England at the end of the century, Locke seems to have brought these together, clearly endorsing the position that Roger Williams and the other residents of Providence had taken; namely, that a woman had a right to liberty of conscience (even if it defied the will of her husband). Further, he agreed that preserving the right of each and every person to liberty of conscience and separating the civil and ecclesiastical functions of government were the best means of maintaining civil order. That these tenets of Western liberal thought had percolated *back* across the Atlantic to the English colonies (and subsequently the United States of America) is embodied in the writings of Thomas Jefferson, particularly in the Declaration of Independence of 1776 and in the Virginia Statute for the Freedom of Religion of 1786 and in James Madison's contributions to the Bill of Rights.[125] Jane Verin, although she is unknown to most Americans, is embedded not only in the fundamental constitution of Rhode Island, but indirectly, in the First Amendment to the Constitution as well.

Notes

1 Teresa M. Bejan, "Evangelical Toleration," *The Journal of Politics*, 77(4), August 13, 2015, 1105.

2 "Archbishop William Laud, 1573–1645," British Civil Wars, Commonwealth, and Protectorate Project, accessed October 9, 2018, http://bcw-project.org/biography/archbishop-william-laud.

3 Martha Nussbaum, *Liberty of Conscience: In Defense of America's Tradition of Religious Equality* (New York: Basic Books, 2008), 45.

4 C.N. Trueman, Declaration of Breda, 1660, full text available at History Learning Site, accessed July 15, 2010, www.historylearningsite.co.uk/text_declaration_breda.htm.

5 Sydney V. James, *John Clarke and His Legacies: Religion and Colonial Law, 1638–1750*, Theodore D. Bozeman, ed. (University Park, PA: The Pennsylvania State University Press, 1999), 82–83.

6 "Sir Edward Coke," in Leslie Stephen, ed., *Dictionary of National Biography*, Vol. XI, 240.

7 Holly Brewer, "The Transformation of Domestic Law," in *The Cambridge History of Law in America Vol. I: Early America, 1580–1815*, Michael Grossberg and Christopher Tomlins, eds. (New York: Cambridge University Press, 2008), 307.

8 Lindsay R. Moore, "Women, Property, and the Law in the Anglo-American World, 1630–1700," *Early American Studies*, Summer 2016. Moore rejects the previous historical interpretation of a "golden age" for colonial women (relative to their peers in England) based on her examination of 3,000 legal cases and 1,100 petitions heard on both sides of the Atlantic. For example, equity law allowed married women to retain control over their real property using trusts, while they were able to control their movable property and inheritances through the use of ecclesiastical law, 542.

9 *Winthrop Papers*, Vol. I, 209, and Chapin, *Documentary History of Rhode Island*, 72.

10 Anne Laurence, *Women in England, 1500–1760: A Social History(s)*, 227.

11 In her analysis of the changes in domestic law during the period from the late sixteenth century to the American Revolution, Holly Brewer describes *The Lawes Resolutions of Womens Rights (1632)* as an obscure text that is not reliable as a report on current law. Brewer argues that the treatise has few citations to later treatises and that it does not appear in the libraries of colonial lawyers, primarily because the author, T.E., was making a fundamentally religious argument. Holly Brewer, "The Transformation of Domestic Law," 308.

12 Ibid., 309. Later, Blackstone's *Commentaries*, published 1765–1769, were also ambiguous on this issue. Blackstone emphasized a husband's right to chastise his wife, again within reasonable bounds. See Susan Dwyer Asmussen, "'Being Stirred to Much Unquietness': Violence and Domestic Violence in Early Modern England," *Journal of Women's History*, 6(2), Summer, 1994, 71.

13 Holly Brewer, "The Transformation of Domestic Law," 307.

14 Thomas Edgar, *The Laws Resolutions of Womens Rights* (London: Miles Flesher, 1632). Book III Section VII, 129 (Accessed April 30, 2010). Early English Books Online (EEBO).

15 Ibid.

16 Ibid.

17 *Second Book of Homilies*, Book Two: "Certain Sermons appointed by the Queen's Majesty to be declared and read by all Parsons, Vicars, and Curates every Sunday and Holy Day in their Churches, and by Her Grace's advice perused and overseen for the better understanding of the simple people" (Paris, 1563). The Anglican Library, www.anglicanlibrary.org/homilies/ (Accessed September 18, 2010), 500–502.

18 Ibid.

19 Ibid.

20 Quoted in Asmussen, "Being Stirred to Much Unquietness," 71–72.

21 "An Homily on the State of Matrimony," 503.

22 Quoted in Asmussen, "Being Stirred to Much Unquietness," 72. Asmussen concludes that "the most generous interpretations of seventeenth-century patriarchal power never gave a husband more than a limited right to correct his wife's behavior through physical force. Such correction was to be used only for serious issues and was distinguished from beating, administered in anger for trivial faults," 72.

23 Richard Baxter, "The Mutual Duties of Husbands and Wives Towards Each Other," *Fire and Ice: Puritan and Reformed Writings*, www.puritansermons.com/baxter (Accessed October 4, 2010).

24 Freeman, 14.

25 Holly Brewer, "The Transformation of Domestic Law," 302.

26 See for example, Elaine Forman Crane, *Ebb Tide in New England*, especially Chap. 4: "A Severe Legislation," for a discussion of women's authority under colonial law where she uses female-authored petitions to analyze both the empowerment of women early in the colonial era followed by the building of patriarchy and a shrinkage of women's legal options by the end of the seventeenth century.

27 Ancestry.com, *Rhode Island court records: records of the Court of Trials of the Colony of Providence Plantations, 1647–1662*. [database online]. (Provo, UT: Ancestry.com Operations Inc., 2005), preface.

28 Howard M. Chapin, *Documentary History of Rhode Island* (Providence: Preston and Rounds Co., 1916), 151. NB: Chapter Five includes the Aquidneck Quarter Court Records, 1641–1646. See also Lyle Koehler, *A Search for Power*, 321.

29 *Rhode Island Court Records: Records of the Court of Trials of the Colony of Providence Plantations, 1647–1670* (Providence: Rhode Island Historical Society, 1922), Vol. 2, 74. NB: Stevens was called at the next session of the court, but he did not appear and the court continued his bond. Ibid., 77.

30 John R. Bartlett, ed., *Records of the colony of Rhode Island and Providence Plantations, in New England* (Providence: A.C. Greene and brother, State printers, 1856–1865), Vol. III, 124.

31 Ibid., 181–182.

32 Jordan quotes the case of Thomas and Dorothy Butler in *Records of Plymouth Colony*, Vol. 3, 191.

33 Ibid.

34 Roger Thompson, *Sex in Middlesex: Popular Mores in a Massachusetts County, 1649–1699* (Amherst, MA: University of Massachusetts Press, 1986), 119.

35 Thompson, *Sex in Middlesex*, 199. See also Jason Jordan, "Domestic Violence in Plymouth Colony," *Historical Ethnography* (Anth. 509, 1998), 1–2.

36 Mark McGarvie and Elizabeth Mensch, "Law and Religion in Colonial America," 333.

37 Richard J. Ross, "The Career of Puritan Jurisprudence," *Law and Historical Review*, 26, Summer 2008, 227.

38 Mark McGarvie and Elizabeth Mensch, "Law and Religion in Colonial America," 333.

39 Ibid., 335.

40 Mark McGarvie and Elizabeth Mensch, "Law and Religion in Colonial America," The authors state "more than in any other colony, the drafters used English law as their source, specifically Dalton's manual for justices of the peace. They estimate that approximately 85 per cent of Rhode Island criminal law had its direct source in England, as contrasted with Massachusetts Bay, which derived its penal law about 40 per cent from England and about 40 per cent from the Bible, 340.

41 Ibid., 339.

42 Isaac Backus, *A History of New England with Particular Reference to the Denomination of Christians called Baptists* (Boston: Edward Draper, 1777), Vol. I, 66.

43 Martha Nussbaum argues that with this text, Williams inaugurated a distinctively American tradition that contributed to America's constitutional heritage, most especially the emphasis on a "mutually respectful civil peace among people who differ in conscientious commitment." See especially Chapter 2 of Martha Nussbaum, *Liberty of Conscience*, 36.

44 Roger Williams, *The Bloudy Tenent of Persecution for Cause of Conscience Discussed: And Mr. Cotton's Letter Examined and Answered*, in E. B. Underhild, ed., The Hanserd Knollys Society (London: J. Haddon, 1848), 37. For an analysis comparing Williams' intent in articulating a "wall of separation" with that of Thomas Jefferson, see W. Clark Gilpin, "Building the 'Wall of Separation': Construction Zone for Historians," *Church History* 79(4), December 2010, 871–880.

45 Roger Williams, quoted in Gilpin, "Building the 'Wall of Separation'," 876.

46 Bejan, "Evangelical Toleration," 1105.

47 Nathanial Ward, *The Simple Cobler of Aggawam in America* (London: Stephen Bowtell, 1647), 5, available at The Project Gutenberg, www.gutenberg.org/files/34974/34974-h/34974-h.htm (Accessed July 13, 2010).

48 Ibid., 10.

49 Ibid.

50 On the Familists, see for example, J.W. Martin, "Elizabethan Familists and English Separatism," *Journal of British Studies*, 20(1) (Autumn 1980), 53–73.

51 David Little, "Roger Williams and the Puritan Background of the Establishment Clause," in *No Establishment of Religion: America's Original Contribution to Religious Liberty*, T. Jeremy Gunn and John R. Witte, eds. (New York: Oxford University Press, 2012), 105.

52 Ibid., 13.

53 Ibid.

54 Ibid.

55 Quoted in Edmund J. Carpenter, *Roger Williams: A Study of the Life, Times, and Character of a Political Pioneer* (New York: The Grafton Press, 1909), 168.

56 John Cotton, letter written from Boston, MA, dated December 3, 1634, to "Some English Clergyman giving Reasons for the Emigration of Puritan

Clergymen," Trent and Wells, eds. *Colonial Prose and Poetry* (New York: Thomas Y. Crowell & Co., 1901). Bartleby.com, www.bartleby.com/163/ (Accessed September 4, 2010).

57 Ibid.

58 John Cotton, "An Answer of Mr. John Cotton of Boston in New England, to the Aforesaid Arguments against Persecution for Cause of Conscience," printed in Williams' *Bloody Tenent*, Ibid.

59 Ibid.

60 Ibid.

61 Quoted in Nussbaum, *Liberty of Conscience*, 39.

62 William Bradford, *History of Plymouth Plantation, 1606–1646*, Vol. 6, William T. Davis, ed. (New York: William Scribner & Sons, 1908), 365–366.

63 *Journal of John Winthrop*, 168.

64 David Little, "Roger Williams and the Puritan Background of the Establishment Clause," reaffirms Williams' central role and traces it back to the Austrian legal scholar Georg Jellinek, who argued the origins of the Establishment Clause of the First Amendment lie in the Reformation and its struggles, not in the Enlightenment ideas underlying the American and French Revolutions, 100ff. See also, Thomas W. Bicknell, *Story of Dr. John Clarke, the founder of the first free commonwealth of the world on the basis of "full liberty in religious concernments"* (Providence, RI: Thomas W. Bicknell, 1915) for an early analysis of Clarke's role in fostering full liberty of conscience in America.

65 Howard M. Chapin, ed., *Documentary History of Rhode Island* (Providence: Preston & Rounds, Co., 1916), 11. See also J. C. Davis, *On Religious Liberty Selections from the Works of Roger Williams* (New York: Belknap Press, 2008). For a recent discussion of William's contributions to liberty of conscience and the separation of church and state, see Martha Nussbaum, *Liberty of Conscience: In Defense of American's tradition of Religious Equality* (New York: Basic Books, 2008); Andrew R. Murphy, *Conscience and Community: Revisiting Toleration and Religious Dissent in Early Modern England and America* (University Park, PA: Penn State University Press, 2010); Edward J. Eberle, "Roger Williams on Liberty of Conscience," *Roger Williams University Law Review*, 10 (2004–2005), 289; Timothy L. Hall, "Roger Williams and the Foundations of Religious Liberty," *Boston University Law Review*, 71(3), May 1991. See also Edmund S. Morgan, *Puritan Political Ideas 1558–1794* (New York: Bobbs-Merrill, 1965).

66 Quoted in Theodore Dwight Bozeman, "Religious Liberty and the Problem of Order in Early Rhode Island," *New England Quarterly*, 45(1), March 1972, 62.

67 Roger Williams, *The Bloudy Tenent, of Persecution, for Cause of Conscience*, in *The Complete Writings of Roger Williams*, Vol. III (Providence: Russell & Russell, 1867; reprint New York, 1963), 425. See also James P. Byrd Jr., *The Challenges of Roger Williams: Religious Liberty, Violent Persecution and the Bible* (Macon, GA: Mercer University Press, 2002). Byrd analyzes the Biblical sources of Williams' conceptions of religious liberty and toleration.

68 *The Bloudy Tenent*, 470.

69 Ibid., 172.

70 Ibid., 135.

71 Ibid., 269.

72 Ibid., 143.

73 Ibid., 358.

74 Cotton Mather, *Magnalia Christi Americana; or The Ecclesiastical History of New-England* (Hartford, 1853), Vol. II, available in its entirety at Making of America Books, a digital project of University of Michigan, http://quod.lib. umich.edu (Accessed September 20, 2010). Mather calls the chapter on Roger

Williams, "Little Foxes; or the Spirit of Rigid Separation in One Remarkable Zealot," 496.

75 Ibid.
76 John Clarke, *Ill Newes from New-England: or A Narrative of New Englands Persecution Wherin is Declared that while Old England is Becoming New, New-England is Become Old.* London: 1652; Collections of the Massachusetts Historical Society, Vol. I, 4th edition (Boston, 1852), 23–24.
77 *Ill Newes from New-England*, 27–61. Clark was accused of preaching and baptizing on the Lord's Day in a conventicle and having professed against the institution of the Church. He was imprisoned and ordered to be fined or whipped. Friends paid his fine.
78 Ibid., 65.
79 Ibid., 103.
80 *Correspondence of Roger Williams*, Vol. I, 534–541.
81 Charter, July 8, 1663, *Records of Rhode Island*, Vol. II, 10.
82 *Correspondence of Roger Williams*, Vol. I, 536.
83 Helena Wall, *Fierce Communion: Family and Community in Early America* (Cambridge, MA: Harvard University Press, 1990), 229.
84 Chapin, *Documentary History of Rhode Island*, 72.
85 Isaac Backus, *A History of New England*, Vol. I, 66.
86 John Winthrop, *The Journal of John Winthrop 1630–1649*, Richard S. Dunn, James Savage and Laetitia Yeandle, eds. (Cambridge, MA: Harvard University Press, 1996), 163–164.
87 Mark McGaarvie and Elizabeth Mensch, "Law and Religion in Colonial America," in Michael Grossberg and Christopher Tomlins, eds., *The Cambridge History of Law in America* (Vol. I: 1580–1815) (New York: Cambridge University Press, 2008), 338.
88 J. Stanley Lemons, "Roger Williams: Not a Seeker but a 'Witness in Sackcloth,'" *The New England Quarterly*, LXXXVIII(4), December 2015, 712.
89 See Entry #25 for 1636 in *The Journal of John Winthrop*, Vol. I, 196.
90 Sanford H. Cobb, *The Rise of Religious Liberty in America: A History* (New York: The Classics, 1968), 180. See also, John G. Palfrey, *History of New England*, Vol. I (Boston: Little, Brown 1858), 279.
91 *Journal of John Winthrop*, 323–324.
92 Ibid.
93 Ibid.
94 Ibid.
95 Quoted in Cobb, *The Rise of Religious Liberty*, 181.
96 Section 80, Massachusetts Body of Liberties (1641) available at Hanover Historical Texts Project, Hanover College; http://history.hanover.edu/texts/masslib.htm (Accessed July 23, 2009).
97 "Sir Edward Coke" in *Dictionary of National Biography*, Leslie Stephen, ed. (New York: Macmillan & Co., 1887), Vol. XI, 229 ff.
98 Cobb, *The Rise of Religious Liberty*, 436.
99 Ibid.
100 Ibid., 437.
101 Mark McGarvie and Elizabeth Mensch, "Law and Religion in Colonial America," 340.
102 Ibid., 338.
103 David D. Hall, *Cultures of Print: Essays in the History of the Book* (Amherst, MA: University of Massachusetts Press, 1996), 49. See especially the chapter entitled, "The Uses of Literacy in New England, 1600–1850."
104 Teresa M. Bejan, "Evangelical Toleration," 1104.

105 To support this argument, Bejan analyzes Williams' *A Key into the Language of America*, his notebook on Narragansett language and customs published in 1643. Bejan focuses on the many references in the *Key* to his attempts to convince the Narragansetts to convert, repent and be saved. She adds that Williams carried a petition from the Narragansetts to Parliament asking for the right to freely practice their religion and complaining about threats by Massachusetts proselytizers in 1651. Ibid., 1108.

106 Perry Miller and Thomas Herbert Johnson, *The Puritans: A Sourcebook of Their Writings* (Mineola, NY: Courier Dover Publications, 2001), 215.

107 Caroline Baker, "An Exploration of Quaker Women's Writing between 1650 and 1700," *Journal of International Women's Studies*, 5(2), March 2004, 8.

108 Christine Faure, *Political and Historical Encyclopedia of Women* (London: Taylor & Francis, 2003), 56.

109 Ibid., 9–10.

110 Ludlow, 93–94.

111 Adrian Chastain Weimer, "Elizabeth Hooton and the Lived Politics of Toleration in Massachusetts Bay," *The William and Mary Quarterly*, 74(1), January 2017, 3rd series.

112 Weimer notes that Hooton arrived in Boston just after Mary Dyer's execution. She quotes Governor Endicott's justification of the hangings on the basis that the Quakers were "open Capital Blasphemers ... open enemies to Government itself." Ibid., 49–50, 75–76.

113 "John Locke," *Dictionary of National Biography*, Leslie Stephen, ed. (London: Smith, Elder & Co., 1885), Vol. 34, 27ff.

114 Tejan, "Evangelical Toleration," 1110.

115 Ibid.

116 John Locke, *The Works of John Locke*, in Nine Volumes (London: C. Baldwin, 1824), Vol. 5, *A Letter Concerning Toleration*, available at Online Library of Liberty: A Collection of Scholarly Works about Individual Liberty and Free Markets; 2014, https://oll.libertyfund.org/titles/locke-the-works-vol-5-four-letters-concerning-toleration (Accessed December 12, 2014).

117 Ibid.

118 Ibid.

119 Anders Schinkel, *Conscience and Conscientious Objections* (Amsterdam: Amsterdam University Press, 2007), 453. Tejan, in "Evangelical Toleration," attempts to restore the evangelical hopes (and religious impulses) to both Williams' and Locke's views on toleration. She concludes "recovering evangelical toleration is an important albeit forgotten tradition in early modern political thought" that is connected to the fundamental rights of religious freedom and free speech inherent in the "First Amendment Faith," 1112.

120 John Locke, *The Second Treatise on Government*, edited by C. B. McPherson (Indianapolis and Cambridge: Hackett Publishing Company, 1980), The Project Gutenberg, www.gutenberg.org/files/7370/7370-h/7370-h.html (Accessed September 15, 2010).

121 Ibid.

122 Ibid.

123 Ibid.

124 Ibid.

125 See for example Ralph Ketcham, "James Madison, Thomas Jefferson, and the Meaning of 'Establishment of Religion' in Eighteenth-Century Virginia," in *No Establishment of Religion: America's Original Contribution to Religious Liberty*, T. Jeremy Gunn and John Witte, Jr., eds. (New York: Oxford University Press, 2012).

Conclusion
Women of obstinate faith

The puritans were "much afflicted with conscience." According to their Calvinist faith, individuals must wrestle with their sinfulness and strive, with the assistance of their families, ministers and the larger community, to live out their faith as "Visible Saints." Many were afflicted with self-doubt, fear, and concern that they were unequal to the task; their faith experiences emboldened them to challenge those whose actions did not accord with their understanding of the Scripture. Acting on their conscience got them in trouble with the Church of England and the Crown, and many puritans suffered all types of officially sanctioned afflictions. In New England, they had an unprecedented opportunity to live out their faith, but they continued to wrestle both individually and collectively with questions of conscience, toleration and civil order.

Jane Verin was a pious woman whose religious convictions drove her to acts of defiance of any authority that would have compelled her to act in a way that she believed contrary to the dictates of her conscience. Jane Verin, not Joshua, was the reason the Verins came to Providence. In her experiences, she was typical of other female dissenters, such as Anne Hutchinson, Mary Dyer, and others who were perceived to be a threat to the established social order in Massachusetts Bay and who would later suffer the consequences. Both Joshua and Jane were admitted to communion in the First Church of Salem; but in the months prior to their arrival in Providence, Jane and her mother, the Widow Reeves, refused to worship with the Congregation and later denied the churches of the Bay Colony were true churches because they had not separated from the Church of England. She was identified subsequently as a follower of Roger Williams, who became one of the most prominent of the newly arrived ministers who challenged the legitimacy of the New England churches. Puritan women were socialized to be modest, submissive and obedient. In defying Church authorities in Salem, and later defying her husband's authority in Providence, Jane Verin not only challenged Puritan notions about appropriate behavior for women, but her obstinate determination threatened to undermine the very basis of family and community structure. It is likely that Jane Verin was also influenced by the preaching of Anne Hutchinson and her supporters. Examining her experiences, and those of others like her, sheds a light on the question of female agency during this pivotal period in English Atlantic history. Using the variety of primary and secondary sources to give voice to a woman who left no written records is one way of trying to understand women like Jane Verin. How was it possible for her, a woman who had been socialized to be humble, meek and obedient and who had been instructed all her life to defer to men who had authority over her, including her husband, minister and magistrates, to find the will and the strength to persevere in face of censure, approbation, and brutal physical abuse that nearly took her life? How could she persist? The only answer that makes any sense is that her obstinate faith inspired her to action. The biographical sketches of the women who helped found Providence reveals that she was not alone or unique. Like their more famous contemporaries, Anne Hutchinson and Mary Dyer, Verin and the members of her spirit group in Providence found ways to exercise agency. They not only acted on their conscience in defiance of male authorities in England and New England, but they also exercised a tacit, indirect influence on at least a majority of men who had the right to vote on whether or not to disenfranchise Joshua Verin for violating Jane Verin's liberty of conscience. Many of them continued to do so long after the Verins returned to Salem. And they continued to do so *knowing* that their actions would result in all sorts of approbation from their male relatives, ministers and magistrates, and others in positions of authority. Nevertheless, they persisted. In this case, examining the actions of those involved *after* the Verin decision had been rendered reinforces the conclusions that were developed by analyzing the biographical sketches of the early founders, especially of the women of Providence.

As English Puritans newly arrived from England, many of the original proprietors and their families would have had experience with active female participation in Church affairs in both Old and New England. Because of the persecution by the Crown, English Puritans often met in conventicles. As members of congregations and as "Visible Saints," women signed church covenants, formed at least half of most congregations, bore either public or private witness to their faith, and sometimes preached in lay ministries. Most of these practices continued in New England churches, although ministers disagreed on the level of female involvement in church affairs and governance. After the Antinomian Controversy, there was a concerted effort by the magistracy in the New England colonies to silence women and restore the traditional order. Anne Hutchinson was representative of these developments. Indeed, the issue split the heads of household in Providence who were deciding on Joshua Verin's fate. At the town meeting, William Arnold supported Joshua Verin's discipline of his wife. He stated that when he had agreed to Roger Williams' edict that no man should be molested for his conscience, "he never intended it should extend to the breach of any ordinance of God, such as the subjection of wives to their husbands ..."[1] He disagreed with the decision to disenfranchise Verin for having violated his wife's liberty of conscience, arguing that, in fact, Verin himself was acting out of conscience.

Joshua Verin was a typical Puritan patriarch. Records from the First Church of Salem and the Town of Salem indicate that he and the other male members of his family were respected members of the church and community. There are no records of any complaints of domestic violence in either the period prior to Verin's arrival in Providence or after his return to Salem. Indeed, after their return to Salem on June 10, 1638, he received several grants of land, and despite the fact that his wife was presented in court at Salem for absence from religious worship in December of 1638, Joshua himself continued within the church. And based on the tasks assigned to him and his kin by the Church, it is clear that he accepted (and was willing to enforce) the attempts by the ministers to enforce puritan orthodoxy, especially when it came to forcing others to attend public worship. In order to understand his "fowle & slanderous & brutish carriage" toward his wife while they resided in Providence, the differences in the structure and form of authority between the colonies of Massachusetts Bay and Providence must be taken into account. As long as the church and hierarchy existed, it served to reinforce traditional norms of female behavior that kept women in a subordinate and submissive position. Jane Verin and other women like her were punished for their challenges to the Church, the Magistracy, and even to their own husbands' authority. However, in Rhode Island, those institutions were not well established or clearly defined. As a result, Joshua Verin, as a puritan male, and governor of his household, had to take on the responsibility for chastising and disciplining his wife. Once he returned to Salem, that role would once again be reinforced by the patriarchy. (His wife was stripped of her church membership in 1640.)

The experiences of the original proprietors of Providence would have predisposed them to be sympathetic to a person's liberty of conscience. Many had been involved either directly or indirectly in the Antinomian Controversy in Massachusetts Bay Colony. Roger Williams personally arranged for Anne Hutchinson and her followers to obtain a land grant in Portsmouth. They arrived in late March 1638, *before* the Verin case was heard. Hutchinson and other women continued to prophesy and preach after their arrival in Rhode Island. In addition to Jane Verin, the wives of several of the original proprietors had been involved in troubles with the respective churches in Salem and Boston prior to their arrival in Providence. Further, the Baptist and Quaker leanings of some of the original proprietors also predisposed them to support Jane Verin. Finally, the beliefs of Roger Williams and John Clarke, who would go on to author the Charter of 1663, giving "each and every person" religious liberty, would also predispose them to be sympathetic to Jane Verin's plight.

Although the Verin Case set no precedent for subsequent legal cases involving women's rights in Rhode Island, it must be examined within the full context of events both in Old and New England. Despite the fact that the colony was very young, the Verin Case forced Williams and other residents to confront the very issues which were perceived to be undermining the quiet and calm of England and the Massachusetts Bay Colony: namely, the right to dissent within the Church of England, the issue of liberty of conscience, the differing positions within Puritanism on the problem of domestic violence, the place of women in Puritan social and religious life, and the role of civil government in responding to these developments. The case reflects that the turmoil of the Antinomian Controversy had affected Providence even before Anne Hutchinson and her followers arrived.

The Verin family reflected in microcosm the forces at work in Plymouth and Massachusetts Bay during the 1630s. In her experiences, Jane Verin was typical of other female religious dissenters, such as Anne Hutchinson, Mary Dyer, and others who were perceived as a threat to the established social order in New England and who would later suffer the consequences. Just as the Hutchinsonians were silenced, so too, women in Rhode Island would lose legal and economic status by the end of the century. Given the experiences in both England and in Massachusetts Bay of several of the original Rhode Island proprietors, there was a predisposition to be sympathetic to a person's liberty of conscience. Further, the Baptist and Quaker leanings of some of the Original Proprietors predisposed them to support Jane Verin. A close analysis of the biographical sketches of these individuals supports these conclusions. Despite Roger Williams' belief in a woman's inferiority and his opposition to female prophesying, he nonetheless supported a woman's full liberty of conscience. While many Puritans expected husbands to discipline their wives, they were divided about whether physical violence was appropriate in that admonishment. Even those who argued it was a husband's duty to punish an unruly wife were divided on how much force was acceptable. The original proprietors had to answer these questions for themselves before they could decide on the disposition of Joshua and Jane Verin's case. They had to weigh his authority and duty as a husband against her duty to follow the dictates of her conscience. They had to determine whether his violent carriage in effect interfered with her liberty of conscience. Clearly, the sustained violence of his rebuke was a central consideration. They chose to disenfranchise Joshua Verin for having violated his wife's liberty of conscience. They decided to deprive him (at least temporarily) of his civil right to vote in response to his having violated her natural right to conscience. Roger Williams, John Clarke and other Rhode Islanders would subsequently apply this same standard to all citizens of the colony. In both the Charter of 1644, obtained from Parliament, and the Charter of 1663, acquired after the restoration of Charles II, the fundamental law of Rhode Island guaranteed that each and every person had a basic and inviolable right to liberty of conscience. The advantage of the microhistorical approach here is that one can flesh out the nuances and unexpected details of these struggles, which might otherwise be overlooked in larger narratives of the period. Those who are familiar with the history of Providence know that Rhode Islanders were a fractious bunch. Few, however, have made the connections between the decision by the proprietors regarding the Verins, a case relating to liberty of conscience, with the fissures that appeared between them over land disputes, relations with the Indians, and arguments about how best to govern the colony. This microhistory, hopefully, will have made a convincing case that all of these factors are interconnected.

In a transatlantic English world, people, goods and ideas travelled back and forth freely on a vast Atlantic highway. The questions that disquieted the residents of the New England colonies were equally disruptive in England during the long seventeenth century. Sectarian violence and civil war intersected with questions of women's roles in religion. Women's religious activism was perceived to be a threat to the traditional order of society and of marriage itself on both sides of the Atlantic. John Locke would reach some of the same conclusions as Roger Williams had decades earlier regarding an individual's right to liberty of conscience, the necessity for tolerance of religious difference, and the emphasis on the limits and separation of church and state.

Jane Verin is also significant because of the fact that she is an unknown. She was a woman of faith and a committed puritan. Although she is virtually unknown, she was not alone. Acting on that faith, she and many of the other women who helped found Providence were willing to defy authority—including their husbands, their ministers and the civil authorities in Massachusetts Bay colony. Jane Verin is important because of the confluence of developments that placed her at the center of controversy at a time when Rhode Islanders were divided on issues such as determining how much government was sufficient to guarantee order and to what extent differences over worship and issues of conscience would be tolerated. In her quiet, but obstinate, faith, she forced those around her to confront issues that would affect the future direction of the colony. Supporters of Joshua Verin, such as William Arnold and William Harris, would leave Providence and attempt to reattach themselves to Massachusetts Bay. A decades-long dispute over property rights, boundaries and the legitimacy of governmental authority ensued. These historical connections would not have been made without utilizing the methodologies of microhistory.

While Jane Verin was an activist, she was *not* a feminist. She did not challenge her place as a woman within the puritan patriarchy. It was only in matters of her conscience that she defied her husband; indeed, despite offers from those in Providence who were sympathetic to her plight to find her a different husband, she remained with Joshua Verin and accompanied him back to Salem. In her actions, she is more similar to many nineteenth-century evangelical Christian women, who compelled by their religious belief, later defied civil authorities and convention in the abolitionist and other social reform movements, many of whom never directly challenged their assigned role as women. It is clear that from the earliest history of America, there have been women, both prominent and virtually unknown, who acted out of conscience, willing to defy and challenge established authority, while at the same time remaining committed to traditional, Biblically-inspired gendered norms. Her actions directly affected her marriage, her family and the future direction of colonial Rhode Island. Her plight reaffirmed for Roger Williams and his supporters the absolute and inviolate liberty that emanates from the individual conscience and confirmed the absolute necessity of keeping church and state separate. These ideas would be re-articulated in the writings of John Locke, who in turn, influenced American political thinkers such as Thomas Jefferson and others, who incorporated these into the foundational documents of the new nation. The issues contributing to the marital dispute between Jane and Joshua Verin had, in effect, come full circle. Much afflicted as they were by conscience, the history of the Verin family is New England history.

Note

1 Quoted in Winthrop, *History*, Vol. I, 340–341.

Works cited

Alderman, J.P., Charles H. *The Ancient Trade Guilds and Companies of Salisbury.* Salisbury, England: Bennett Brothers Printers, 1912.

Allen, Thomas. "The Call of Christ Unto Thirsty Sinners, to Come to Him and Drink of the Waters of Life. As It Was Preached by that Holy Man of God, and Faithful Servant of Christ." Evans Early American Imprint Collection, 1608–1673.

Anderson, Robert Charles. "Communications: On English Migration to Early New England," *New England Quarterly,* 59(3), September 1986, 406–407.

Anderson, Robert Charles. *The Great Migration: Immigrants to New England, 1634–1635,* 7 volumes. Boston: New England Historic Genealogical Society, 1999–2011.

Anderson, Virginia Dejohn. "Migrants and Motives: Religion and the Settlement of New England, 1630–1640," *New England Quarterly,* 58, 1985, 339–383.

Apple, Rima D. and Golden, Janet, eds. *Mothers and Motherhood: Readings in American History.* Columbus, OH: Ohio State University Press, 1997.

Arnold, Samuel Greene. *History of the State of Rhode Island and Providence Plant-ations,* Vol. I, 1636–1700. New York: D. Appleton & Co., 1859.

Asmussen, Susan Dwyer. "'Being Stirred to Much Unquietness': Violence and Domestic Violence in Early Modern England," *Journal of Women's History,* 6(2), Summer 1994, 70–89.

Austin, John O. *The Genealogical Dictionary of Rhode Island: Comprising Three Generations of Settlers Who Came before 1690: With Many Families Carried to the Fourth Generation.* Albany, NY: J. Munsell's Sons, 1887.

Backus, Isaac. *A History of New England with Particular Reference to the Denomin-ation of Christians Called Baptists.* Boston: Edward Draper, 1777.

Baker, Caroline. "An Exploration of Quaker Women's Writing between 1650 and 1700," *Journal of International Women's Studies,* 5(2), March 2004, 8–20.

Banks, Charles E. *Topographical Dictionary of 2885 English Emigrants to New England, 1620–1650,* Edited, indexed and published by Brownell, Elijah Ellsworth. Philadelphia: Bertram Press, 1937.

Banner, Michael. *Christian Ethics and Contemporary Moral Problems.* Cambridge, England: University of Cambridge Press, 1999.

Barker-Benfield, Ben. "Ann Hutchinson and the Puritan Attitude toward Women," *Feminist Studies,* 1(2), 1972, 65–96.

Barnes, Viola F. *The Winthrop Papers, Vol. IV, 1638–1644.* Boston: Massachusetts Historical Society, 1944.

Barry, Heather E. "Naked Quakers Who Were Not so Naked: Seventeenth Century Quaker Women in the Massachusetts Bay Colony," *Historical Journal of Massachusetts*, 43(2), Summer 2015, 116–135.

Barry, John M. *Roger Williams and the Creation of the American Soul: Church, State and the Birth of Liberty*. New York: Penguin Books, 2012.

Bartlett, John R., ed. *Colonial Records of Rhode Island, Vol. I, 1636–63*. Providence: A.C. Greene & Brothers, 1856.

Bartlett, John R., ed. *Letters of Roger Williams, 1632–1682, Now First Collected*. Providence: The Narragansett Club, 1874.

Baxter, Richard. "The Mutual Duties of Husbands and Wives Towards Each Other," *Fire and Ice: Puritan and Reformed Writings*, Available at www.puritan sermons.com/baxter.

Bejan, Teresa M. "Evangelical Toleration," *The Journal of Politics*, 77(4), August 13 2015, 1103–1114.

Belleisles, Michael A., ed. *Lethal Imagination: Violence and Brutality in American History*. New York: New York University Press, 1999.

Berkin, Carol. *First Generations: Women in Colonial America*. New York: Hill and Wang, 1996.

Bicknell, Thomas Williams. *The Story of Dr. John Clarke, the Founder of the First Free Commonwealth of the World on the Basis of "Full Liberty in Religious Concernments*. Providence, RI: Thomas W. Bicknell, 1915.

Bicknell, Thomas Williams. *The History of the State of Rhode Island and Providence Plantations*, Vol. 1. New York: American Historical Society, 1920.

Bloch, Ruth H. *Gender and Morality in Anglo-American Culture, 1650–1800*. Berkeley and Los Angeles: University of California Press, 2003.

Boughton, Lynne Courter. "Choice and Action: William Ames's Concept of the Mind's Operation in Moral Decisions," *Church History*, 56, 1987, 188–203.

Bozeman, Theodore Dwight. "Religious Liberty and the Problem of Order in Early Rhode Island," *New England Quarterly*, 45(1), March 1972, 44–64.

Bozeman, Theodore Dwight. *To Live Ancient Lives: The Primitivist Dimension in Puritanism*. Williamsburg, VA: Institute of Early American History and Culture, 1988.

Bozeman, Theodore Dwight. *The Precisionist Strain: Disciplinary Religion and Antinomian Backlash in Puritanism to 1638*. Chapel Hill: University of North Carolina Press, 2004.

Bradford, William. *History of Plymouth Plantation*, Collection of Massachusetts Historical Society, Vol. III. Boston: Wright & Potter Printing Co., 1898.

Breen, T.H. and Foster, Stephen. "Moving to the New World: The Character of Early Massachusetts Immigration," *William and Mary Quarterly*, 30(2), 1973, 3rd Series, 189–222.

Bremer, Francis J. "'To Tell What God Hath Done for Thy Soul': Puritan Spiritual Testimonies as Admissions Tests and Means of Edification," *The New England Quarterly*, 87(4), December 2014, 625–665.

Byrd, Jr, James P. *The Challenges of Roger Williams: Religious Liberty, Violent Persecution and the Bible*. Macon, GA: Mercer University Press, 2002.

Carpenter, Edmund J. *Roger Williams: A Study of the Life, Times, and Character of a Political Pioneer*. New York: Grafton Press, 1909.

Chapin, Howard M. *Documentary History of Rhode Island: Being the History of the Towns of Providence and Warwick to 1649 and of the Colony to 1647*. Providence: Preston & Rounds, Co., 1916.

Christian, John T. *A History of the Baptists, of the Unites States from the First Settlement of the Country to the Year 1845,* Vol. II. Nashville, TE: Broadman Press, 1926.

Clarke, John. *Ill Newes from New-England: Or A Narrative of New Englands Persecution Wherin Is Declared that while Old England Is Becoming New, New-England Is Become Old*, London: 1652, Collections of the Massachusetts Historical Society, Vol. I, 4th ed. Boston: Massachusetts Historical Society, 1852.

Cleaver, Robert. *A Godly Forme of Household Government.* London: Thomas Creede, 1603. Early English Books Online (database).

Cobb, Sanford H. *The Rise of Religious Liberty in America: A History.* New York: MacMillan Company, 1968.

Cohen, Charles L. *God's Caress: The Psychology of Puritan Religious Experience.* New York: Oxford University Press, 1986.

Cohen, Charles L. "The Post-Puritan Paradigm of Early American Religious History," *William and Mary Quarterly*, LIV(4), October 1997, 3rd Series, 903–990.

Coldham, Peter Wilson. *The Complete Book of Emigrants: 1607–1660: A Comprehensive Listing Compiled from English Public Records of Those Who Took Ship to the Americas for Political, Religious, and Economic Reasons; of Those Who Were Deported for Vagrancy, Roguery, or Non-Conformity; and of Those Who Were Sold to Labour in the New Colonies.* Baltimore: Genealogical Publishing, 1987.

Como, David R. "Women, Prophecy, and Authority in Early Stuart Puritanism," *Huntington Library Quarterly*, 61(2), 1998, 203–222.

Como, David R. *Blown by the Spirit: Puritanism and the Emergence of an Antinomian Underground in Pre-Civil-War England.* Stanford, CA: Stanford University Press, 2004.

Cooke, Kathy J. "Generations and Regeneration: 'Sexceptionalism' and Group Identity among Puritans in Colonial New England," *Journal of the History of Sexuality*, 23(3), September 2014, 333–357.

Crane, Elaine Forman. *Ebb Tide in New England: Women, Seaports, and Social Change, 1630–1800.* Boston: Northeastern University Press, 1998.

Crane, Elaine Forman. *Witches, Wife Beaters, and Whores: Common Law and Common Folk in Early America.* Ithaca, NY: Cornell University Press, 2011.

Crawford, Patricia. *Women and Religion in England.* London: Routledge, 1993.

Davis, J.C. *On Religious Liberty: Selections from the Works of Roger Williams.* New York: Belknap Press, 2008.

Davis, William T. and Bradford, William. *History of Plymouth Plantation, 1606–1646.* New York: William Scribner & Sons, 1908.

Demos, John. *A Little Commonwealth: Family Life in Plymouth Colony.* New York: Oxford University Press, 1971.

DeWeese, Charles W. *Women Deacons and Deaconesses: 400 Years of Baptist Service.* Macon, GA: Mercer University Press, 2005.

Dow, George F., ed. *Records and Files of the Quarterly Courts of Essex County, Vol. III, 1662–1667.* Essex, MA: Essex Institute, 1913.

Duke, William. *Memoirs of the First Settlement of the Island of Barbados and Other the [Sic]Caribbee Islands, with the Succession of the Governors and Commanders in Chief of Barbados to the Year 1742,* Extracted from the ancient records, papers, and accounts, taken from Mr. William Arnold, Mr. Samuel Bulkly and Mr. John Summers. London: E. Owen & W. Meadows, 1743.

Dunn, Richard S., Savage, James and Yeandle, Laetitia, eds. *The Journal of John Winthrop 1630–1649*. Cambridge, MA: The Massachusetts Historical Society, 1996.

Eberle, Edward J. "Roger Williams on Liberty of Conscience," *Roger Williams University Law Review*, 10, 2004–2005, 289–323.

Edgar, Thomas. *The Laws Resolutions of Womens Rights*. London: Miles Flesher, 1632. Early English Books Online (Database).

Edwards, Rev., Thomas. *The First and Second Part of Gangraena: Or a Catalogue and Discovery of Many of the Errors, Heresies, Blasphemies, and Pernicious Practices of the Sectaries of This Time*, 3rd ed. London: T.R. and E.M. for Ralph Smith, 1646. Massachusetts Historical Society.

Essex Institute. *Town Records of Salem, 1634–1659*, Essex Institute – Historical Collections, Second Series, Vol. I, Part I. Salem, MA: Essex Institute, 1868.

Faure, Christine. *Political and Historical Encyclopedia of Women*. London: Taylor & Francis, 2003.

Felt, Joseph B. *Annals of Salem, from Its First Settlement*. Salem, MA: W & SB Ives, 1827.

Field, Jonathan Beecher. "The Governor's Two Bodies," *Early American Literature*, 52(1), January 2017, 29–52.

Foster, Stephen. *The Long Argument: English Puritanism and the Shaping of New England Culture 1570–1700*. Chapel Hill, NC: Omohundro Institute and University of North Carolina Press, reprint edition, 1996.

Freeman, Curtis W. *A Company of Women Preachers: Baptists Prophetesses in Seventeenth-Century England*. Waco, TX: Baylor University Press, 2011.

Gale Research. *Passenger and Immigration Lists Index, 1500s-1900s* [database online]. Provo, UT: The Generations Network, Inc., 2006. Original data: Filby, P. William, ed., *Passenger and Immigration Lists Index, 1500s-1900s*. Farmington Hills, MI, USA: Gale Research, 2006.

Geree, John. *The Character of an Old English Puritan, or Non-Conformist*. London: W. Wilson, 1646.

Gillespie, Katharine. *Domesticity and Dissent in the Seventeenth Century: English Women Writers and the Public Sphere*. Cambridge, England: Cambridge University Press, 2004.

Gilpin, W. Clark. "Building the 'Wall of Separation': Construction Zone for Historians," *Church History*, 79(4), December 2010, 871–880.

Godbeer, Richard. "'Your Wife Will Be Your Biggest Accuser': Reinforcing Codes of Manhood at New England Witch Trials," *Early American Studies, an Interdisciplinary Journal*, 15(3), Summer 2017, 474–504.

Goodwin, John A. *Pilgrim Republic: An Historical Review of the Colony of New Plymouth*. Boston: Houghton, Mifflin & Co., 1888.

Gouge, William. *Of Domesticall Duties*. London: William Bladen, 1622. The British Library, Available at www.bl.uk/collection-items/of-domesticall-duties-by-william-gouge-1622.

Greaves, Richard L., ed. *Triumph over Silence—Women in Protestant History*. Greenwood, CT: Praeger, 1985.

Grossberg, Michael and Tomlins, Christopher, eds. *The Cambridge History of Law in America, Vol. I – Early America (1580–1815)*. New York: Cambridge University Press, 2008.

Gunn, T. Jeremy and Witte, John R., eds. *No Establishment of Religion: America's Original Contribution to Religious Liberty*. New York: Oxford University Press, 2012.

Hall, David D. *The Antinomian Controversy, 1636–1638: A Documentary History*, 2nd ed. Durham, NC: Duke University Press, 1990.

Hall, David D. *Cultures of Print: Essays in the History of the Book*. Amherst: University of Massachusetts Amherst Press, 1996.

Hall, David D. *Puritans in the New World: A Critical Anthology*. Princeton, NJ: Princeton University Press, 2004.

Hall, David D. "The Experience of Authority in Early New England," *The Journal of American and Canadian Studies*, (23), 2005, 3–32.

Hall, Timothy L. "Roger Williams and the Foundations of Religious Liberty," *Boston University Law Review*, 71, May 1991, 3.

Hardy, Nathaniel. *Love and Fear, the Inseparable Twins of a Blest Matrimony: Characterized in a Sermon Occasioned by the Late Nuptialls between Mr. William Christmas and Mrs. Elizabeth Adams/Preached in St. Dionis Backe-Church*. London: Printed for TC for National Webb and William Grantham, 1658. Box 1658, Massachusetts Historical Society.

Hughes, Ann. "Anglo American Puritanisms: Introduction," *Journal of British Studies*, 39, January 2000, 1–7.

Hughes, Richard T. and Allen, Crawford L. *Illusions of Innocence: Protestant Primitivism in America, 1630–1875*. Chicago: University of Chicago Press, 1988.

Irwin, Raymond D. "Cast Out from the 'City upon a Hill': Antinomian Exiles in Rhode Island, 1638–1650," *Rhode Island History*, 52(1), 1994, 2–19.

James, Janet Wilson, ed. *Women in American Religion*. Philadelphia: University of Pennsylvania Press, 1980.

Johnson, Edward. *Wonder-Working Providence, 1628–1651*. New York: Charles Scribner's Sons, 1910.

Jordan, Jason. "Domestic Violence in Plymouth Colony," *Historical Ethnography*, (Anth. 509, 1998). The Plymouth Colony Archive Project, Available at www.his tarch.illinois.edu/plymouth/Domestic.html.

Kamensky, Jane. "Talk like a Man: Speech, Power, and Masculinity in Early New England," *Gender and History*, 8(1), April 1996, 22–47.

Keary, Ann. "Retelling the History of the Settlement of Providence: Speech, Writing, and Cultural Interaction on Narragansett Bay," *The New England Quarterly*, 69 (2), 1996, 250–286.

Kimball, Gertrude Selwyn. *Providence in Colonial Times*. Boston: Houghton Mifflin Co., 1912.

King, Henry Melville. *Historical Catalogue of the Members of the First Baptist Church in Providence, Rhode Island*. Providence: F.H. Townsend, 1908.

Koehler, Lyle. "The Case of the American Jezebels: Anne Hutchinson and Female Agitation during the Years of Antinomian Turmoil, 1636–1640," *William and Mary Quarterly*, 31(1), 1974, 55–78.

Koehler, Lyle. *A Search for Power: The "Weaker Sex" in Seventeenth-Century New England*. Champaign, IL: University of Illinois Press, 1980.

LaFantasie, Glen W., ed. *The Correspondence of Roger Williams, Volume I, 1629–1653*. Providence: RI Historical Society, 1988.

LaPlante, Eve. *American Jezebel: The Uncommon Life of Anne Hutchinson, the Woman Who Defied the Puritans*. New York: Harper One, Reprint edition, 2005.

Laurence, Anne. *Women in England, 1500–1760: A Social History*. New York: Palmgrave Macmillan, 1994.

Lemons, J. Stanley. "Roger Williams: Not a Seeker but a 'Witness in Sackcloth'," *The New England Quarterly*, LXXXVIII(4), December 2015, 693–714.

Lindley, Susan Hill. *"You Have Stept Out of Your Place": A History of Women and Religion in America*. Louisville, KY: Westminster John Knox Press, 1996.

Locke, John. *A Letter Concerning Toleration*, in Locke, John, ed. *The Works of John Locke*, 9 volumes. London: C. Baldwin, 1824.

Locke, John. *The Second Treatise on Government*. McPherson, C. B., ed. Indianapolis and Cambridge: Hackett Publishing Company, 1980, The Project Gutenberg, Available at www.gutenberg.org/files/7370/7370-h/7370-h.html.

Mack, Phyllis. *Visionary Women: Ecstatic Prophecy in Seventeenth-Century England*. Berkeley, CA: University of California Press, 1994.

Manchester, Margaret M. "A Family 'Much Afflicted with Conscience': The Verins and the Puritan Order," *Journal of Family History*, 42(3), July 2017, 211–235.

Marsh, Margaret and Ronner, Wander. *The Empty Cradle: Infertility in America from Colonial Times to the Present*. Baltimore: Johns Hopkins University Press, 1996.

Mather, Cotton. *Magnalia Christi Americana; or the Ecclesiastical History of New-England*. Hartford: Silas Andrus & Son, 1853, Available in its entirety at Making of America Books, a digital project of University of Michigan at http://quod.lib.umich.edu.

May, Elaine Tyler. *Barren in the Promised Land: Childless Americans and the Pursuit of Happiness*. New York: Basic Books, Inc., 1995.

McDowell, Nicholas. *The English Radical Imagination: Culture, Religion, and Revolution, 1630–1660*. Oxford: Clarendon Press, 2003.

Miller, Perry. *The New England Mind: The Seventeenth Century*. Cambridge, MA: Harvard University Press, 1954.

Miller, Perry and Johnson, Thomas Herbert. *The Puritans: A Sourcebook of Their Writings*. Mineola, NY: Courier Dover Publications, 2001.

Morgan, Edmund S. *The Puritan Family: Religion and Domestic Relations in Seventeenth Century New England*. New York: Harper & Row, 1944.

Morgan, Edmund S. *Puritan Political Ideas 1558–1794*. New York: Bobbs-Merrill, 1965.

Morgan, Edmund S. *Roger Williams: The Church and the State*. New York: W.W. Norton & Co., 2007.

Morris, M. Michelle Jarrett. *Under Household Government: Sex and Family in Puritan Massachusetts*. Cambridge, MA: Harvard University Press, 2013.

M.R. *The Mothers Counsell Or, Liuve within Compasse. Being the Last Will and Testament to Her Dearest Daughter*, M.R. London: John Wright, 1630. Early English Books Online (database).

Murphy, Andrew R. *Conscience and Community: Revisiting Toleration and Religious Dissent in Early Modern England and America*. University Park, PA: Penn State University Press, 2010.

Nevitt, Marcus. *Women and the Pamphlet Culture of Revolutionary England, 1640–1660*. Aldershot, England: Ashgate Publishing, Ltd., 2006.

Noble, Supervisor, John. *Records of the Court of Assistants of the Colony of Massachusetts Bay 1630–1692*. Boston: Massachusetts Historical Society, 1904.

Norton, Mary Beth. *Founding Mothers and Fathers: Gendered Power and the Forming of American Society*. New York: Vintage, 1997.

Nussbaum, Martha. *Liberty of Conscience: In Defense of America's Tradition of Religious Equality.* New York: Basic Books, 2008.

Olney, James H. *A Genealogy of the Descendants of Thomas Olney: An Original Proprietor of Providence, RI Who Came from England in 1635.* Providence: Press of E.L. Freeman, 1889.

Palfrey, John Gorham. *History of New England.* Boston: Little, Brown, 1858, e-book Available at https://archive.org/details/historynewengla23palfgoog/page/n11.

Perkins, William. *The Golden Chain, or the Description of Theology, Containing the Order of the Causes of Salvation and Damnation.* Cambridge: John Legat, 1600 Available at https://archive.org/details/goldenchaineorde00perk/page/n1.

Perley, Sidney. *The History of Salem, Massachusetts.* Salem, MA: S. Perley, 1924–1928.

Pierce, Richard D., ed. *The Records of the First Church in Boston.* Portland, ME: The Anthoensen Press, 1961.

Pierce, Richard D., ed. *The Records of the First Church in Salem.* Salem, MA: Essex Institute, 1974.

Pleck, Elizabeth. *Domestic Tyranny: The Making of American Social Policy against Family Violence from Colonial Times to the Present.* Urbana-Champaign: University of Illinois Press, 2004.

Pope, Charles Henry. *The Pioneers of Massachusetts: A Descriptive List, Drawn from the Records of the Colonies, Towns, and Churches, and Other Contemporaneous Documents.* Baltimore: Genealogical Publishing Co., Inc., 1998.

Porterfield, Amanda. *Female Piety in Puritan New England: The Emergence of Religious Humanism.* New York: Oxford University Press, 1992.

Porterfield, Amanda. *Mary Lyon and the Mount Holyoke Missionaries.* New York: Oxford University Press, 1997.

Providence Home Lots, 1636–1650, Providence. VMO11_02_01043. Providence, RI: John Hitchens Cady Research Scrapbooks Collection, Providence Public Library.

Providence Record Commissioners. *The Early Records of the Town of Providence,* Vol. I. Providence: Snow & Farnham, City Printers, 1892.

Pulsifer, David. "Extracts from Records Kept by the Rev. John Fiske, during His Ministry at Salem, Wenham, and Chelmsford" Historical Collections of the Essex Institute (Vol. I(#2), May 1859). Salem: Essex Institute, 1859.

Reardon, Matthew J. "A Fraternity of Patriarchs: The Gendered Order of Early Puritan Massachusetts," *Historical Journal of Massachusetts,* 42(2), Summer 2014, 122ff.

Rhode Island, Court of Trials. *Rhode Island Court Records: Records of the Court of Trials of the Colony of Providence Plantations, 1647–1670.* Providence: Rhode Island Historical Society, 1922.

Ross, Richard J. "The Career of Puritan Jurisprudence," *Law and Historical Review,* 26, Summer 2008, 227–258.

Sainsbury, Esq., W. Noel, ed. *Calendar of State Papers, Colonial Series, 1574–1660.* London: Longman, Green, Longman, & Roberts, 1860. TNA.

Salerno, Anthony. "The Social Background of Seventeenth-Century Emigration to America," *Journal of British Studies,* 29(1), 1979, 31–52.

Sanders, Joanne McRee. *English Settlers in Barbados, 1637–1800.* Baltimore: Genealogical Publishing Co., 2009.

Savage, James. *Genealogical Dictionary of the First Settlers of New England.* Boston: Little, Brown & Co., 1860.

Schinkel, Anders. *Conscience and Conscientious Objections*. Amsterdam: Amsterdam University Press, 2007.

Schomburgk, Robert H. *The History of Barbados Comprising A Geographical and Statistical Description of the Island; A Sketch of the Historical Events since the Settlement, and an Account of Its Geology and Natural Productions*. London: Longman, Brown, and Longmans, 1848.

Schwartz, Kathryn. *What You Will: Gender, Contract, and Shakespearean Social Space*. Philadelphia, PA: University of Pennsylvania Press, 2011.

Shurtleff, Nathaniel B., ed. *Records of the Governor and Company of the Massachusetts Bay in New England, 1628–1686*, 5 volumes. Boston: William White, 1853.

Stephen, Leslie, ed. *Dictionary of National Biography*, 63 volumes. London: Smith, Elder & Co., 1885–1900.

Strong, Robert, ed. "Two Seventeenth-Century Conversion Narratives from Ipswich, Massachusetts Bay Colony," *The New England Quarterly*, 82(1), March 2009, 136–169.

Tepper, Michael, ed. *Passengers to America: A Consolidation of Ship Passenger Lists from the New England Historical and Genealogical Register*. Baltimore: Genealogical Pub. Co, 1978.

Thomas, Keith. "Women and the Civil War Sects," *Past and Present*, 13, 1958, 42–62.

Thompson, Roger. *Sex in Middlesex: Popular Mores in a Massachusetts County, 1649–1699*. Amherst, MA: University of Massachusetts Press, 1986.

Thompson, Roger. "State of the Art: Early Modern Migration," *Journal of American Studies*, 25, 1991, I: 59–69.

Threlfall, John B. "The Verin Family of Salem, Massachusetts," *The New England Historical and Genealogical Register*, 131, April 1977, 100–112.

Torrey, Clarence Almon. *New England Marriages Prior to 1700*, 3 volumes. Baltimore: New England Historic Genealogical Society, 2004.

Traister, Bruce. *Female Piety and the Invention of American Puritanism*. Columbus, OH: The Ohio State University Press, 2016.

Trent and Wells, eds. *Colonial Prose and Poetry*. New York: Thomas Y. Crowell & Co., 1901. Available at www.bartleby.com/163/.

Ulrich, Laurel T. *Good Wives: Image and Reality in the Lives of Women in Northern New England*. New York: Knopf Doubleday Publishing Group, 1982.

Van Engen, Abram C. *Sympathetic Puritans: Calvinist Fellow Feeling in Early New England*. New York: Oxford University Press, 2015.

Wall, Helena. *Fierce Communion: Family and Community in Early America*. Cambridge, MA: Harvard University Press, 1990.

Ward, Nathaniel. *The Simple Cobler of Aggawam in America*. London: Stephen Bowtell, 1647, Available at The Project Gutenberg www.gutenberg.org/files/34974/34974-h/34974-h.htm.

Weimer, Adrian Chastain. "Elizabeth Hooton and the Lived Politics of Toleration in Massachusetts Bay," *The William and Mary Quarterly*, 74(1), January 2017, 3rd series, 43–76.

Westercamp, Marilyn J. "Anne Hutchinson, Sectarian Mysticism, and the Puritan Order," *Church History*, 59(4), 1990, 482–496.

Williams, Roger. *George Fox Digg'd Out of His Burrowes, Or, an Offer of Disputation on Fourteen Proposals Made This Last Summer 1672 (So Cal'd Unto G. Fox, Then Present on Rhode-Island in New England* by R. Williams). Boston: John

Foster, 1676, Available at https://quod.lib.umich.edu/e/eebo/A66448.0001.001? view=toc.

Williams, Roger. *The Bloudy Tenent of Persecution for Cause of Conscience Discussed: And Mr. Cotton's Letter Examined and Answered*, Underhill, Edward B., ed. The Hanserd Knollys Society. London: J. Haddon, 1848.

Williams, Roger. *The Bloudy Tenent of Persecution*, in Caldwell, Samuel L., ed. *Publications of the Narragansett Club*, First Series, Vol. III. Providence, RI: The Narragansett Club, 1867.

Williams, Selma R. *Divine Rebel: The Life of Anne Marbury Hutchinson*. New York: Henry Holt & Co., 1981.

Winship, Michael P. *Making Heretics: Militant Protestantism and Free Grace in Massachusetts, 1636–1641*. Princeton, NJ: Princeton University Press, 2002.

Winship, Michael P. *The Times and Trials of Anne Hutchinson: Puritans Divided*, (Landmark Law Cases and American Society). Lawrence, KS: University Press of Kansas, 2005.

Winship, Michael P. *Godly Republicanism: Puritans Pilgrims, and a City on a Hill*. Cambridge, MA: Harvard University Press, 2012.

Wright, Louis B. "William Perkins: Elizabethan Apostle of 'Practical Divinity'," *Huntington Library Quarterly*, 3(2), January 1940: 171–196, Available at JSTOR www.jstor.org/stable/3815898.

Yates Publishing. *U.S. And International Marriage Records, 1560–1900* [database on-line]. Provo, UT: The Generations Network, Inc., 2004.

Index

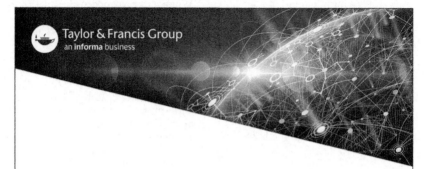